o o o o o

The Complete Guide to Investing in Exchange Traded Funds:

How to Earn High Rates of Return — Safely

By Martha Maeda

THE COMPLETE GUIDE TO INVESTING IN EXCHANGE TRADED FUNDS:
HOW TO EARN HIGH RATES OF RETURN — SAFELY

Copyright © 2009 by Atlantic Publishing Group, Inc.
1405 SW 6th Ave. • Ocala, Florida 34471 • 800-814-1132 • 352-622-1875–Fax
Web site: www.atlantic-pub.com • E-mail: sales@atlantic-pub.com
SAN Number: 268-1250

ISBN-13: 978-1-60138-290-0   ISBN-10: 1-60138-290-1

Library of Congress Cataloging-in-Publication Data

Maeda, Martha, 1953-
  The complete guide to investing in exchange traded funds : how to earn high rates of return--safely / by Martha Maeda.
       p. cm.
  Includes bibliographical references and indexes.
  ISBN-13: 978-1-60138-290-0 (alk. paper)
  ISBN-10: 1-60138-290-1 (alk. paper)
  1. Exchange traded funds. 2. Stock index futures. 3. Exchange traded funds--United States. I. Title.
  HG6043.M34 2008
  332.63'27--dc22
                                   2008035554

INTERIOR LAYOUT DESIGN: Nicole Deck ndeck@atlantic-pub.com

Printed in the United States

○ ○ ○ ○ ○
Table of Contents

Chapter 4: Anatomy of an ETF   31

Chapter 5: What Are the Advantages of ETFs?   39

Chapter 6: ETFs and Mutual Funds   45

Chapter 7: The Indexes   53

Chapter 8: The ETF Providers   69

Chapter 9: The ETFs   73

Chapter 10: International Investing
Global Equity ETFs
117

Chapter 11: Doing the Research
131

Section 2: Investing with ETFs
138

Chapter 12: Choosing Your Investment Strategy
139

Chapter 13: Building Your Buy-and-Hold Portfolio
145

Chapter 14: Getting Started: Choosing a Brokerage
165

Chapter 20: What Does the Future Hold for ETFs?   239

Appendix A: Exchange Traded Funds   253

Appendix B: Where to Find Information   313

Appendix C: Glossary   319

Bibliography   331

Dedication   333

Author Biography   334

Index   335

○ ○ ○ ○ ○

Foreword

As waves of losses from financial instruments wash over markets across the globe, an investor cannot help but ask whether exchange traded funds (ETFs) are not just another fad invented by slick Wall Street firms to extract fees. Collateralized debt obligation (CDO) and mortgage-backed security (MBS) are just some of the three-letter acronyms that put the U.S. financial system on the brink of disaster.

Happily, ETFs are quite a different animal for reasons made abundantly clear in *The Complete Guide to Investing in Exchange Traded Funds: How to Earn High Rates of Return — Safely.* If ETFs are a fad, then they are unlike any other investment fad seen in decades. They have grown more than 20 percent per year during good years and bad for over 15 years. This period includes some of the wildest stock market gyrations in decades during the Tech Boom. Nearly every conceivable asset class is now represented by ETFs. At over $600 billion in assets, they represent a sizable portion of American investor wealth. Size, of course, is no guarantee of solvency or indicator of common sense, as the near collapse of Fannie Mae demonstrated.

Fads typically do not have a solid competitive edge. As you will learn from *The Complete Guide to Exchange Traded Funds,* ETFs are cheap to buy and own; they delay taxes; and their instant liquidity ensures flexibility of strategy. These are no small feats. For the vast majority of investors, ETFs constitute a considerable advance from stock picking and a noticeable advance from mutual funds.

Stock picking helps keep stock prices in line with valuations, but it is time consuming. Also, because so many experts do it, the likelihood of capturing some edge against them is difficult even for the full-time professional.

Mutual funds are a wonderful innovation but, on average, have high fees and mediocre performance — a deadly combination.

After having written hundreds of articles and analysis pieces on ETFs and their indexes, I have come to appreciate the more subtle aspects of exchange traded funds. Transparency is what sets ETFs apart from many investment vehicles.

ETFs are utterly transparent in what they hold, why they hold it, and how they may change holdings in the future. At all times, ETF managers must declare the holdings of an ETF and the methodology used to create and modify it. What sank mortgage-backed securities was the opacity and complexity of their holdings. Mortgages of various qualities were cobbled together into bonds whose quality was determined by hurried ratings analysts. Even professionals did not pretend to really know what was in them. Everyone assumed that because real estate values would continue to go up, all would be well. Mutual funds are somewhat transparent in that they reveal their funds quarterly or perhaps more often, but their holdings are certainly not known minute-to-minute. Many ETFs track volatile asset classes, but this is always explicitly stated.

From an operational point of view, the economic advantages of ETFs stem from their transparency. The very creation of an ETF is a highly public affair whereby institutional investors trade or loan baskets of stocks for ETF securities. It turns out that this process is quite inexpensive because many institutional investors have such baskets ready to trade or loan. Because the resulting security is extremely transparent, it trades at the same price as a stock. And because no actual purchasing has been made, no taxation is triggered. These benefits all flow from transparency.

For even the casual student of international affairs, some obvious points emerge. The dominant economic model in the modern world, free-market capitalism, is predicated on transparency of how companies conduct business. The dominant political model in the modern world, democracy, depends on transparency of how government taxes and governs. Most of the world's peace and prosperity comes from them. Transparency of ETFs should not be taken lightly.

In making investment decisions clearer and simpler, ETFs enhance awareness. ETF investors or their advisors may buy only a few funds a year, but they do so with an understanding of what they are buying and why. By staying at the asset class level, ETFs are quite comprehensible. Mutual funds often stray wildly from their targets as they pick and choose stocks. This makes knowing how many large versus small or domestic versus international companies you own quite difficult. ETFs, on the other hand, make things tidy.

Academics tout ETFs as the latest expression of acknowledgement of their work. A cottage industry of economics researchers have pounded out study after study showing that trying to beat the market does not work for most investors. The question remains: If you are trying to simply match the market, what market is it that you are trying not to beat? There are many fine indexes to choose from, and there are just as many ETFs tracking them.

Some investors come to think of ETFs as the end of investment decision making. "Just buy the market" is the mantra of the narrow-minded. One can "just buy the market," but decision making will never disappear. Some investors may simply not realize they are making decisions. Blindly buying a broad market ETF involves making an implicit decision not to buy something else. ETFs do their part by helping to simplify and crystallize decisions. For instance, one must still pick and choose from among the innumerable asset classes. There is no way around this. Classically, this involves deciding one's risk tolerance and time horizon and allocating appropriately. Then, where the rubber meets the road, one must pick individual ETFs to represent the desired asset classes. ETFs follow asset classes closely so that making a list of candidate funds to buy is easy.

Are investors up to the task of educating themselves for all these decisions? It partly depends on the difficulty of that task. Because ETFs match up with nearly every conceivable asset class, they present investors with clear choices for deciding the most important investment decision: "What asset classes do I want to be exposed to?" While complicated, this question has finite parameters. There are only so many asset classes, and their histories and behaviors are well-known. ETFs help make the task manageable by matching up with them cleanly. In contrast, mutual funds with active stock picking managers add a maddening layer of subjective judgment. Investors wander a hall of mirrors trying to determine who the best manager is because it is often not until the end of the game that one can show that a manager has unusual skill and not blind luck. There is always a new star manager to consider, too. Meanwhile, investors do not spend the time getting to know the asset classes that they are going to hitch their wealth wagon to. Even if investors do find time to study asset classes, mutual funds often do not match up cleanly with them. No matter how much the task of education is focused and simplified, at some point, it cannot be made any simpler. Investors simply have to do a little homework and consult reference works from time to time.

There are many reasons to read, and then always keep on hand, a comprehensive book on ETFs such as *The Complete Guide to Exchange Traded Funds*. It is useful to understand why ETFs are efficient and in what ways; it is important to understand their composition, underlying indexes, and methodologies; it is helpful to see how major investment strategies pair with various ETF product lines; and it saves time to be able to look up fund names, tickers, and data tables in a compact tome.

The ETF revolution has just begun. An increasing number of ETFs are targeting niche products which afford the investor an opportunity to beat an index by over- or underweighting one of its subindexes. These funds tend to carry slightly higher fees than plain vanilla index ETFs, but they are still cheap by mutual fund standards. For the knowledgeable investor, they present an intriguing set of potential benefits at a reasonable cost.

John Bogle, founder of the Vanguard Group and inventor of the index mutual fund, has lambasted niche funds as a siren calling unsophisticated investors to their doom. In early 2007, he predicted they would abandon inexpensive broad-based ETFs in favor of higher cost niche market ETFs. Bogle has been right on most trends in indexing, but this prediction is proving wildly wrong. Investors are buying up niche ETFs in large numbers but not at the expense of broad-based ETFs, which still dominate the landscape. And it is clearly the most sophisticated investors who are gravitating towards the most sophisticated ETFs. Investors are pairing up with appropriate offerings.

Not since the elaboration of the public stock exchange have such wildly different types come together to make an investment vehicle serve them well. Individual investors with long-term, passive portfolios are huge buyers of ETFs, but so, too, are hedge funds with hair-trigger trading schemes and just about every other type of investor in between. The presence of institutional investors of ETFs irks Bogle, who is a fan of the small, buy-and-hold investor. But institutional investors are not to be feared. The diversity of the community of ETF investors probably contributes more to the success of ETFs than anything except transparency. All contribute to keeping costs in their various forms down, and everyone is the better for it.

Just as an educated workforce is critical to a growing economy and an educated citizenry is critical to a thriving democracy, education is ultimately the key to a successful investor community. One cannot understand all the asset classes, follow every investment strategy, or keep track of every new ETF in the world today; with some exertion, though, one can gain a general understanding of key asset classes, focus on those that seem most appropriate to one's situation, and keep an eye on specific ETFs of interest. This volume will surely help.

Will McClatchy, M.B.A.
www.ETFzone.com

Will McClatchy is the editor of **www.ETFzone.com**, an independent Web site devoted entirely to exchange traded fund investment research, data, and commentary. He has authored hundreds of articles for ETFzone.com and previously for **www.IndexFunds.com**, which he founded. He is the author of two investment books, *Strategies for Investment Success: Index Funds* and *Exchange Traded Funds: An Insider's Guide to Buying the Market*. He holds a B.A. from Stanford and an M.B.A. from the University of Texas at Austin.

We recently lost our beloved pet "Bear," who was not only our best and dearest friend but also the "Vice President of Sunshine" here at Atlantic Publishing. He did not receive a salary but worked tirelessly 24 hours a day to please his parents. Bear was a rescue dog that turned around and showered myself, my wife Sherri, his grandparents Jean, Bob and Nancy and every person and animal he met (maybe not rabbits) with friendship and love. He made a lot of people smile every day.

We wanted you to know that a portion of the profits of this book will be donated to The Humane Society of the United States. *–Douglas & Sherri Brown*

The human-animal bond is as old as human history. We cherish our animal companions for their unconditional affection and acceptance. We feel a thrill when we glimpse wild creatures in their natural habitat or in our own backyard.

Unfortunately, the human-animal bond has at times been weakened. Humans have exploited some animal species to the point of extinction.

The Humane Society of the United States makes a difference in the lives of animals here at home and worldwide. The HSUS is dedicated to creating a world where our relationship with animals is guided by compassion. We seek a truly humane society in which animals are respected for their intrinsic value, and where the human-animal bond is strong.

Want to help animals? We have plenty of suggestions. Adopt a pet from a local shelter,

join The Humane Society and be a part of our work to help companion animals and wildlife. You will be funding our educational, legislative, investigative and outreach projects in the U.S. and across the globe.

Or perhaps you'd like to make a memorial donation in honor of a pet, friend or relative? You can through our Kindred Spirits program. And if you'd like to contribute in a more structured way, our Planned Giving Office has suggestions about estate planning, annuities, and even gifts of stock that avoid capital gains taxes.

Maybe you have land that you would like to preserve as a lasting habitat for wildlife. Our Wildlife Land Trust can help you. Perhaps the land you want to share is a backyard— that's enough. Our Urban Wildlife Sanctuary Program will show you how to create a habitat for your wild neighbors.

So you see, it's easy to help animals. And The HSUS is here to help.

THE HUMANE SOCIETY OF THE UNITED STATES.

2100 L Street NW • Washington, DC 20037 • 202-452-1100 • www.hsus.org

○ ○ ○ ○ ○

Introduction

Just as the Internet has made the stock market universally accessible, exchange traded funds, or ETFs, have opened opportunities to private investors that were not even imaginable a decade ago. Originally conceived by institutional investors who needed to quickly move large blocks of assets, ETFs have become an exciting trading vehicle that allows individuals to participate in almost every sector of the financial markets. They can be bought and sold like individual stocks, yet they offer the broad exposure and diversity of mutual funds. Since 2000, when ETFs began to attract the interest of private investors, more than 775 ETF products have appeared on the United States market. Almost 300 new ETFs were launched during 2007 and the early months of 2008. According to the Investment Company Institute, as of November 30, 2007, ETF assets made up more than $572 billion of the more than $1 trillion in stock index funds. Today, private investors account for more than 60 percent of ETF ownership.

This book will introduce you to an exciting new world. You will learn what exchange traded funds are, how they function, how you can use them to provide for your financial future, and even how to play the stock market with them. You will learn how to establish your financial goals, evaluate risk and return, build a portfolio, and protect yourself against financial loss. You will also get a peek into the future of investing and learn how you can be a part of the economic development taking place all over the globe.

○ ○ ○ ○ ○

Section 1

Understanding ETFs

Chapter 1

o o o o o

What Is an
Exchange Traded Fund?

An ETF is a fund, containing assets which attempt to track the performance of a particular index or commodity in the stock market, which trades like a stock. Shares of an ETF can be bought and sold throughout the day on the stock market, just like shares of stock. Each share of an ETF represents a share of the underlying stocks or assets held by the fund. As the prices of those underlying stocks or assets rise and fall, the value of the ETF shares rise and fall with them.

ETFs are open-ended, meaning that as the demand for shares of the fund increases, new shares are created, and the holdings of the fund are enlarged. When the price of ETF shares rises above the value of their underlying securities, a process called arbitrage is used to bring the price back into line with the net asset value (NAV) of the ETF shares. If demand for an ETF should decline, outstanding shares are redeemed, and the underlying securities are sold.

ETFs make it possible for an individual investor to own a share of a broad range of stocks, rather than investing in just one or two individual companies. Private investors can enjoy the same advantages as large institutional investors: exposure to a variety of markets and the protection offered by a diverse portfolio of holdings. If one or two individual stocks drop in value, the loss is offset by gains from other securities.

ETFs offer other advantages, too. Management costs are lower because

ETFs are frequently passively managed, meaning that they track an index of securities selected according to a fixed set of rules rather than employing fund managers to make investment decisions. Securities are bought and sold only when necessary to maintain integrity with the fund index, thereby reducing expenses. ETFs are legally required to provide a prospectus listing their holdings and detailing their investment objectives. This transparency allows investors to understand clearly what risks and returns they can expect when they purchase shares in an ETF. ETFs are also tax-efficient because investors are not liable for capital gains when stocks held by the fund are sold for a profit.

ETFs also provide a means of quickly putting excess cash to productive use and of immediately adding a new industrial or geographic sector to a portfolio. With one or two transactions, investors are able to move large amounts of capital from one market sector to another. The market price of ETF shares is updated regularly throughout the day, and they can be bought and sold quickly. Active traders can attempt to increase their returns by buying and selling ETFs, using the same strategies as with individual stocks.

Chapter 2

o o o o o

History of ETFs

Mutual Funds

Exchange traded funds are a modification of the mutual fund, a concept that originated in Amsterdam in the 1770s with the establishment of the first investment trust by Adriaan van Ketwich. A group of investors pooled their money, invested it in various businesses, and shared the profits. The first investment trust in the United Kingdom, the Foreign and Colonial Government Trust, was founded in 1868, and by 1875, there were 18 investment trusts in London. During the 1890s, investment trusts began to appear in the United States. The first modern, open-ended U.S. mutual fund, the Massachusetts Investment Trust (MIT), was founded in 1924 by the faculty and staff of Harvard University. The MIT was the first fund to allow the investment company to continually create and redeem shares at a price proportional to the value of the stocks held by the fund. After the markets closed each trading day, the company computed the NAV of their assets and determined a fair price for shares of the fund. New shares were created or outstanding shares were redeemed, according to investor demand.

When investors bought shares of a mutual fund, they paid a commission to the salesperson who sold them the shares. During the 1920s, banks became the leading issuers of open-ended mutual funds and closed investment trusts. Bank tellers sold shares to bank customers, and some banks loaned money to their depositors to buy shares. The stock market crash of 1929 wiped out many mutual funds and highlighted the abuses in the mutual fund industry. In 1933, Congress passed the Glass-Steagall Act to separate commercial banking from investment activities. The United States Securities and Exchange Commission (SEC) was created by the Securities Exchange Act of 1934 to regulate the stock market and prevent corporate abuses relating to the sale of securities and financial reporting.

Investment Act of 1940

After the passage of the Investment Act of 1940 to regulate the mutual fund industry, the number of mutual funds increased dramatically. Almost 50 new funds were introduced during the 1950s as the economic boom following World War II and the expansion of investment firms led to an increase in the number of investors. Nevertheless, few mutual fund managers were able to bring in returns as high as the average stock market returns, and those that succeeded one year rarely maintained their success through the next year. Investors began to recognize the impact of high mutual fund management costs on their returns and, therefore, demanded low-cost alternatives. The financial sector began to consider a new type of low-cost mutual fund that would not rely on the luck or skill of an active fund manager but that would simply emulate the stock market indexes as closely as possible. In 1971, Wells Fargo Bank established the first low-cost index fund.

John Bogle, the founder of Vanguard, and Dr. Burton Malkiel, a professor of economics at Princeton University, developed a plan for the Vanguard 500 Index Fund in the spring of 1976. It was designed to track the Standard & Poor's 500 Stock Index, and it launched on August 31, 1976.

Black Monday, October 19, 1987

On October 19, 1987, now known as Black Monday, the Dow Jones Industrial Average fell more than 20 percent. The drop was not triggered by any particular event; some economists believe it was caused by "program trading," an automated buy/sell mechanism that triggers instantaneous execution of large orders based on computerized tracking of the market. The events of Black Monday made it clear that large institutional investors did not have the liquidity to quickly hedge positions and protect against losses. A simple way was needed to hedge a portfolio of stock against rapidly falling stock prices with an exchange traded vehicle.

In 1989, in an effort to stimulate trading, the Toronto Stock Exchange launched Toronto Stock Exchange Index Participation Shares (TIPS) that were designed to track the Toronto 35 Index. Proportionate numbers of shares of the 35 stocks in the index were held in a trust, and TIPS trust receipts were bought and sold on the trading floor of the Toronto Stock Exchange.

Acting on a request by the law firm of Hayne Leland, John O'Brien, and Mark Rubinstein (LOR), the United States Securities and Exchange Commission began rewriting securities regulations and, in 1990, issued the Investment Company Act Release No. 17809 to allow for a new type of mutual fund that could create and redeem shares during the day. Large investors could create "SuperTrusts," which allowed them to buy or sell an entire basket of Standard & Poor's stocks in a single trade. The first "SuperTrust" was launched by LOR in December 1992, but it was not reissued after it matured because it did not appeal to individual investors.

First U.S. ETF

In January 1993, the American Stock Exchange took advantage of the Investment Company Act Release No. 17809 to launch the first Standard &

Poor's Depository Receipts (SPDRs, known as SPDRs S&P 500) managed by State Street Global Advisors. SPDRs S&P 500 were immediately successful because they were affordable for individual investors, with individual units selling for one-tenth the value of the S&P 500 Index. They also provided stockbrokers with an alternative means of rapidly transferring their clients' assets at a time when many companies were investing their cash in the low-cost Vanguard 500 mutual fund. During the first year, SPDRs S&P 500 brought in assets of nearly $500 million, and it remains the most popular ETF today, with assets now over $60 billion.

In 1996, Morgan Stanley and Barclays Global Investors launched a series of 13 ETFs, called World Equity Benchmark Shares (WEBS), on the American Stock Exchange. Each represented a different world equity market. While the SPDRs S&P 500 were organized as a unit investment trust (UIT) and were required to strictly replicate the S&P 500 Index, WEBS were organized as investment companies. This structure gave fund managers the freedom to modify the fund holdings to work around difficulties in the indexes the funds were tracking. Dividends paid by stocks in the fund could be reinvested. For the first time, the Securities and Exchange Commission agreed to allow WEBS to use the words "index fund" and "ETF" together in their prospectuses.

In 1997, State Street Global Advisors (SSGA) introduced Diamonds (DIA), an ETF indexed to the Dow Jones Industrial Average and organized as a unit investment trust. Public familiarity with the Dow Jones made this fund attractive to investors, and it now holds approximately $8 billion in assets. In 1998, State Street Global Advisors organized Sector SPDRs, nine ETFs benchmarked to nine S&P 500 industry sectors:

- Materials

- Energy

- Healthcare

- Financial

- Consumer staples

- Industrial

- Consumer discretionary

- Utilities

- Technology

During the technology boom of the late 1990s, the most popular ETF was a National Association of Securities Dealers Automated Quotation (NASDAQ) 100 index-tracking stock, QQQ, nicknamed Cubes. It was immediately popular with individual investors seeking to speculate in technology and communications. After technology crashed in 2000, individual investors became less interested in ETFs, but many new ETF companies and products were created. Cubes was renamed PowerShares QQQ (symbol: QQQQ) in 2007.

In 2001, Vanguard launched its first ETF, Vanguard Index Participation Equity Receipts (VIPERS), linked to its existing Total Stock Market Index Fund. In 2002, Vanguard offered a second ETF, Vanguard Extended Market VIPERS, tracking the Wilshire 400 Index. Early in 2007, Vanguard launched fixed-income ETFs, which are shares of existing fixed-income funds, and dropped the name VIPERS. Vanguard has patented the structure of an ETF as a share class of an existing index fund.

In May 2000, Barclay's Global Investors (BGI) introduced 50 new iShares ETF products in a single day, indexed to a wide variety of U.S., foreign, and global benchmarks. This began a new trend of flooding the market with as many new products as possible, even though the future of some of them is uncertain. In 2006, Rydex set a record by filing for almost 100 new funds in one day. A boom in commodity prices beginning in 2005 attracted the attention of investors, and ETF companies launched new funds that tracked commodities indexes, or the prices of individual commodities such as oil or gold.

In 2005, the introduction of Rydex CurrencyShares ETFs signaled the entry of ETFs into the currency market. Rydex introduced additional currency market ETFs in 2006 and 2007. During 2007 and the early months of 2008, almost 300 new ETFs were launched, many of them tracking increasingly specialized market sectors, individual commodities, or custom indexes.

In 2006, Barclays Bank PLC released the first series of iPaths exchange traded notes (ETNs). ETNs do not represent ownership of underlying stocks held by a fund; they are debt notes issued by a bank promising to pay investors the total return of a specific index or benchmark over a specified time, minus fees. Purchasers of ETN shares can hold them until the note matures or sell their shares on the secondary market. Units of ETN shares can also be redeemed for cash by large institutional investors.

Chapter 3

o o o o o

Creation of an ETF

The creation of a new ETF involves three entities: a sponsor, authorized participants, and a trust company. The sponsor is normally a bank or other large financial institution; major sponsors of ETFs include Vanguard, Barclay's Global Investors, and State Street Global Advisors. Authorized participants are large institutional investors, specialists, or market makers, who are given the authority to create and redeem ETF shares. The trust company is a third party, commonly a bank, which physically holds the securities underlying an ETF in trust.

Defining Objectives and Licensing an Index

To set up an ETF, an investment company first defines the fund's investment objectives and then submits a proposal to the Securities and Exchange Commission (SEC), which contains legal details such as fees, objectives, risks, names and symbols, the index to be used and the securities to be included in the fund, methodology, and how the fund will be administered. Most ETFs track securities indexes, many of which are licensed from outside vendors, such as Standard & Poor's, Dow Jones, Russell, Morgan Stanley Capital International, and providers that create niche indexes. Sometimes the price of a single commodity, such as oil or gold, serves as the index or benchmark.

A good index uses clear procedures for selecting and weighing the relative importance of the components that make up the index and a consistent method for maintaining it. The provider of the index charges a licensing fee, which is part of the expenses of the ETF. The amount of a licensing fee is frequently not disclosed, but it is based on a percentage of the assets in the ETF. Some ETF sponsors avoid these licensing fees by creating their own in-house index, but in that case, the SEC requires them to hire an outside fund manager to oversee the fund, adding to the expenses of the fund.

Authorized Participants

The new ETF signs participant agreements with several authorized participants (APs), regularly well-known, market-making firms, such as Goldman Sachs, Merrill Lynch, and Smith Barney, as well as some less familiar market specialists. The APs act as middlemen, buying or borrowing a "basket" of stocks — which replicates the index of the new ETF — and delivering them to the ETF manager in exchange for a large block of newly created ETF shares, known as a "creation unit." Creation units vary in size but are characteristically made up of between 20,000 and 50,000 shares of the new ETF. The previous day's published NAV is used to determine the value of the securities and cash delivered by the authorized participant.

When the authorized participant has received a creation unit, or large block of shares, it can hold the block of shares, trade it to another authorized participant, or break it up into individual ETF shares that can be purchased by the public on the open market. Individual investors who purchase shares of these larger units are essentially indirect owners of shares of stock held by a third party.

An AP can also redeem a creation unit by buying up the requisite number of ETF shares (redemption unit) on the stock market and turning them into the fund company in exchange for individual securities and cash valued at exactly the NAV of the redemption unit. The ETF sponsor charges the AP a relatively small fee every time a creation unit is created or redeemed. Because the exchange of securities for ETF shares is an in-kind transaction, no tax liabilities are created.

Fund Management

The ETF fund manager forwards the securities to the Depository Trust Company (DTC), part of the United States Depository Trust and Clearing Corporation, which holds them and arranges for electronic delivery of the shares to the custodial bank, transfer, and settlement of shares. A custodial bank is required to physically hold the fund's securities. The custodial bank processes and records all transactions and exchanges of securities within the fund and earns a small fee normally based on the amount of assets in the ETF.

After the stock market closes each day, the exact NAV of the ETF is calculated based on the net asset values of all the individual securities held by the fund. The ETF fund manager then publishes a portfolio composition file (PCF), listing the exact names and quantities of underlying securities and cash that must be submitted by an authorized provider to receive one creation unit. The cash part of the package represents unpaid stock dividends or investments in nonliquid securities, such as bonds. ETF managers are responsible for sending their PCF files to the National Securities Clearing Corporation (NSCC), which processes and distributes the PCFs to all authorized participants before the opening of the next market day.

If the composition of the index underlying the fund changes, authorized providers are responsible for making similar changes to the creation units they hold by purchasing and delivering the new stocks to the ETF company and receiving in exchange the old securities, which have been removed from the index.

As demand for an ETF grows, additional shares are created by the APs, who purchase the requisite additional securities and deliver them to the fund sponsor. Should demand for the ETF decline, the APs can redeem units of outstanding shares for the underlying securities. The value of an ETF share rises and falls with the prices of the underlying stocks. When consumer demand causes the share price of an ETF to rise too far above the value of the underlying securities (selling at a premium) or market forces cause the price to drop below the actual value of an ETF share (selling at a discount), arbitrage is carried out by the APs to maintain the price of ETF shares close to the NAV of its underlying securities.

CASE STUDY: EXCHANGE TRADED FUNDS (ETFS)

The following is excerpted from the U.S. Securities and Exchange Commission Web site: **http://www.sec. gov/answers/etf.htm**.

Exchange traded funds, or ETFs, are investment companies that are legally classified as open-end companies or unit investment trusts (UITs), but that differ from traditional open-end companies and UITs in the following respects:

- ETFs do not sell individual shares directly to investors, and only issue their shares in large blocks (blocks of 50,000 shares, for example) that are known as "creation units."

- Investors generally do not purchase creation units with cash. Instead, they buy creation units with a basket of securities that generally mirrors the ETF's portfolio. Those who purchase creation units are frequently institutions.

- After purchasing a creation unit, an investor often splits it up and sells the individual shares on a secondary market. This permits other investors to purchase individual shares, instead of creation units.

- Investors who want to sell their ETF shares have two options: they can sell individual shares to other investors on the secondary market, or they can sell the creation units back to the ETF. In addition, ETFs generally redeem creation units by giving investors the securities that comprise the portfolio instead of cash. Because of the limited redeemability of ETF shares, ETFs are not considered to be — and may not call themselves — mutual funds.

CASE STUDY: EXCHANGE TRADED FUNDS (ETFS)

An ETF, like any other type of investment company, will have a prospectus. Some ETFs deliver a prospectus to secondary market purchasers. ETFs that do not deliver a prospectus are required to give investors a document known as a Product Description, which summarizes key information about the ETF and explains how to obtain a prospectus. All ETFs will deliver a prospectus upon request. Before purchasing ETF shares, you should carefully read all of an ETF's available information, including its prospectus.

An ETF will have annual operating expenses and may also impose certain shareholders fees that are disclosed in the prospectus.

Currently, all ETFs seek to achieve the same return as particular market indexes. Such an ETF is similar to an index fund in that it will primarily invest in the securities of companies that are included in a selected market index. An ETF will invest in either all the securities or a representative sample of the securities included in the index.

Regulating the Price: Arbitrage

The earliest funds were investment trusts, or close-ended funds, first introduced to American investors during the 1890s. In a close-ended fund, shares are initially offered to the public for a limited time before being closed to new investors. Original investors in the fund cannot withdraw money, but they can trade their shares of the fund on the stock exchange. To protect investors from price manipulation by fund managers, the SEC does not allow a closed-end fund to create new shares or to redeem shares from investors when their price is lower than the value of the stocks owned by the fund. As a result, shares of closed-end funds often sell for prices that are considerably higher (selling at a premium) or lower (selling at a discount) than the value (NAV) of the shares' underlying securities. If an article in a popular money magazine recommends a particular closed-end fund, investors rushing to buy shares of that fund may drive up demand and pay more than the shares are truly worth. The fund manager has no mechanism for bringing the share prices into line with their actual value (NAV).

To avoid a similar problem with ETFs, their early creators petitioned the SEC to allow arbitrage, the creation or redemption of shares of the fund throughout the trading day. If shares of a fund are selling at a price higher than their actual value, an independent third party, called an "authorized participant" (AP), can create additional fund shares and sell them in the market to lower the price. The AP then uses the proceeds from selling these new shares to buy more stocks for the fund. This brings the fund's underlying value into line with the selling price of its shares and also realizes a profit for the authorized participant. If shares of a fund are selling for less than the value of its underlying stocks, the authorized participant purchases large quantities of them, turns them into the fund company in exchange for the underlying stocks, and sells those shares of stocks at a profit. This process is repeated several times, until ETF share prices are close to the actual value (NAV) of the underlying shares and profits can no longer be made from arbitrage.

Every ETF has several authorized participants who compete with each other for business, ensuring transparency and keeping profits within reasonable margins. The Depository Trust Clearing Corporation (DTC), the United States government agency that records securities transactions, provides oversight.

Chapter 4

o o o o o

Anatomy of an ETF

The Investment Company Act of 1940, often referred to as the 40 Act, was passed by Congress to regulate the mutual funds industry and restore investor confidence in the stock market. It mandated regular reporting procedures for mutual funds, established minimum requirements for diversification, set standards for advertising, and gave the SEC oversight. The 40 Act made it a legal requirement that each investment company disclose the material details of its operation and provide public information about its financial health.

Two types of ETFs are organized under the 40 Act: unit investment trusts (UITs) and regulated investment companies (RICs). Both types of funds are eligible to pass taxes on capital gains, dividends, or interest payments on to individual investors.

UITs: SPDRs S&P 500 Trust

The first ETF to be sold in the American market, the SPDRs S&P 500 Trust (symbol: SPY) is organized as a UIT (unit investment trust). It is a nonmanaged entity; the manager of the fund has no discretion in selecting which securities go into the fund and which do not. The fund must own all the securities, which are tracked by the S&P 500 Index. None of the stocks in the S&P 500 can be excluded from, and no additional stocks outside that index can be included in, the fund. Dividends paid by stocks held in the fund are not reinvested to buy additional shares but are placed in a non-interest-bearing escrow account and distributed to shareholders on a quarterly basis.

Fund managers are allowed some flexibility to make practical decisions — such as when to buy and sell stocks — aimed at maintaining a balance of underlying securities, which reflects the S&P 500 Index as closely as possible. A trustee oversees the execution of the managers' strategies and ensures that they are in compliance with the 40 Act.

Since its inception in 1993, the SPDRs S&P 500 Trust has remained the most popular ETF. As of November 30, 2007, it held almost $74 billion in assets, with almost 477 million shares outstanding.

UITs dissolve on a mandatory termination date, ranging from 1 to 30 years, established when the UIT is created. However, some UITs may terminate more than 50 years after they are created.

Regulated Investment Companies: RICs

Most ETFs are structured as regulated investment companies (RICs). The manager of a RIC is not required to hold all the stocks in an index but can select sample stocks from the index and then optimize the portfolio so that it follows the performance of the index it is tracking as closely as possible. The manager of a RIC may also add securities, including other stocks, bonds, futures, options, and other derivatives, that are not included in the index, to the portfolio. A RIC can hold bonds and other illiquid assets that could not ordinarily be included in a fund, and it can compensate by selecting other tradable bonds to track the performance of an index, such as the Lehman Brothers Aggregate Bond Market Index.

When dividends are paid by underlying stock, a RIC manager can reinvest these funds in the purchase of additional securities, rather than leaving the cash idle in an escrow account. Dividends are paid out to the shareholders on a quarterly basis.

An ETF structured as a RIC is allowed to participate in securities lending programs as a means of generating extra revenue to offset the expenses of administering the fund. These expenses often cause the performance of an ETF to lag behind the index it is tracking. Under the RIC structure, an ETF can also file as a nondiversified fund to track a specialized market. (A UIT cannot invest more than 50 percent of its holdings in a specialized industry or sector.)

The oversight of a RIC is carried out by a board of directors, elected by authorized participants, who hold shares as part of a creation unit, and by the individual ETF shareholders.

The discretion allowed to a RIC manager in selecting securities for the fund portfolio can be a disadvantage. If the manager's strategy is unsuccessful, the fund may develop discrepancies with its underlying index and no longer track it accurately.

Vanguard ETFs (VIPERs)

Vanguard has patented the concept of an ETF that is a separate share class of an existing open-ended mutual fund: Vanguard ETFs are RICs. Vanguard's first ETF, Vanguard Index Participation Equity Receipts (VIPERs), was linked to its existing Total Stock Market Index Fund. This structure allows short-term investors to buy and sell shares of its index funds on the stock market instead of incurring expenses and capital gains by obliging the fund managers to sell the fund's securities to meet redemption requests. Vanguard dropped the name "VIPERs" in 2007.

Vanguard ETFs are exceptionally low-cost but may incur capital gains taxes because the Internal Revenue Service requires that capital gains generated by other shareholders be distributed across all share classes of a mutual fund. The ETF improves the tax efficiency of the fund as a whole because short-term investors buy and sell ETF shares instead of requiring the fund to sell its underlying stocks every time they make a trade.

Exchange Traded Notes (ETNs)

Exchange traded notes (ETNs) are debt obligations issued by a bank, which promises to pay investors the total return of a specific index or benchmark, minus annual fees, when the note matures. Ownership of shares in an ETN does not represent ownership of securities tracked by the index. The bank may invest in the index, or it may choose to invest the funds in other assets. ETNs do not pay interest or offer protection of principal. They simply pay the return of the specific index that is being tracked.

ETNs, like ETFs, trade on stock exchanges; their returns are linked to a market index; and they can be shorted like stocks. Investors in ETNs sell their shares for cash. They do not receive any interest or any dividends from securities in the index. This could make ETNs more tax efficient than ETFs because an investor incurs no capital gains until the ETN shares are sold or redeemed.

Barclay's Bank PLC released the first series of iPaths exchange traded notes in 2006. Purchasers of iPath ETN shares can hold them until the note matures after 30 years or sell their shares on the secondary market. Once a week, units of 50,000 or more ETN shares can be redeemed for cash. If the price of the ETN shares on the stock market drops below their cash value, institutional investors or market makers can buy them and redeem them for a profit. This arbitrage process keeps the ETN market price in line with intraday values of the index they are tracking.

An ETN guarantees the same return as its index, but it carries credit risk, or the risk that the bank issuing the notes might fail and default on payment. An ETF carries the risk that the fund's returns might not match the returns of the index because of tracking error. Both ETNs and ETFs carry the risk that the index they track might have negative returns over time, resulting in the loss of capital.

HOLDRs: Exchange Traded Grantor Trusts

A grantor trust is organized under the Securities Act of 1933 as a nonmanaged investment pool. A basket of securities is selected from an index, and the securities are equal-weighted, meaning that the same number of shares of each stock is placed in the trust. Shares are traded on the stock exchanges like shares of ETFs. The trust is never rebalanced, and the stocks it holds are never updated as the index changes.

Grantor trusts are structured so that shareholders are treated as actual owners of the stocks held by the fund. Cash dividends paid by the stocks in a grantor trust are immediately paid out to investors instead of being held until the end of each quarter. Investors retain voting rights in the stocks and receive annual reports. Individual investors can redeem shares of a grantor trust and receive actual stock certificates for each company.

An example of grantor trusts are Holding Company Depository Receipts (HOLDRs), a series of investment trusts indexed to various narrow industry sectors, launched by Merrill Lynch early in 2000; 20 large stocks were initially selected for each HOLDR. Owners of HOLDRs retain voting rights in the stocks held by the fund and receive annual reports for each of the 20 holdings. Individual investors can turn in 100 units in exchange for the underlying stocks, allowing them to sell individual stocks rather than just shares of the fund. There are no management costs, but an annual fee of $2 per 100 units is paid to the Bank of New York from stock dividends.

HOLDRs offer an additional tax advantage because investors can avoid capital gains tax by redeeming their shares for the underlying stocks instead of selling the shares outright. They can then choose which stocks to sell and which ones to keep to reduce tax liability.

A disadvantage of grantor trusts is that their holdings eventually become less diversified, as some companies grow larger and as others are sold or go out of business.

Investment Trusts: StreetTRACKS Gold Trust

Many commodity ETFs are organized as investment trusts under the Securities Act of 1933. An investment trust may hold stocks, bonds, hard assets such as precious metals, or derivatives such as commodity futures. Individual investors do not have voting rights and cannot redeem their shares for the underlying assets. Shares are traded on the stock exchanges.

StreetTRACKS Gold Trust (GLD) is an example of an investment trust. It is sponsored by World Gold Trust Services LLC and marketed by State Street Global Markets. Its trustee, the Bank of New York, holds gold bullion for the trust. Authorized participants can deposit "baskets" of gold worth 100,000 shares of GLD in exchange for shares to sell on the open market. They can also redeem a basket of 100,000 shares of GLD for gold. When the price of GLD shares deviates from the actual price of gold bullion, this process allows authorized participants to earn a profit while bringing the prices back into line. The investment objective of GLD is to follow the performance of the price of gold bullion, minus expenses.

Investors profit by buying GLD shares when the price of gold is low and selling when it is high as well as by owning gold, which is considered a hedge against inflation. Ownership of GLD shares has a tax disadvantage; gold is considered a collectible by the IRS, and profit from the sale of GLD is taxed at the long-term capital gains rate of 28 percent instead of the normal capital gains rate of 15 percent.

Types of ETFs	SEC Regis- tration Act	Role of Manager	Type of Risk	Pays Divid- ends	Divid- ends Rein- vested	Allows redemp tion in kind
Unit Investment Trust (UIT)	1940	Has restricted discretion; fund must contain all stocks in index	Tracking error	Some- times	No	No
Regulated Investment Compan- ies (RICs)	1940	Has discretion to sample and optimize	Tracking error	Some- times	Yes	No
RIC Vanguard ETFs	1940	ETF is a share class of an actively managed mutual index fund	Tracking error	Some- times	Yes	No
Exchange Traded Notes (ETNs)	1933	None	Credit risk	No	Included in calcul- ation of returns	No

Types of ETFs	SEC Registration Act	Role of Manager	Type of Risk	Pays Dividends	Dividends Reinvested	Allows redemption in kind
Investment Trusts	1933	Manager has discretion in fulfilling investment objectives	Tracking error	Sometimes	No	No
Exchange Traded Grantor Trusts	1933	Non-managed after initial selection of securities	Tracking error	Sometimes	No	Yes

TAKE NOTE: ALL ETFS ARE NOT ALIKE

Be wary of ETF hype. Investment Web sites and literature often oversimplify the benefits of owning ETFs and make extravagant promises. You can only succeed in investing with ETFs if you understand what you are buying. ETFs are only as rewarding as the assets they hold. There are differences in the ways ETFs are structured. Some ETFs pay dividends or interest. Some grow in value because of increasing returns, and some grow because the prices of their underlying assets increase. Some investments are more tax-efficient than others. Before you jump in, study the prospectus and understand the type of investment you are making.

Chapter 5

o o o o o

What Are the Advantages of ETFs?

Diversification

Exchange traded funds represent an assortment of securities selected from a particular index, or benchmark. Their objective is to follow the market performance of the index as a whole. An investor purchasing a share in an ETF is purchasing a share of a whole basket of stocks instead of placing all his or her capital in the shares of a single company. The market price of an individual stock is affected by countless factors apart from the actual value of the company itself. Economic news, predictions about the future, news of natural disasters and political conflicts in other parts of the world, and the beliefs and emotions of other investors cause prices to fluctuate constantly. A company that has been doing well for years can suddenly encounter difficulties and plunge in value, causing its shareholders to lose a large part of their capital. Investing in an ETF offers individual investors the same kind of safety cushion that is available to large investors with expansive portfolios.

An ETF makes it easy to diversify a portfolio by adding exposure to an entire market sector, style, or asset class with a single purchase. Broad market index ETFs, such as the SPDRs S&P 500 Trust (SPY), are still the most popular, ETFs tracking a wide spectrum of investment styles, geographical regions, and market sectors are available. The newest ETFs follow highly specialized market indexes. It is possible to add bonds and Treasury notes (T-notes) to your portfolio by purchasing fixed-income ETFs, though they are not nearly as numerous as those tracking the equity markets. ETFs also offer participation in the ownership of hard assets, such as gold, and in commodity futures trading.

Transparency

By definition, an ETF is required to make available at all times information about the underlying stocks that it holds. A share of an ETF represents a share in the ownership of specific securities, and the investor can, at any time, look at a prospectus online or request a printed copy of a prospectus, which shows exactly which stocks are included in the ETF and what fees and expenses are incurred by the fund. ETF shares are traded on the stock market throughout the day, and an investor can watch prices and track the intraday value of the fund. The exchange on which an ETF is trading is responsible for calculating its estimated NAV — the actual value of its underlying securities — throughout the day. The estimated NAV of all ETFs is calculated every 15 seconds and is posted on a number of stock exchange and investment Web sites, including those of the ETF companies. The NAV of an ETF is not necessarily the market price of an ETF, but it indicates the estimated price at which the ETF should be selling. Investors can easily detect when an ETF is selling at a premium (the market price is higher than the actual value of the ETF) or selling at a discount (the market price is lower than the actual value of the ETF) and make investment decisions accordingly.

Mutual funds are notoriously vague about their holdings because fund managers do not wish to publicly disclose their trademark investment strategies. Over time, fund managers may make investment decisions that significantly change the character of their fund, a phenomenon known as "style drift." Investors may be unaware that the actual holdings of the funds no longer reflect their stated objectives and that the asset allocations in their portfolios have been affected. ETFs such as S&P 500 SPDRs, which are organized as UITs, are strictly required to maintain holdings that reflect the composition of the index they are tracking. ETFs organized as RICs contain only a representative sampling of the securities tracked by the index and can be manipulated to accommodate difficulties, such as illiquid assets, but are still required to publish a daily account of all their holdings.

Even the actively managed ETFs launched by PowerShares in April 2008, which follow the investment strategies of active fund managers, list their holdings daily on the PowerShares Web site.

Lower Fees and Commissions

After an ETF has been set up, it is "passively managed." It simply aims to maintain the same composition as the index it is tracking by occasionally adding or selling off shares of its underlying stocks. The portfolios of actively managed mutual funds experience a high turnover of stocks and bonds as their managers strive to execute investment strategies, generating additional expenses, such as trading costs for buying and selling stocks and bonds on the stock exchange (estimated to average about 0.08 percent). Managers of actively managed mutual funds must keep some cash out of circulation to use in executing trades; the "opportunity cost" of maintaining this cash reserve instead of investing it is estimated to be around 0.04 percent.

In addition to commissions, many mutual funds have "load" or "exit" fees, amounts that an investor pays to enter or exit the fund, which must be subtracted when calculating returns from an investment. Shares of an ETF are not sold directly by the company sponsoring it, but they are sold through a brokerage on the open market. To purchase or sell shares in an ETF, an investor pays a single, low transaction fee to the brokerage. The brokerage does the work of bookkeeping and customer service, keeping administration costs for the fund low.

Because an ETF is linked to an index and is not actively managed, it is not paying the salaries of market analysts and active fund managers, only a licensing fee to the provider of the index (such as S&P).

Tax Efficiency

ETFs are tax-efficient because they are structured to minimize capital gains tax. If a mutual fund sells some of its assets for a profit, the individual investors in that fund are required to pay capital gains tax (about 15 percent in most cases) even if the fund as a whole loses value during the year. An individual investor who owns shares of an ETF is not liable for capital gains tax if the underlying securities are sold by the fund for a profit because those securities are effectively owned by a third party. When an authorized provider (AP) creates or redeems shares of an ETF, it performs an in-kind exchange, not a cash transaction, with the ETF sponsor.

ETFs are not tax-free. Securities held by an ETF may pay dividends, which are taxable. An investor pays capital gains tax when he or she sells shares of an ETF at a higher price than he or she paid for them, unless the ETFs are held in a tax-free or tax-deferred account, such as an Individual Retirement Account (IRA).

ETFs can also be used to carry out strategies to reduce taxes; look for an explanation of tax-loss harvesting in "Chapter 19: Special Uses of ETFs."

Ease of Purchase

ETF shares can be bought and sold anywhere, and shares of ETFs from different providers can be managed in a single brokerage account. Comparable low-cost index mutual funds are often available only from a single provider so that an investor who wishes to hold more than one index mutual fund in his or her portfolio has to maintain several separate accounts. Some index mutual funds charge a substantial "load fee" to initiate an investment. International ETFs allow U.S. investors to buy into foreign markets using U.S. dollars by making simple transactions through a U.S. brokerage.

Investor Strategies

Shares of ETFs are sold on the stock exchanges throughout the day and can be employed in all the investment strategies that are used with stocks: options, buying on margin, market timing, hedging, and leveraging. This has made them a popular investment vehicle with investors of all types. Long-term investors benefit from the diversity and low costs of ETFs, while active traders are able to speculate with entire market sectors rather than the stocks of individual companies.

TAKE NOTE: YOU ARE RESPONSIBLE

All the advantages offered by ETFs are only beneficial if you, as an investor, use them in the right way. Easy access to detailed information about ETFs and their estimated intraday values may tempt an investor to trade too frequently and run up trading fees, which eat into returns. It is your responsibility to read the prospectus of each fund and determine whether it fits your investment goals. Some ETFs have a relatively high expense ratio, which should be taken into consideration.

Chapter 6

○ ○ ○ ○ ○

ETFs and Mutual Funds

Although many ETFs are registered as open-ended mutual funds, ETF companies have agreed with the SEC not to advertise or market their products as mutual funds. Shares of an ETF are offered to investors on the stock exchanges by third-party authorized participants who deal directly with the fund company. Because investors in ETFs do not deal directly with the mutual fund companies, the SEC has decided that ETF shares should not be called mutual funds in any marketing materials.

Management

Mutual funds are managed by professional fund managers, highly trained specialists who use various types of market analysis to select and manage investments. Surprisingly, statistics show that mutual funds have produced lower returns than indexed funds and significantly lower returns over time than many of the larger indexes themselves. Why? No fund manager can be right all the time. While one transaction might result in a substantial gain, it can be easily offset by losses on another security. Also, fees on stock transactions and the commissions charged by fund managers consume a portion of the returns, resulting over time in less income for the investor.

ETFs are created to replicate an index, and they require relatively little management. Securities are bought and sold only to rebalance the fund portfolio so that it continues to track the index, keeping expenses low. The new, actively managed ETFs may be an exception.

ETFs Trade on the Stock Exchanges

An investor buys shares of an open-ended mutual fund directly from the company that manages the fund or through a broker. The fund receives money from the investor and issues new, open-ended shares. Shares of an ETF, on the other hand, trade directly on the stock market and are bought and sold by investors, not by the fund company. Shares of ETFs are purchased through a brokerage on the stock exchanges. An individual investor is purchasing ETF shares that already exist in another investor's portfolio. An investor wishing to purchase shares in several mutual funds may have to open accounts with two or three mutual fund companies. Shares of numerous ETFs can be held in a single brokerage account.

Tax Liability

When an investor cashes out of a mutual fund, the fund must sell the underlying shares of stock and deliver the cash to the investor. If those shares sell for more than their original purchase price, the investor must pay capital gains tax on the difference. All investors in a mutual fund are liable for capital gains tax on securities sold by the fund during the year, even if the total returns of the fund have been negative for that year. During most years, an investor who owns an ETF pays capital gains tax only on the sale of the ETF shares; however, there are some exceptions.

Calculation of Net Asset Value (NAV)

A mutual fund company issues new shares and settles all transactions at the end of the business day. The price of the mutual fund for that day is its NAV, calculated by adding the current market value of the fund's underlying securities and any cash or other assets it holds, subtracting fund liabilities, and dividing the result by the number of outstanding shares. The NAV is the price at which shares of the fund are bought and sold for that day.

$$\frac{\text{Underlying value of assets held by a fund}}{\text{Number of shares outstanding}} = \text{Net Asset Value (NAV)}$$

ETF shares are bought and sold on the stock market all day long at varying prices. The true NAV of all ETFs is calculated once a day, after the markets have closed, but an estimated NAV of all ETFs is calculated by the stock exchanges and posted every 15 minutes. This intraday value estimate may not coincide with the market price of an ETF for various reasons. The value of some of the underlying securities may not be readily available because they trade in another time zone or because they have not traded that day. It could also be that the market price of an ETF is a more accurate assessment of the value placed on the underlying securities by investors than the prices at which those securities last traded. ETFs normally trade at a discount or premium to their intraday value.

Settlement Period

ETFs have a longer settlement period than open-ended mutual funds, whose purchase or sale is often transacted on the next business day. The account for the sale or purchase of ETFs is not settled until three business days after the order is placed. This may create difficulties for an investor wishing to sell ETFs and buy securities on the same day because funds from the sale of the ETF will not become available until three days later.

Trading Symbols

Symbols for open-ended mutual funds are five letters, ending in X. Symbols for ETFs are three letters if they trade on the New York Stock Exchange (NYSE) or the American Stock Exchange (AMEX). They are four letters, ending in Q, if they trade over-the-counter on the NASDAQ.

Disadvantages of Investing in Mutual Funds

The average investor in a mutual fund does not have the skill and inside knowledge to take advantage of the potential benefits mutual funds offer, and regularly achieves a rate of return much lower than that of the stock market at large. Mutual fund investors may sometimes pay a high fee to have their investments actively managed because they do not have a clear understanding of the fund's components. They also tend to invest in a fund when a particular sector is receiving glowing publicity in the media, after its price has already risen, and to sell when a sector turns cold, forfeiting the opportunity to profit from a later upturn. Commissions and fees also eat into the returns generated by mutual funds by reducing the amount of cash available for reinvestment.

Are ETFs for Me?

ETFs have many advantages that make them attractive investments, such as low costs, transparency, tax efficiency, and the ease with which they can be purchased and sold. However, this does not mean that you should sell all your mutual funds and replace them with ETFs. Many low-cost index mutual funds offer respectable returns. Several factors should be considered in the decision to invest in ETFs.

How Much Do You Plan to Invest?

How much are you investing, and how often? Each time you purchase or sell shares of an ETF, you pay a brokerage fee of between $10 and $20. $10 is 0.5 percent of $2,000; consequently, the cost of buying and selling $2,000 worth of ETF shares would amount to 1 percent of your investment, a substantial cut of your returns. However, if you are investing $15,000, trading fees would amount to only 0.14 percent of your total investment, a much more worthwhile proposition. A mutual fund that charges a one-time entry fee (load fee) or charges higher management fees is still a better investment for someone who plans to invest small amounts regularly over time. If you are investing larger sums at longer intervals, an ETF is an attractive investment.

What Type of Investor Are You?

The ability to check prices and to buy and sell shares of an ETF throughout the day on the stock exchange is useful for an active investor, such as a day trader or an institutional investment manager, but it is meaningless to the average investor who is executing a "buy-and-hold" strategy and who reviews his portfolio once or twice a month. Still, the low cost, diversity, and tax efficiency of ETFs make them attractive to long-term investors and provide a quick means of filling in gaps in a portfolio or adding exposure to a new sector.

Liquidity

How soon will you need access to your money? How much can you afford to invest? In calculating returns from an ETF, it is important to consider the trading fees for buying and selling the investment and also the expense ratios. If you sell shares of an ETF only a short time after buying them, you may get a lower rate of return than if you simply purchased a short-term Certificate of Deposit.

Over time, the higher management fees of a mutual fund would surpass the one-time trading costs of buying an ETF with lower management fees. However, if you intend to buy $1,000 worth of shares and sell them two years later, the mutual fund is most likely a better choice.

Overall, a portfolio composed entirely of ETFs is cost-effective only if you plan to invest more than $50,000. If your investment capital is less than $50,000, a mix of mutual funds and ETFs is a better choice.

TAKE NOTE: WATCH YOUR TRADING COSTS

ETFs have many characteristics that make them attractive investment tools. Before you rush to buy ETFs, though, take a careful look at your investment strategy and at the expense ratios and trading costs in relation to the expected returns. If you plan to regularly invest small amounts over a long period, an ETF may not be the best option.

CASE STUDY: JOE FICALORA

Joe Ficalora is Vice President of Technology for Sigma Breakthrough Technologies, Inc. (**www.sbtionline.com**). The following is an excerpt from Mr. Ficalora's "Exchange Traded Funds."

ETFs are more volatile, may rise and fall faster than an index mutual fund, and may need more of your time to actively manage them. In effect, you are purchasing a piece of a pre-set group of stocks representing a certain slice of the market. You have the advantages of stocks for higher returns with some amount of diversification. These may have better overall return than a mutual fund in the short term and cost less, as they are not actively managed like a mutual fund. However, since ETFs are traded like stocks and other securities, commissions are charged. So, to be fair, expense-adjusted returns must be used when making comparisons to index mutual funds or other types of investment vehicles. A typical ETF may have an expense fee of 0.4 percent of assets, while the average mutual fund fees are 1.4 percent, or three times higher. This makes ETFs attractive for the long-term, buy-and-hold investor.

ETFs may be shorted, or bought on low margins, and may be bought or sold throughout the trading day. When breaking news occurs in your selected market sector, good or bad, you have the opportunity to quickly change your investment position, unlike a mutual fund. ETFs exist for market indexes like the Dow Jones Industrials, NASDAQ composite, real estate investment trusts (REITs), large U.S. companies, small U.S. companies, and even gold. If there is a particular market sector you have researched or of which you are intimately knowledgeable, chances are you can invest in ETFs that will allow knowledge and savvy timing to be turned into profits. If index investing or buying part or all of the market is in your strategy, ETFs may be right for you.

Disadvantages of ETFs

The primary disadvantage of ETFs over mutual funds is one of increased volatility, or

CASE STUDY: JOE FICALORA

increased risks in a market or sector downturn. A secondary disadvantage of ETFs is the cost of trading commissions. These can be minimized with online brokers, which generally have lower security buy-and-sell commissions.

Potential ETF Strategies:

- For investors with accounts likely to be managed with a "buy-and-hold" strategy, ETFs offer advantages because they have lower cost over a long term, yielding a better overall return on the investment.

- If you are interested in broad market investing, ETFs offer a simple and convenient way to "buy the market" at lower cost than mutual funds. Many indexes tend to equal or exceed managed fund returns, which have higher operating expenses as well.

- Many mutual funds have a minimum entry purchase amount. These initial amounts can be a barrier, as some exceed thousands of dollars. ETFs offer a way to get into indexing for smaller investors or those just getting started.

- For the sector-focused investor or specialty-focused investor, chances are there is an ETF that is available with the right focus. A technology-focused ETF, for example, would allow a tech-savvy investor to time his or her investments and withdrawals around the technology sector's ups and downs. If you have great and current knowledge in a key sector, specialty-focused ETFs can allow you to turn that knowledge into profits.

- Some investment sectors provide returns that must be timed well in order to lock in profits. Quick turns on the investing road require investment vehicles that can be bought or sold quickly like stocks; ETFs provide this flexibility to timing-sensitive sectors.

Chapter 7

○ ○ ○ ○ ○

The Indexes

Every ETF is designed to track the performance of a particular index, which is specified when the fund creators apply for approval from the SEC. An index is a method used to measure the performance of a financial market. You are perhaps familiar with two of the most famous indexes because they are mentioned every day in the stock market news: the Dow Jones Industrial Average and the S&P 500. An index takes the prices of a selection of stocks and applies a formula to gauge the relative performance of the stock market and the economy as a whole, or of a particular industry or market sector. ETFs and mutual funds attempt to duplicate the performance of an index by purchasing all the securities included in that index and holding them over a specific period.

An ETF provider may pay a fee to license a well-known, established index from a company such as S&P or Dow Jones, or it may design a customized index to track a specific market sector or commodity. The use of an established index attracts the confidence of investors, who can analyze the past performance of that index when making decisions. Fund sponsors who design their own indexes are required by the SEC to designate a third party to monitor the fund's compliance with its stated investment objectives.

Difference Between an Index and a Fund

For several reasons, an ETF or a mutual fund can never duplicate the performance of an index exactly. An index is simply a measurement tool, using existing data to measure the performance of a particular market. A fund has operating expenses, such as licensing fees and administration costs, which must be subtracted from its returns. ETFs organized as UITs are required to hold dividends paid by underlying stocks in non-interest-bearing escrow accounts so that they cannot be reinvested to earn additional returns. RICs, on the other hand, are permitted to utilize dividends until they are due to be paid out and to participate in securities lending programs to generate extra revenue, which helps to pay the fund's expenses. A fund that tracks futures or commodities or that tracks an index containing thinly traded stocks, illiquid securities, or bonds may encounter periods of discrepancy with the index until the fund manager can adjust the portfolio to compensate for the difference. Securities trading on foreign stock exchanges in different time zones may make significant moves up or down while stock exchanges in the United States are closed for business.

Two Different Animals: Market Indexes and Custom Indexes

There are two basic types of indexes: market indexes and custom indexes. Market indexes follow the broad price levels and value of a specific financial market. A custom index is more like an investment strategy, a method for managing a portfolio that is used as the basis of an ETF or mutual fund.

Market Indexes

The earliest market index was the Dow Jones Average, first published on May 26, 1896. It was an average of the stock prices of 12 companies representing major American industries. Only one of those companies, General Electric, is still included among the 30 companies that comprise the Dow Jones Average today. Many economists criticize the Dow Jones Average for being primitive and for giving too much weight (importance) to higher-priced stocks. In the mid-1900s, value-weighted methods for measuring financial markets were introduced. A value-weighted measure multiplies the stock price of a security by its number of outstanding shares. Value-weighted measures are used around the world to gauge market levels and values.

Market indexes track the changes in value and price of a broad range of securities representing a specific financial market. Securities in the index are selected and weighted according to the natural state of the market; automatic, unbiased criteria are used to select a sampling of securities, and each one is weighted according to its market value relative to all the other securities in the index. Market indexes are used as financial indicators all over the world, not only by the financial markets, but also by academic researchers and by government entities, such as the United States Federal Reserve. Market indexes are the benchmarks used by institutional and private investors in judging the performance of their portfolios and in the management of index funds.

STYLES AND SECTORS

Broad market indexes take a representative sample of the entire financial market. Broad market indexes are frequently divided into smaller indexes, representing styles, industry sectors, or types. A style is a group of securities classified according to certain shared characteristics, such as the value of outstanding shares (capitalization) or whether a company's stock is considered to be a growth or a value investment. Market sectors include the stocks of companies operating in a particular geographic region or of companies involved in a particular field, such as technology, healthcare, real estate, or energy. Types single out specific investment vehicles, such as corporate bonds and mortgages. The smaller indexes combined equal the broad market index.

Custom Indexes

Custom indexes are designed to achieve a specific investment strategy. This is accomplished by using a specified methodology to select the securities to be included in the index, by a method of modified security weighting, or both. While market indexes are created to measure and track the financial market, and can be used for research and analysis, custom indexes are created primarily as financial products. The providers of customized indexes are concerned with rules-based management of investment products. Their methodologies are so diverse that little academic research is done on their performance. Market indexes can be studied and analyzed using a vast public history of economic data. The data available for custom indexes is provided mostly by the companies creating them, who receive licensing fees from investment management companies, such as the sponsors of ETFs.

TAKE NOTE: CUSTOM INDEXES HAVE DIFFERENT RISKS AND RETURNS

Market indexes track a broad range of passively selected, capitalization-weighted securities. Custom indexes are rules-based investment strategies. ETF firms sometimes promote ETFs based on custom indexes by inferring that the old definition of a market index is outdated or inferior. A custom index is specifically designed not to track the broad market. The risk and returns of an ETF tracking a custom index are different from those of an ETF tracking a broad market index. An investor should be aware of these differences when choosing ETFs to match his or her own investment goals.

Weighting

After the individual securities have been selected for an index, various methodologies are used to determine how many shares of each will be included. Weighting is the method used to determine the weight, or influence, of an individual stock in an index. Several types of weighting are used in indexes: capitalization weighting, price weighting, equal weighting, equal-dollar weighting, and weighting according to fundamentals.

Capitalization Weighting

In capitalization weighting, the share price of each stock is multiplied by the total number of outstanding shares of that stock. This method gives more weight to large-cap (large capitalization) stocks, which have large numbers of outstanding shares, than to small- or mid-cap stocks; it also gives more weight to higher-priced stocks. Capitalization weighting is used for the majority of indexes. There are four types of capitalization weighting: full cap, free-float, liquidity, and capped.

- **Full cap** weighting is calculated using the total number of outstanding shares of a particular stock.

- **Free-float** weighting considers only the number of shares available for sale on the market and disregards shares that are out of circulation because they are held by company employees or pension funds.

- **Liquidity** weighting goes even further; it is based on the number of shares that actually trade regularly on the market, disregarding shares that are held by private investors for long periods or shares of a thinly traded, emerging market.

- **Capped**: When one or more of the securities in a free-float index are dominant because large numbers of its shares are available on the market, the weight of those dominant securities may be capped at a certain percentage, and the remaining "weight" is allocated proportionately to the other securities in the index.

Price Weighting

In price weighting, a stock's share price determines its influence in an index with no regard for its number of outstanding shares. In a price-weighted index, a small company with expensive shares would outweigh a large company with low-priced shares.

Equal Weighting

All stocks receive the same weight in the index, regardless of share price or the number of shares outstanding.

Equal-Dollar Weighting

The index is constructed as though the same amount of money had been invested in each stock. Expensive stocks would have less weight than low-priced shares because more shares of the low-priced stock could be bought for the same amount of money.

Fundamental Selection and Weighting

After value stocks performed well between 2000 and 2006, fundamental selection and weighting methods were introduced to create a strong bias toward value stocks in an index. Value stocks are those whose prices are considered low in relation to the actual value of the company. Fundamental weighting uses factors other than market capitalization to determine the weight of securities in an index. Stocks are selected and weighted according to data from the companies' financial reports or other quantifiable characteristics, which are associated with a company's potential for success.

Fundamental weighting may use a single factor, such as the dividend yield of each company, to assign weight, or it may use a complex equation incorporating several factors. Weight may also be assigned to companies according to some social or political rating, such as their degree of commitment to environmental protection, involvement in the community, or human rights record.

FACTORS OFTEN USED IN FUNDAMENTAL WEIGHTING

Dividend growth rate
Dividend yield
Earnings growth rate
Earnings yield
Estimate change momentum
Number of employees
Price momentum
Price-to-book ratio

Price-to-cash flow ratio
Price-to-earnings ratio
Price-to-sales ratio
Ratio of employees to sales
Ratio of number of employees to earnings
Return on equity
Social responsibility ratings
Stock price

Fundamental weighting requires periodic rebalancing to keep the index in line with changing fundamental conditions. This rebalancing is accompanied by a large turnover of stocks in the index, which can incur substantial trading costs for an ETF and reduce its tax efficiency.

What Makes a Good Index?

The Chartered Financial Analysts (CFA) Institute, an organization with more than 83,000 members worldwide, advocates fair and transparent capital markets and sets a high standard of ethics and education. In 1990, the CFA Institute published a set of guidelines for market indexes:

- **Simple and objective selection criteria:** The inclusion of securities, markets, or bonds in the index should be governed by a clear set of rules. Based on these rules, investors should easily be able to forecast and agree on changes in the composition of the index when the markets change.

- **Comprehensive:** An index should be made up of all the securities that fit the criteria of the index and are available for purchase to all investors under normal market conditions. Prices of securities in the index should be frequently updated so that their value can be computed accurately.

- **Replicable:** Market participants should be able to replicate the total returns reported by the index, using readily available information about the composition and historical returns of the index. Over time, an index should represent a realistic baseline strategy that a passive investor could have followed.

- **Stability:** The index should maintain its composition consistently, and any changes to it should be predictable and easily understood by investors familiar with the market. The index should not be subject to opinion-driven fluctuations. However, its composition should change, when necessary, to reflect the market. An index is intended to provide a passive benchmark.

- **Relevance:** An index should track the markets and market segments that are of the greatest interest and relevance to investors.

- **Free of barriers to entry:** The components of an index should be free of significant barriers to entry. For example, an international index should not include a country that has regulations against foreign participation in its equity market.

- **Expenses:** The expenses associated with investing in a particular market or market sector should be consistent and clearly understood and accounted for so that they do not interfere with the index's measurement of market performance.

BEST INDEXES FOR ETFS

An ideal index for an ETF should have:

- **Broad diversity:** The index should consist of a variety of stocks and should not be dominated by a small number of large companies to protect a passive investor against risk associated with the downturn of a single stock.

- **Low index turnover:** The composition of an index should change infrequently to avoid trading expenses for the ETF tracking it and to ensure that the index maintains its investment objectives.

- **Capitalization weighting:** An ETF is intended to reflect the behavior of a particular market or market segment. Capitalization weighting provides the most realistic approximation of actual market conditions.

- **Strict rules for changing the composition of the index:** An ETF is structured to be passively managed, and its authorized participants (APs) are responsible for ensuring that the composition of the ETF mirrors the index it is tracking. Both APs and investors should be able to easily foresee any changes that will occur in the composition of the fund.

The Index Providers

The majority of indexes are created by a handful of major index providers.

Standard & Poor's (www.standardandpoors.com/indices)

Standard & Poor's, owned by McGraw-Hill, maintains hundreds of indexes, including the most famous market index of all, the Standard & Poor's 500. More ETFs are based on indexes provided by S&P than by any other provider. S&P indexes include those used by the Barclay's broad-based international ETFs, Select Sector SPDRs that track various market sectors, and the iShares S&P Growth and Value ETFs.

STANDARD & POOR'S 500

The Standard & Poor's 500 broad market index is classified as "passively selected" because it contains a large number of stocks, has a low rate of turnover, and correlates closely with the returns of competing indexes. The S&P 500 includes 500 major companies, most of which are American. The criterion for inclusion is that the company must be a leader in an important industry. Though the S&P indexes have strict rules to determine which companies will be included or deleted, the final decision is made by a team of analysts. The S&P 500 does not contain all the large-cap stocks in the market; about 10 percent of the stocks included in it are mid-cap companies.

STANDARD & POOR'S CUSTOMIZED INDEXES

The Equal Weighted S&P 500 comprises all the stocks in the S&P 500 Index in equal amounts, rather than weighting them by market capitalization. Rebalancing of the index is done each quarter. The Rydex S&P Equal Weight ETF (symbol: RSP) tracks this index.

The Standard & Poor's/Citigroup Pure Style Index Series uses a variety of factors to assign each company a growth or value score. About one-third of all companies are identified as pure growth and another third as pure value; the remainder is excluded. Each security is weighted according to its growth or value score, not according to its market capitalization.

Dow Jones and DJ Wilshire Equity Indexes (www.djindexes.com)

Dow Jones licenses over 3,000 market indexes, including the world's oldest stock indicator, the Dow Jones Industrial Average. ETFs based on Dow Jones indexes include iShares industry; sector ETFs; and streetTRACKS large-, mid-, and small-cap ETFs. Dow Jones publishes *The Wall Street Journal* and *Barron's*.

The Dow Jones Total Market Index, launched in 2000, represents the top 95 percent of the free-float value of the United States stock market. It follows a range of only 1,850 stocks, the smallest range for any index labeling itself "total market."

In 2004, Dow Jones partnered with Wilshire Associates, a privately owned investment firm and index provider, to increase its depth in the market. The DJ Wilshire 5000 Index, established in 1974, was the first U.S. equity index to track the return of the entire U.S. stock market. The DJ Wilshire 5000 includes all U.S.-headquartered securities with available price data; the actual number of stocks is not restricted to 5,000 and varies from week to week. An ETF benchmarked to the DJ Wilshire 5000 provides the broadest possible breadth of stocks in the United States markets. However, some of the smallest stocks cannot be included in an ETF because not enough of them are available for purchase by an authorized participant.

The Wilshire 4500, created in 1983, follows the performance of the small- and mid-cap stocks within the Wilshire 5000. It essentially excludes the securities in the S&P 500, providing an excellent study of the performance of the rest of the stock market in relation to the S&P 500.

DJ Wilshire Style Indexes separate the DJ Wilshire 5000 into four capitalization groups (large-, mid-, small-, and micro-cap) and then into growth and value indexes using six factors.

Morgan Stanley Capital International (www.morganstanley.com)

Morgan Stanley Capital International (MSCI) provides a wide variety of indexes. Its indexes underlie the domestic and international Vanguard ETFs and the Barclay iShares individual country ETFs.

MSCI indexes were created in 2003 when Vanguard was seeking an alternative to S&P indexes. MSCI defines "large-cap" as the 300 largest companies in the investable market, weighted by full market capitalization. Mid-cap is comprised of the next 450 companies, and small-cap of the remaining 1,750. A separate index combines the 750 large- and mid-cap companies. MSCI uses a system of buffer zones to transfer companies from one size category to another, minimizing portfolio stock turnover and thwarting front runners — traders who attempt to take advantage of index investors by jumping into the market just before a stock price moves up or down.

Russell U.S. Equity Indexes (www.russell.com/Indexes)

The Russell 3000 Index measures the performance of the 3,000 largest U.S. companies, based on total market capitalization, and represents 98 percent of the United States equity market. A number of Russell indexes are subsets of the Russell 3000, including the Russell 1000, tracking the 1,000 largest U.S. stocks, and the Russell 2000, tracking the next 2,000 largest U.S. stocks. The Russell Micro Cap Index is not a subset of the Russell 3000; it tracks the performance of stocks occupying the positions from 2,001 to 4,000 in order of size.

Russell indexes are used for more than a dozen of the iShares domestic ETFs and for the Rydex Russell Top 50 Index. The most popular is the iShares Russell 2000.

Russell indexes are reconstructed annually. Using market values on May 31 of every year, the largest 3,000 stocks are selected and ranked strictly according to size. Russell U.S. indexes are capitalization-weighted, representing only the free-float value of U.S. stocks rather than all outstanding shares. They include only companies headquartered in the United States and its territories.

Lehman Brothers (www.lehman.com)

Lehman Brothers is the leading provider of fixed-income benchmarks. Five of Barclay's fixed-income ETFs are based on Lehman Brothers indexes. Lehman Brothers produces some of the most widely followed benchmarks in the global debt markets, including the United States Aggregate, Euro Aggregate, Global Aggregate, and U.S. Universal Index.

Morningstar Indexes (www.morningstar.com)

Morningstar has 16 size and style indexes, based on the methodology used in their Morningstar Style Boxes, targeting 97 percent of the free-float U.S. equity market. Morningstar uses ten factors, five for growth and five for value, to define the style characteristics of a stock.

Morningstar defines large-cap as the largest 70 percent of the investable market cap, mid-cap as the next 20 percent, and small-cap as the next 7 percent. The final 3 percent are micro-cap stocks. Within these sizes, each stock is classified by style as value, growth, or core, depending on its value and growth scores. Stocks are reclassified only when they move sufficiently beyond the parameters that define size and style, and buffer zones are used to move stocks gradually among size and style categories.

Exchange-Specific Indexes

Exchange-specific indexes are custom indexes that track the stocks traded primarily on one particular stock exchange.

AMERICAN STOCK EXCHANGE (WWW.AMEX.COM)

The American Stock Exchange (AMEX) calculates and publishes a wide variety of indexes to support various index-based products, such as ETFs, index options, and structured products. It also provides third-party index calculation services for custom indexes.

NASDAQ (WWW.NASDAQ.COM)

The NASDAQ Composite index tracks only companies that trade primarily on the NASDAQ, and it is the basis for the Fidelity NASDAQ Composite ETF (symbol: ONEQ). The NASDAQ 100 tracks only companies that traded on the NASDAQ and excludes financial companies. PowerShares QQQ (symbol: QQQQ), which tracks the NASDAQ 100, is popular because of its emphasis on technology stocks and now has almost $20.5 billion invested in it. First Trust has two ETFs based on customized NASDAQ-100 indexes: an equal-weighted NASDAQ-100 (QQEW) and a NASDAQ-100 that specifically excludes the technology stocks (symbol:QQXT).

NEW YORK STOCK EXCHANGE (WWW.NYSE.COM)

The iShares NYSE Composite Index (symbol: NYC) tracks all the stocks that trade on the NYSE. The iShares NYSE 100 Index (symbol: NY) tracks the 100 largest companies on the NYSE.

Fundamental Selection and Weighting Indexes

RESEARCH-AFFILIATED FUNDAMENTAL INDEXES (RAFI)

FTSE Group (**www.ftse.com**) partnered with Research Affiliates to create RAFI indexes. They use a combination of several factors to rank securities in a passively selected basket and then assign a percentage to each security according to its rank.

DIVIDEND INDEXES

Wisdom Tree Dividend Indexes (**www.wisdomtree.com**) eliminate all stocks that do not pay a regular cash dividend and then weight the rest using dividend data. During 2007, there were 1,500 stocks (from a universe of 3,500) that paid dividends. Wisdom Tree ETFs track several indexes, which separate these 1,500 securities by size. Companies that pay higher dividends by cash value are given a higher percentage in each index.

S&P and Merchants also have dividend indexes. All the selection and weighting is based on dividend payments, but each index differs in the weight it gives to factors such as the relation of dividend payments to earnings and the length of time that a company has been paying dividends.

EARNINGS INDEXES

Wisdom Tree Earnings ETFs select companies according to their earnings over the past four quarters.

QUANTITATIVE INDEXES

Intellidex indexes, originally initiated by Bruce Bonds, the founder of PowerShares (**www.powershares.com**), are now maintained by AMEX, while PowerShares administers the Intellidex ETFs. Stocks are selected and reallocated every quarter. Twenty-five criteria are used to rank securities according to risk factors, momentum, fundamental growth, and stock valuation. The top-ranking securities are then selected for an index. A modified equal weighting system assigns a higher fixed weighting to the larger stocks and a lower percentage to the smaller stocks. A detailed description of the selection and weighting process is not available to investors or authorized providers.

First Trust AlphaDEX ETFs track a group of equity indexes created by S&P using an equally complicated methodology.

The Dow Jones Industrial Average (DJIA) is composed of 30 large U.S. companies. Although these companies are selected by a committee, the

DJIA is categorized as passive because the securities adequately represent the United States' large capitalization market. The selected securities are price-weighted. A small company with a high stock price carries more weight than a large company with a low stock price, giving the index a value bias. Several billion dollars have been invested in the Diamonds Trust (symbol: DIA), mostly by private investors.

The Dow Jones Select Micro-Cap Index tracks particularly small stocks trading on the United States stock exchanges with reasonable liquidity. It is a custom index that screens out the smallest stocks and those that exhibit poor operating profit margins, inadequate price-to-earnings or price-to-sales ratios, low earnings momentum, and poor performance when compared with other micro-caps.

Other Important Indexers

The S&P Goldman Sachs Commodity Index (GSCI) (**www2. goldmansachs.com**) tracks a broadly diversified, unleveraged, long-only investment in commodity futures. Individual components qualify for inclusion in the S&P GSCI on the basis of liquidity and are weighted by their respective world production quantities. It is the basis for a variety of commodity ETFs.

FTSE Group calculates over 100,000 indexes, covering more than 48 countries and all major asset classes. FTSE indexes provide the basis for a number of market-sector and geographic-sector ETFs.

Chapter 8

o o o o o

The ETF Providers

Barclays Global International

Barclays Global Investors (BGI) is one of the largest asset managers in the world, with more than $2 trillion in assets (June 2007) for over 2,900 clients in more than 50 countries around the world. BGI created the first index strategy in 1971 and the first quantitative active strategy in 1978. It is the global leader in assets and products in the exchange traded funds business, offering more than 190 funds, and is the world's second largest manager of U.S. institutional tax-exempt assets.

Barclays offers the iShares series of ETFs (**www.iShares.com**) and iPath ETNs (**www.ipathetn.com**). Barclays also manages Canadian ETFs (**www.iShares.ca**). iShares Canadian ETF information is managed by Barclays Global Investors.

Claymore Securities

Claymore Securities (**www.claymore.com/etfs**) manages $18.5 billion in assets and offers a lineup of ETFs that track key market segments and indexes that seek to best capture the investment potential of unique strategies.

Deutsche Bank

Partnering with PowerShares and State Street Global Advisors, Deutsche Bank (**www.dbcfund.db.com**) is the sponsor of a series of ETFs tracking indexes in commodity and currency futures.

Merrill Lynch

Merrill Lynch (**www.totalmerrill.com**) sponsors HOLDRS (**www.holdrs.com**), a group of unmanaged sector portfolios in which the investor retains ownership benefits related to the underlying stocks.

PowerShares

Invesco PowerShares Capital Management LLC (PowerShares.com) offers a family of 110 quantitative ETFs, including BLDRS (**www.adrbnymellon.com/bldrs_ overview.jsp**), a series of ETFs based on The Bank of New York ADR Index.

ProShares

ProShares (**www.proshares.com**) offers leveraged and inverse ETFs and is a unit of ProFunds Group.

Rydex

Rydex Investments (**www.rydexfunds.com**) offers a lineup of ETFs that track key market segments.

State Street Global Advisors

State Street Global Advisors (**www.ssgafunds.com**) manages a diverse lineup of ETFs tracking a variety of style and sector indexes. SPDR ETFs are managed by State Street Global Advisors.

Vanguard ETFs

Vanguard (**www.vanguard.com**) ETFs are a share class of Vanguard index mutual funds.

Wisdom Tree

Wisdom Tree (**www.wisdomtree.com**) offers ETFs that fundamentally select and weight global equities.

Other Suppliers

Ameristock Funds (**www.ameristock.com**) offers ETFs that track the Ryan Indexes, the first daily bond indexes, which follow the most recently auctioned Treasury securities.

ELEMENTS (**www.elementsetn.com**) are exchange traded notes designed to track the returns of commodity and currency indexes.

Fidelity Management & Research Company (**www.nasdaq.com/oneq**) manages the "ONEQ" ETF-tracking NASDAQ Composite Index, a market capitalization-weighted index representing the performance of over 3,000 stocks.

First Trust (**www.ftportfolios.com**) ETFs track market segments and fundamentally weighted, quantitative indexes.

FocusShares (**www.focusshares.com**) ETFs follow custom indexes intended to target "real world" events.

Greenhaven Commodity Services LLC sponsors the Greenhaven Continuous Commodity Index Fund (GCC), tracking the Continuous Commodity Total Return Index (CCI-TR), a basket of 17 commodities: wheat, corn, soybeans, live cattle, lean hogs, gold, silver, platinum, copper, cotton, coffee, cocoa, orange juice, sugar, crude oil, heating oil, and natural gas.

HealthShares, Inc. (**www.healthsharesinc.com**) offers themed ETFs in pharmaceuticals, health services, life sciences, and biotechnology.

Lehman Brothers (**www.optaetn.com**) offers ETNs tracking commodities, agriculture, and private equity.

NETS Trust (**www.northerntrust.com**) collaborates with Lehman Brothers and also offers the NETS DAX Index Fund (DAX), tracking the price and yield performance of the 30 largest and most actively traded companies in the German market.

RevenueShares Investor Services (**www.revenuesharesetfs.com**) offers three ETFs following revenue-weighted indexes.

SPA (**www.spa-etf.com**) offers ETFs that track fundamentally driven indexes by MarketGrader.

Swedish Export Credit Corp sponsors the ELEMENTS SPECTRUM Large Cap U.S. Sector Momentum ETN (EEH), tracking the SPECTRUM Large Cap U.S. Sector Momentum Index, which attempts to profit from the different performances of the ten S&P industry sectors by applying a "momentum investing" strategy to the sectors.

UBS (**www.ubs.com**) sponsors the E-TRACS UBS Bloomberg CMCI Index ETN (UCI), tracking the UBS Bloomberg Constant Maturity Commodity Index, which measures long-term commodity performance.

Van Eck Global (**www.vaneck.com**) is the sponsor of market vector ETFs, tracking global industry sectors, municipal bonds, and Chinese and Indian currencies.

XShares (**www.xsharesadvisors.com**) offers ETFs tracking custom indexes that categorize real estate and global industry sectors according to functional characteristics.

Victoria Bay Asset Management (**www.unitedstatesoilfund.com**) sponsors four ETFs following U.S. oil and natural gas prices.

Ziegler Capital Management (**www.ziegler.com**) sponsors the NYSE Arca Tech 100 ETF, tracking a price-weighted index comprised of 100 technology ADRs (American Depository Receipts) and common stocks listed on U.S. exchanges.

Chapter 9

○ ○ ○ ○ ○

The ETFs

At the beginning of 2008, more than 600 ETFs were trading on the market, and new offerings appear almost monthly. There is a dizzying selection to choose from, and many ETFs follow similar indexes or investment strategies. When deciding which ETFs to invest in, always keep your target asset allocations foremost in your mind. How will the ETF fit your investment goals? Will it complement other investments in your portfolio or fill in areas that are underexposed? After you have selected several candidates from a particular style or market category, compare them by looking at their underlying securities, expense ratios, index strategies, and historical performance to determine which is the best choice for your portfolio. (See "Chapter 11: Doing the Research" for more information.)

CASE STUDY: SIMON MAIERHOFER

Simon Maierhofer is the cofounder of **ETFguide.com**. After graduating with a degree in banking from the prestigious German Sparkasse Bank, he moved to the U.S. in 1997. Before cofounding ETFguide.com in 2003, he worked with individual investors in the capacity of a Registered Investment Advisor (RIA).

ETFguide.com is the information leader in exchange traded funds. Its content is distributed through licensing agreements with Schwab, Scottrade, Institutional Investor, and others. ETFguide.com (and its founders, Maierhofer and Ron DeLegge) are consistently featured in the media.

Mr. Maierhofer offers the following advice to investors interested in buying ETFs:

CASE STUDY: SIMON MAIERHOFER

ETFs, although superior to mutual funds in many ways, are based on a different product structure. Become familiar with ETFs, and "look under the hood" of your favorite ETFs. Perhaps start out with simple, market-cap–weighted, passively selected ETFs that track well-known indexes (i.e., SPY) before you move into more complex ETFs.

Investors new to ETFs may feel like a "kid in the candy store." There are so many different ETFs and so many different ways to use them. ETFs are a great investment vehicle when used in combination with a disciplined asset allocation approach. Because ETFs trade like stocks, they are also easily used as a speculation vehicle. As with any other investment vehicle, a "day-trading" approach to ETFs opens you up to a world of hurt.

ETFs have changed the investing landscape by reintroducing a certain amount of integrity and credibility into the marketplace. Fees and holdings are transparent. Performance usually is closely tied to the underlying index. From an asset allocation standpoint, ETFs provide incredible flexibility. Through ETFs, investors now have access to stocks, bonds, commodities, currencies, real estate, and short and leveraged investments. Asset allocation models can be exercised with razor-sharp precision.

The filing for the first so-called, "actively managed" ETF has been approved by the SEC. Even though this set of already approved ETFs is far away from the active management style known from mutual fund companies, it is the beginning of a trend that will shift billions of dollars from actively managed mutual funds into ETFs.

Broad U.S. Equity and Style ETFs

Broad market ETFs track broad market indexes, also referred to as all cap or total market indexes, that measure the performance of the securities market as a whole or of a broad subsector of the market. Broad market indexes are made up of passively selected securities, weighted according to market capitalization. Passive selection means that securities are chosen for inclusion in the index strictly according to predetermined rules. Capitalization weighting multiplies the price of a single share of each security times the number of outstanding shares of that security, and it assigns representation in the index in proportion to each company's size.

Broad market indexes contain hundreds and even thousands of securities. The Dow Jones Wilshire indexes include over 5,000 U.S. stocks, Russell Indexes include 4,000 stocks, the MSCI follows 3,500 stocks, and the S&P 1500 tracks 1,500 stocks. There is at least one ETF tracking each of these broad market indexes.

All index providers use relatively similar criteria to divide broad markets into components, tracking companies of different sizes. Large-cap indexes track predominantly large companies, mid-cap and small-cap indexes track medium-sized companies, and micro-cap indexes track the smallest companies. To maintain the integrity of indexes based on company size, reallocation of companies to the various-sized components is carried out at regular intervals. Providers may reallocate companies by size annually, quarterly, monthly, or as needed. When reallocation is carried out at longer intervals, there is less turnover of the stocks in each size index; however, the reallocations usually result in portfolio changes when they do occur. More frequent reallocation enables an index to stay current with a rapidly changing economy. Index providers do not all follow the same rules to move companies from one size allocation to another. The prospectus for each ETF includes a detailed description of the index it follows, and more information is available from the index provider.

Style indexes divide broad market indexes into growth and value components. Each provider has its own method for determining whether a stock is "growth" or "value." Russell uses two factors to separate value from growth; Dow Jones uses six; S&P and S&P/Citigroup uses seven; MSCI uses eight; and Morningstar uses ten. Each provider usually reallocates companies in its style indexes when size reallocation is carried out. Because these reallocations are performed at different time intervals, the composition and performance of one growth index can be considerably different from another.

Broad market ETFs provide exposure to the entire stock market, or to broad market sectors, and can be expected to yield similar returns. The expense ratio for broad market ETFs tends to be lower than for other types of

ETFs and lower than most mutual funds. For these reasons, broad market ETFs are an essential component of any portfolio. The most popular ETFs follow the S&P 500.

A list of broad U.S. equity and style ETFs can be found in Appendix B of this book and on Web sites such as **www.etfguide.com** and **www. morningstar.com**.

Industry-Sector ETFs

Historically, long-term investors have tended to diversify their portfolios by style while short-term, active investors diversified by industry sector, hoping to find one or more industries that would outperform the stock market as a whole. Many investors buy into sectors that have been performing well, expecting the trend to continue. Others look for low-priced investments in industry sectors that are underperforming, believing in the theory that they must eventually begin to rise again, just as every sector has done in the past.

There are now more than 180 industry-sector ETFs, covering every major U.S. industry sector and subsector and many foreign industry sectors. Many of the newest ETFs track some kind of industry sector.

The first industry-sector ETFs, Select Sector Standard & Poor's Depository Receipts ("spiders"), were launched in 1998 by State Street Bank and Trust Company, and they remain the most popular. Select SPDRs divide the S&P 500 into nine industry sectors, and each SPDR tracks the price performance, before expenses, of one sector. The American Stock Exchange calculates the value of Select Sector Indexes every day. Many ETF providers offer ETFs that follow industry sectors, and some track global industry sectors.

Some industry-sector ETFs are based on customized indexes designed to outperform market-industry indexes. PowerShares offers a series using quantitative methods and another using a fundamental weighting scheme. Wisdom Tree has dividend-weighted industry indexes; Rydex and State

Street offer equal-weighted industry ETFs; and First Trust has a quantitative AlphaDEX series.

Categorizing Industry Sectors

ELEVEN MAJOR SECTORS

The various index providers use different methodologies to classify companies according to industry, but they all recognize ten or eleven major industry groups. As new technologies are developed, new types of businesses are listed on the stock exchange, creating new industry sectors and subsectors while old, established industries disappear.

11 MAJOR INDUSTRY SECTORS	
Computer Technology	Financial Services
Healthcare	Industrial materials
Energy	Utilities
Telecommunications	Consumer Services
Business Services	Consumer Goods

If you are diversifying a portfolio by industry sector, it is important to include representatives of all the sectors so that your portfolio can benefit from growth and development in any of them.

Global Industry Classification Standard

The Global Industry Classification Standard (GICS) was introduced in 2000 by Morgan Stanley Capital International in collaboration with Standard & Poor's. It classifies over 34,000 publicly traded companies worldwide into 10 sectors, 24 industry groups, 67 industries, and 147 subindustries. Thousands of MSCI global industry indexes classify industries at each level, globally, by region and by country.

10 GICS SECTORS	
Basic Materials	metals, mining, forest and paper products, chemicals
Consumer Discretionary	auto, appliances, retail, leisure, home building, media

10 GICS SECTORS	
Consumer Staples	food and drug retail, tobacco, household products
Energy	energy equipment, oil, oil and gas exploration, refining, storage
Financials	banks, financial services, real estate investment trusts, insurance
Healthcare	managed care, medical products, drugs, biotech
Industrials	capital goods, building, defense, aerospace, transportation
Information Technology	hardware, software, telecom equipment, consulting
Telecommunication Services	fixed line, mobile, integrated services
Utilities	electric, gas, water, and multi-utilities

The nine Select Sector SPDRs classify the S&P 500 according to the GICS sectors, with Information Technology and Telecommunications combined under the Technology SPDR.

Vanguard industry-sector ETFs also use the GICS to divide the MSCI U.S. Investable Market 2500 Index into industry sectors. Because this index tracks 2,500 stocks, it includes small-cap and mid-cap companies. Vanguard ETFs are formed under the Investment Company Act of 1940, allowing them to use a sample of the stocks in their indexes rather than including every stock in the index. This sometimes results in discrepancies between the performance of the ETF and the performance of the index.

iShare Global Sector Industry ETFs also follow the GICS classification.

Industry Classification Benchmark (ICB)

Dow Jones Indexes and FTSE use a competing classification system called the Industry Classification Benchmark (ICB). The ICB Universe Database contains more than 40,000 companies and 45,000 securities around the world, and it classifies them according to revenue, not earnings.

The ICB uses 10 industries, 18 supersectors, 39 sectors, and 104 subsectors.

Even though the ICB uses a similar terminology to the GSCI, the terms do not have the same meaning. Some of the subsectors are divided differently; for example, ICB classifies airline transportation as Consumer Services, but GSCI places it under Industrials.

Barclays Global Investors (BGI) offers a series of 22 sector iShares based on the ICB.

Morningstar Sector Classification

Morningstar assigns each company to one of 129 industry categories, according to the business activity that represents its primary source of revenue. The 129 industries are grouped into 12 sectors, organized under 3 supersectors: information economy, service economy, and manufacturing economy.

The three supersectors are intended to reflect the developmental stages of an economy, from dependence on physical production, to service industries, to information exchange. Each stock in an index is weighted according to the number of shares available for trading on the market (free-float).

Industry-Sector ETFs
Merrill Lynch HOLDRS

Early in 2000, Merrill Lynch launched HOLDRS, a series of unit investment trusts (UITs). Twenty large stocks were initially selected for each HOLDR using an MSCI Industry Index based on GICS. The securities were equal-weighted at the beginning, but the trust is never rebalanced, and the stocks it holds are never updated as the index changes.

Individual investors can turn in 100 units in exchange for the underlying stocks, which allows them to sell individual stocks rather than just shares of the fund. Owners of HOLDRS retain voting rights in the stocks held by the fund and receive annual reports for each of the 20 holdings. There are no management costs, but an annual fee of $2 per 100 units is paid to the Bank of New York from stock dividends.

Customized Industry Indexes

Customized industry indexes attempt to create a methodology that will produce better returns than the industry sector or the broad market. New ETFs based on customized indexes are appearing regularly.

Rydex created the RYDEX S&P Equal Weight Sector ETFs, holding the same securities as Select SPDR ETFs but giving each stock in the index equal weight instead of using capitalization weighting. The fees for these are twice the fees of Select SPDR ETFs.

State Street offers narrowly focused S&P industry SPDR ETFs using equal-weighted indexes to capture markets, such as biotech, home builders, and semiconductors.

In 2007, Wisdom Tree released international industry ETFs weighted according to the level of dividends paid by each company.

PowerShares offers almost 40 industry ETFs, some using quantitative analysis and some using a multifactor fundamental weighting method. The PowerShares Dynamic Industry Sector Portfolio uses the AMEX Dynamic Intellidex indexes, which evaluate companies using criteria, such as fundamental growth, stock valuation, investments, and risk factors. Securities that appear to possess the greatest potential for capital appreciation are placed in an index and given a fixed weight based on their size.

First Trust AlphaDEX ETFs are based on AMEX StrataQuant index. The stocks from the Russell 1000 are ranked according to several growth and value factors. The top 75 percent are selected for the StrataQuant industry indexes. The stocks in the indexes are equal-weighted, but the top 25 percent receive more weight than the next 25 percent, which receive more weight than the lowest 25 percent.

Some narrow sector ETFs contain only a limited number of stocks; in that case, the weight of any individual stock in the fund is capped at 5 to 10 percent.

Fixed-Income ETFs

The average private investor invests approximately 50 percent of long-term savings in fixed-income assets, which offer stability and a source of income. Fixed-income securities involve an investor loaning money to a government entity or a corporation for a specified time and provide interest earnings and the return of principal at maturity. There are many types of fixed-income assets, including Treasury notes, government agency issues, mortgages, corporate bonds, municipal bonds, asset-backed securities, and inflation-protected securities. Because bonds typically have a predictable stream of payments and repayment of principal, many people invest in them to preserve and increase their capital or to receive dependable interest income. The public U.S. fixed-income market (nearly $30 trillion) is much larger in size than the public U.S. equity market.

Why Are Fixed-Income Assets Important in a Portfolio?

Lower volatility: Bonds are an important investment, not because of their rate of return, but because of their lower volatility, which provides a safety net in difficult times. Historically, investments in stocks have brought in higher returns than investments in bonds. Over the past 80 years, the average annualized return of the S&P 500 Index has been about 10 percent, while the average annualized return of long-term U.S. government bonds has been approximately 5.5 percent. Adjusted for inflation, the real return on stocks has averaged 7 percent, while the real return on bonds has averaged 2.4 percent. However, during their worst year, 1967, volatile U.S. government bonds returned -9.2 percent. In contrast, during its worst year, 1931, the stock market returned -43 percent. There is no guarantee that historical trends will repeat themselves, but two factors affect the performance of bonds during periods of economic difficulty. Demand for bonds increases because they are considered a safer investment than stocks. During periods of economic decline, the interest rate is often lowered, making older bonds with higher interest rates more valuable and causing the prices of these older bonds to escalate.

- **No correlation to stocks:** Most bonds have a slightly negative correlation to the performance of stocks. Factors related to poor performance of the stock market tend to raise the returns on bonds.

- **Income:** Bonds and asset-backed securities, such as mortgages, provide income from interest. Preferred stocks promise regular dividend payments, although these may be eliminated if the board of directors finds it necessary.

Nature and Risk of Bonds

Bonds are essentially promissory notes issued by a government, agency, or company that promises to pay interest on the money it borrows from you. Purchasing a company's stock carries the risk that the company may operate at a loss or go bankrupt, and your capital may be lost. Bonds carry different kinds of risk:

- **Default:** The risk that the agency or company issuing the bonds will not be able to pay you back.

- **Interest rate risk:** If the prevailing interest rate jumps to 10 percent, and you purchased a bond at an earlier prevailing interest rate of 5 percent, you will be stuck with an investment that returns only 5 percent when you could be getting much better returns somewhere else. If you try to sell the bond, you will have to accept a deeply discounted price and take a loss. If you hold the bond to maturity, you will suffer a loss of opportunity — the chance to earn much higher returns by investing your money elsewhere. The longer the maturity of a bond, the greater the likelihood that interest rates will rise before it matures (interest rate risk). A three-year bond will have a far lower interest rate risk than a 20-year bond.

- **Inflation risk:** If the rate of inflation exceeds the rate of interest on your bonds, in terms of actual value, they will be worth less when they mature than they were worth when you bought them. Inflation risk is greatest for low-yielding bonds. Inflation-protected bonds are immune to this risk, but they offer a much lower interest rate. If deflation occurs, the protection they offer becomes meaningless and you are left holding low-interest bonds.

Fixed-Income Indexes

Bonds are classified by type, maturity, and credit rating.

Type: Fixed-income assets include T-notes, government agency issues, mortgages, corporate bonds, municipal bonds, asset-backed securities, and inflation-protected securities.

U.S. Treasury securities, used to finance the federal government debt, are considered to have the bond market's lowest risk because they are guaranteed by the U.S. government's "full faith and credit" or, in other words, its authority to tax the citizens of the United States.

Government agencies, such as the Government National Mortgage Association (Ginnie Mae), issue debt to support their role in financing mortgages. As divisions of the government, their securities are also backed by the full faith and credit of the United States.

Government-sponsored enterprises (GSEs) are financing entities created by Congress to fund loans to certain groups of borrowers, such as homeowners, farmers, and students. Though GSEs are sometimes referred to as federal agencies or federally sponsored agencies, their debt is sponsored but not guaranteed by the federal government. They are considered a greater credit risk than agencies of the federal government, and their bonds often offer a higher yield than U.S. Treasury bonds with the same maturity. Student Loan Marketing Association (Sallie Mae), Federal National Mortgage Association (Fannie Mae) and Federal Home Loan Mortgage Corporation (Freddie Mac) are privately owned corporations established with a public purpose. The Federal Home Loan Banks and the Federal Farm Credit Banks are systems comprising regional banks.

Treasury inflation protection securities (TIPS) are securities issued by the U.S. government and carry its full-faith-and-credit backing. TIPS have a fixed interest rate, indexed to inflation through adjustments to their principal amount made on the basis of changes in the Consumer Price Index-U (CPI-U). (The Consumer Price Index-U is a monthly measurement of the price for a fixed basket of goods and services bought regularly by U.S. urban consumers, including professional and self-employed people.) At maturity, investors receive the greater of the inflation-adjusted principal or the par amount. To compensate for the guaranteed protection against inflation, the interest rate on these bonds is lower.

Corporate bonds are debts issued by industrial, financial, and service companies to finance capital investment and operating cash flow. The corporate bond market is bigger than each of the markets for municipal bonds, U.S. Treasury securities, and government agency securities. Corporate bonds have a wide range of bond structures, coupon rates, maturity dates, credit quality, and industry exposure.

Mortgage-backed securities (MBS) represent an interest in pools of loans, typically first mortgages on residential properties. They are primarily issued by a government agency, such as Ginnie Mae, or a government-sponsored enterprise, such as Fannie Mae or Freddie Mac, which typically guarantee the interest and principal payments on their securities. The MBS market also includes "private-label" mortgage securities issued by subsidiaries of investment banks, financial institutions, and home builders.

Asset-backed securities (ABS) also represent an interest in a pool of asset-backed loans, such as credit card receivables, auto loans and leases, or home-equity loans. ABS carry some form of credit enhancement, such as bond insurance, to make them attractive to investors.

Maturity:

Indexes divide maturities into three ranges:

- **Short-term:** Bonds that have an average maturity of three years or less

- **Intermediate:** Bonds that have an average maturity of four to nine years

- **Long-term:** Bonds that have an average maturity of ten years or longer

When an index has an average maturity of five years, all the bonds in that index do not necessarily mature in five years. The maturity of individual bonds in the index may range from one year to ten years, with the total average maturity being five years.

The average maturity of an index is a measure of interest rate risk. When interest rates rise, ETFs benchmarked to indexes with longer durations will decrease in value more than those benchmarked to indexes with shorter durations. Because of the higher risk associated with long-term bonds, they are expected to generate a higher total return.

CREDIT RATING

Credit risk is a reflection of the financial strength of the government, agency, or company issuing a bond. The greater the chance of a default, the higher the interest rate must be to compensate for the risk. The U.S.

government and its agencies are low credit risks. Investment-grade corporate bonds are higher. The highest-yield bonds, called junk bonds, are issued by companies whose financial future is uncertain. The greater the credit risk and the longer the duration of the bonds in an index, the higher the expected long-term rate of return.

Bonds are rated by rating agencies, private companies that evaluate a bond issuer's financial health and assess its ability to repay its obligations in a timely manner. A rating is an evaluation of the likelihood that an issuer will repay the principal and interest of a particular bond on time and in full. In the United States, the major rating agencies are Moody's Investor Service, Standard and Poor's Ratings Services, and Fitch IBCA.

Bond prices are determined by investors in the marketplace, and investor confidence is influenced by credit ratings. When bond ratings are lowered, their price often goes down. When ratings are raised, prices go up. Investors do not rely wholly on credit ratings; price changes often precede ratings changes because investors' assessment of risk has been altered based on other factors, such as economic news.

FIXED-INCOME INDEXERS

Lehman Brothers (**www.lehman.com**) constructs hundreds of fixed-income indexes, covering all the global bond markets. Many of these serve as the basis for fixed-income ETFs. In order to be included in a Lehman index, a bond must have a minimum issue of $100 million.

Lehman Brothers Treasury indexes measure the performance of fixed-rate, U.S. dollar-denominated, nonconvertible U.S. Treasury securities that have $250 million or more of outstanding face value. They are classified by maturities. The 1-3 Year Treasury Index includes all publicly issued U.S. Treasury securities with a remaining maturity of between one and three years. The 3-5 Year Treasury Index includes those with remaining maturities of between 3 and 5 years, and so on. The indexes are market capitalization-weighted, and the index is updated at the end of every month.

Ryan ALM (**www.ryanindex.com**) indexes are bullet indexes: they are isolated to one bullet maturity year instead of an average of maturity years. The Ryan Five-Year Treasury Index includes only five-year Treasury notes.

Markit iBoxx (**www.indexco.com**) indexes measure the performance of U.S. dollar-denominated, fixed-income, investment-grade issues. In addition to overall indexes for U.S. Treasury, agency, and corporate issues, separate indexes are published for domestic and Eurodollar issues, as well as for maturity, rating, and sector. The selection criteria include only the part of the market that is tradable and thus are available to investors and asset managers.

Dorchester Capital Management Company (**www.cpmkts.com**), launched the Capital Markets Index (CPMKTS) in December 2006, a real-time, market-weighted index including 9,673 equity, fixed-income, and money market instruments. It is the first to measure the total return of U.S. stocks, investment-grade bonds, and fixed-income securities with maturities less than one year (liquidity). Dorchester utilizes market data and government statistics to adjust weights used in calculating the index, thereby ensuring it accurately reflects the total return of the markets, based on actual asset allocation. Other indexes within the CPMKTS family measure subsegments of the market.

Other index providers for bond ETFs include Merrill Lynch (**www. ml.com**) and Vanguard (**www.vanguard.com**).

Bond ETFs

Most bond indexes were created as a means for economists and financial analysts to measure the fixed-income marketplace and as a way to measure the performance of active bond management strategies. They were not intended as benchmarks for ETFs, and it is difficult for ETFs to track most of these indexes. Many of the bonds included in traditional indexes are not available on the market, and there is a high turnover of the bonds in an index as they mature or are redeemed and replaced by other bond issues.

Fund managers are not able to replicate a bond index exactly; instead, they use a complicated sampling methodology. Each bond in an index is assigned to a quadrant, based on a number of factors, including credit rating, issue size, industry, maturity, and bond coupon. A few liquid bonds (bonds that are easily available on the market) are then selected to represent each quadrant. After a portfolio of bonds has been created and optimized, it is tested to see if the past performance of those bonds follows the performance of the index closely enough. If there is too great a discrepancy (tracking error) between the performance of the selected bonds and the actual index, the bonds in the portfolio are replaced with other bonds and more tests are done. The process is repeated until the performance of the portfolio mimics the index within an acceptable margin of error. A few hundred bonds are sufficient to create a portfolio that tracks the index.

Adding Bonds to Your Portfolio with ETFs

Bond ETFs offer a quick way to add fixed-income assets to your portfolio. Like stock ETFs, fixed-income ETFs offer the advantage of owning a share of hundreds of bonds instead of a few individual bonds, decreasing overall interest risk. Bond ETFs can be bought and sold on the stock market at any time, allowing rapid reallocation of the assets in a portfolio. When the bonds underlying a bond ETF mature, they are redeemed and replaced with other, similar bonds; the investor retains shares in the ETF and does not have to seek out new opportunities for reinvestment.

Though the public U.S. fixed-income market is much larger than the public U.S. equity market, fewer than 60 of the approximately 700 ETFs on the market in early 2008 were bond ETFs. Both bond issuers and bond providers have recognized the potential for selling bonds through ETFs and are now creating new financial products that will be easier to market.

Ultimately, it is up to you to choose the bond ETFs that best fit your investment objectives. Detailed information, historical data, rates of return, and prospectuses can be found on the Web sites of fund providers, stock exchanges, financial analysts, and brokers.

TAKE NOTE: COSTS ARE EVEN MORE IMPORTANT FOR FIXED-INCOME ETFS

Because bonds offer a lower rate of return than stock investments, it is important to look at the cost of a bond ETF in relation to its rate of return. The real return on bonds, adjusted for inflation, has historically been only 2.5 percent. Even a moderate expense ratio could seriously diminish your returns.

Treasury Bond ETFs

The U.S. Treasury bond market is the most liquid fixed-income market in the world; trillions of dollars in U.S. Treasury bonds are traded every year. The Lehman Brothers Treasury indexes are most popular as benchmarks for bond ETFs. Barclays iShares offers six Treasury bond ETFs, benchmarked to Lehman indexes.

Five Ameristock ETFs track Ryan ALM Treasury Indexes. The PowerShares 1-30 Laddered Treasury (PLW) is based on the Ryan/Mergent 1-30-Year Treasury Laddered Index, which measures the potential return of U.S. Treasury securities with a yield curve based on 30 U.S. Treasury bonds with fixed interest rates, scheduled to mature in an annual sequential (laddered) structure.

State Street Global Advisors offers three U.S. Treasury ETFs, including the short-term SPDR Lehman 1-3 Month T-bill ETF, based on Lehman Brothers 1-3 Month U.S. Treasury Bill Index.

Sovereign bonds are issued by national governments. The SPDR Lehman International Treasury Bond ETF tracks the performance of the Lehman

Brothers Global Treasury ex-U.S. Index, which includes Treasury bonds of investment-grade countries outside the U.S., such as Austria, Italy, Germany, Belgium, Canada, Denmark, and France.

TAKE NOTE: INTEREST IS TAXABLE
Interest paid on U.S. Treasury notes is taxed by the federal government but not by state governments.

Municipal Bond ETFs

State Street Global Advisors offers four SPDR Municipal Bond ETFs. PowerShares offers PowerShares Insured National Municipal Bond Portfolio, PowerShares Insured California Municipal Bond Portfolio, and PowerShares Insured New York Municipal Bond Portfolio, which track the performance of top-rated, insured municipal bonds.

Corporate Bonds

Barclays launched the first corporate bond ETF, iShares iBoxx $ Investment Grade Corporate Bond ETF, in July 2002. It measures the performance of approximately 100 investment-grade, highly liquid corporate bonds. Several of them are Yankee bonds, issued by foreign companies but trading on U.S. exchanges. Several ETFs provided by Vanguard and Barclays are benchmarked to the Lehman Brothers Short-Term Credit Index, Intermediate-Term Credit Index, and Credit Index, which holds investment-grade corporate bonds along with some asset-backed securities.

The iShares iBoxx $ High Yield Corporate Bond ETF (HYG), PowerShares High Yield Corporate Bond Portfolio (PHB), and SPDR Lehman High Yield Bond ETF (JNK) track the performance of less-than-investment-grade corporate bonds, or junk bonds. Junk bonds offer higher interest payments because of the increased risk of default. Although high-yield corporate bond ETFs offer higher returns than other bond ETFs, they offer lower returns than the stock market in general.

Composite Fixed-Income ETFs

Composite fixed-income indexes combine different types of bonds into one index. Lehman Brothers has several investment-grade government/credit indexes, classified according to the average maturity of the bonds. These indexes do not contain mortgages. Several Barclays and Vanguard ETFs track these indexes by sampling ranges of securities that approximate key risk factors and other characteristics of the indexes as a whole.

The Lehman Aggregate Bond Index tracks more than 7,000 U.S. fixed-income securities and measures the performance of the U.S. investment-grade bond market. The Vanguard Total Bond Market ETF (BND), SPDR Lehman Aggregate Bond ETF (LAG), and the iShares Lehman Aggregate Bond ETF (AGG) all use sampling methodologies to follow the Lehman Aggregate Bond Index.

The Claymore U.S. Capital Markets Bond ETF (UBD) follows Dorchester Capital Management Company's Capital Markets Index (CPMKTS), a market-weighted index including 9,673 equity, fixed-income, and money market instruments.

> **TAKE NOTE: HIGHER YIELDS MEAN HIGHER RISK AND HIGHER EXPENSES**
>
> The higher yield of junk bond ETFs comes along with higher risk and higher expense ratios. While most bond ETFs have expense ratios ranging from 0.15 to 0.25 percent, the expense ratio for high-yield bond ETFs is between 0.4 and 0.5 percent.

Preferred Stock ETFs

Financial companies frequently issue preferred stock, which provides a fixed dividend and gives its holders priority over other shareholders. The dividend may be cut or eliminated by the issuer's board of directors without defaulting on the issue, but in such cases, the preferred stock holders always receive dividends before anything is paid out to common shareholders. The dividends from preferred stock offer a higher income than bonds because of the increased risk. Some preferred stock pays qualified dividend income (QDI), which is taxed at the lower federal tax rate of 15 percent.

PowerShares Financial Preferred Portfolio (PGF) follows the Wachovia Hybrid & Preferred Securities Index and tries to include only QDI preferred stocks, but its expense ratio is 0.60 percent. The iShares S&P U.S. Preferred Stock Index (PFF) tracks the S&P U.S. Preferred Stock Index, and only about 50 percent of its holdings are QDI stocks; its expense ratio is 0.48 percent. With an expense ratio of 0.50 percent, the PowerShares Preferred Portfolio ETF (PGX) is based on the Merrill Lynch Fixed Rate Preferred Securities Index and designed to replicate the total return of a diversified group of investment-grade preferred securities.

TIPS ETFs

Treasury Inflation Protection Securities (TIPS) are securities issued by the U.S. government and are protected against inflation by making adjustments to their principal amount based on changes in the Consumer Price Index-U (CPI-U). TIPS have a fixed interest rate, which naturally increases returns as the capital is increased to counter inflation. To compensate for the guaranteed protection against inflation, the interest rate on these bonds is lower. SPDR Barclays TIPS ETF (IPE) aims to track the Barclays U.S. government inflation-linked bond index. iShares Lehman TIPS Bond ETF (TIP) follows the performance of the inflation-protected sector of the United States Treasury market as defined by the Lehman Brothers U.S. TIPS index.

Special Equity ETFs

A number of ETFs follow unique investment strategies based on customized indexes. Some of these are designed to make the most of a particular economic trend or to bank on progressive technology and scientific breakthroughs. Others are a response to investor interest, such as FocusShares ISE Revere Wal-Mart Supplier Index Fund, launched in November 2007, which tracks

30 companies that generate most of their sales supplying Wal-Mart. Social and environmental responsibility appeals to some investors. An increasing number of new ETFs employ various leveraged investment strategies to achieve higher returns than broad market, style, or sector indexes.

Special equity ETFs are based on custom indexes, and, therefore, their expense ratios are on average three times higher than those of market indexes. It is assumed that higher returns will more than make up for increased expenses. The costs of comparable open-end mutual funds with similar investment strategies are almost double those of special equity ETFs.

Themed ETFs

Thematic investing follows popular social, economic, corporate, or demographic themes. If increasing interest draws large numbers of investors towards a particular theme, a thematic portfolio can benefit in two ways: share prices will be driven up by the increased demand, and the infusion of capital may boost the performance of the companies in the thematic indexes.

Critics characterize thematic investing as a marketing gimmick that can be harmful to investors, enticing them to follow the latest fad and exposing them to economic risk when the trend changes. An example is the technology funds that attracted so much investment in the late 1990s and wiped out many individual investors. Supporters believe that thematic investing helps to drive investment towards innovative and little-understood sectors, which are then able to flourish.

SOCIALLY RESPONSIBLE

An increasing number of investors are following ethical and moral parameters, screening out companies that profit from tobacco or weapons of mass destruction, use child labor, or generate heavy pollution. By rewarding companies with good ethical standards, they hope to influence other companies to follow suit.

According to the *Report on Socially Responsible Investing Trends in the United States*, published in March 2008 by the nonprofit Social Investment Forum (SIF), SRI (Socially Responsible Investment) assets increased more than 18 percent while all investment assets under management edged up by less than 3 percent from 2005 to 2007. The report identifies $2.71 trillion, up from $2.29 trillion in 2005, in total assets under management using one or more of the three core SRI strategies: screening, shareholder advocacy, and community investing. Assets in socially and environmentally screened mutual funds and ETFs rose to $201.8 billion in 260 funds in 2007, a 13 percent increase over the $179.0 billion in the 201 funds tracked in 2005. By the end of 2006, eight socially and environmentally screened ETFs with $2.25 billion in total net assets were available. In February of 2008, Claymore closed several of its lightly followed ETFs, including Claymore/LGA Green ETF (GRN) and Claymore/KLD Sudan Free Large-Cap Core ETF (KSF).

The Barclays iShares KLD Select Social Index (KLD) invests in companies in the KLD Select Social Index, which is composed of around 200 to 300 companies from the S&P 500 and Russell 1000 indexes, excluding tobacco companies. Top recent holdings included Texas Instruments, Hewlett-Packard, and Procter & Gamble.

CLEAN ENERGY

The Power-Shares WilderHill Clean Energy Portfolio (PBW) attempts to track the WilderHill Clean Energy Index, which is designed to deliver capital appreciation through the selection of companies that focus on greener and generally renewable sources of energy and technologies that facilitate cleaner energy. Its top holdings include Zoltek, Cree, and Emcore. By mid 2008, it held assets totaling almost $1.5 billion.

PowerShares Global Clean Energy Portfolio Fund (PBD), launched in June 2007, is based on the WilderHill New Energy Global Innovation Index, comprised of companies worldwide whose "innovative technologies and services focus on generation and use of cleaner energy, conservation, efficiency, and advancing renewable energy generally." Included are companies whose lower-carbon approaches are relevant to climate change and whose technologies help reduce emissions relative to traditional fossil fuel use." The index is calculated using a modified equal-dollar weighting methodology. All components are limited individually to 5 percent of the index by weight.

Market Vectors Global Alternative Energy ETF (GEX) follows the Ardour Global Index (Extra Liquid). The index is a 30-stock, capitalization-weighted, float-adjusted index and includes companies that derive over 50 percent of total revenues from the global alternative energy industry. By the beginning of 2008, it held $222.5 million in assets.

> ### TAKE NOTE: LOOK CAREFULLY AT SOCIALLY RESPONSIBLE ETFS
>
> Socially responsible ETFs have higher expense ratios than market index ETFs. In a portfolio that is already diversified by capitalization and industry sectors, they may overlap with other funds and ETFs.

FIGHTING DISEASE

HealthShares (**www.healthsharesinc.com**) ETFs comprise a combination of small-, mid-, and large-cap companies that focus on curing, diagnosing, or treating a specific disease, such as heart disease, cancer, or diabetes. The idea is to allow individual investors to invest in the technologies that will specifically affect their health in the future and for insurance companies to profit from the same companies to whom they will be issuing payments for those treatments.

Some healthcare ETFs may bring in higher returns than the market as a whole, but they are much more volatile. Each ETF has only 22 to 25 holdings of equal weight. If several companies in the fund are competing, for example, to patent a drug for the same disease, profits from the success of one company could be negated by the decline of the others.

CORPORATE ACTION

Several ETFs track corporate actions, the decisions made by boards of directors that affect a company's structure.

The First Trust IPOX-100 Index Fund (FPX) tracks the IPOX-100 U.S. Index, which measures the average performance of U.S. initial public offerings (IPOs) during the first 1,000 trading days. The index includes the 100 largest, typically best performing, and most liquid IPOs in the U.S. IPOs are added to the index upon their seventh trading day after "going public" and automatically exit the index after 1,000 trading days.

The PowerShares Buyback Achievers Portfolio Fund (PKW) follows Mergent, Inc.'s Share BuyBack Achievers Index. To be included in the index, a company must be incorporated in the U.S., trade on a U.S. exchange, and have repurchased at least 5 percent of its outstanding shares for the trailing 12 months. The index is weighted by modified market cap; constituents are capped at 5 percent.

The Claymore/Sabrient Insider ETF (NFO), based on the Sabrient Insider Sentiment Index, aims to actively represent a group of stocks that reflect favorable corporate insider buying trends or Wall Street analyst earnings estimate increases, giving them the potential to outperform on a risk-adjusted basis the S&P 500 Index and other broad market indexes.

CORPORATE QUALITY

A group called IndexIQ has filed for 20 new ETFs that track indexes based on intangible qualities, such as customer loyalty, productivity, effective corporate governance, elite workforces, and sustainability. The concept is that these qualities, often overlooked by traditional measures, are the strongest drivers of corporate growth and equity returns. IndexIQ Exchange Traded Funds is a subsidiary of XShares Group LLC, the same company that launched HealthShares ETFs.

Actively Managed ETFs

A number of ETFs track custom indexes that employ methodologies similar to those used by active managers of open-ended mutual funds, such as fundamental analysis and sector rotation. You can invest in an ETF that carries out active strategies for you.

ETFs Based on Stock Analyst Research

The First Trust Value Line Equity Allocation Index Fund (FVI) is based on the Value Line Equity Allocation Index, designed to objectively identify and select those stocks that appear to have the greatest potential for capital appreciation. Value Line gives a timeliness, safety, or technical ranking of #1 or #2 using the Value Line Ranking Systems. The universe of stocks is separated into large-, mid-, and small-cap categories, and stock that do not meet certain liquidity and size requirements are eliminated. The remaining stocks are then classified into growth and value. Value Line determines the equity allocations among the six resulting style classifications and ranks each stock using several factors, including price-to-cash flow, price-to-book, return on assets, and price appreciation. The 25 highest-ranked stocks in each of the six style classifications are selected and are equally weighted within each classification. The stock selection process is reapplied semiannually, and the index is rebalanced in August and February of every year.

The PowerShares DWA Technical Leaders Portfolio Fund (PDP) corresponds generally to the performance, before fees and expenses, of the Dorsey Wright Technical Leaders Index, which includes approximately 100 U.S.-listed companies that demonstrate powerful relative strength characteristics. Among other factors, Dorsey Wright proprietary methodology takes into account the performance of each of the 3,000 largest U.S.-listed companies as compared to a benchmark index and the relative performance of industry sectors and subsectors. The index uses relative strength as the only factor in selecting securities and employs a modified equal weighting methodology. More weight is assigned to securities with better relative strength characteristics. Essentially, stocks that have performed better in the past get a higher weighting in the portfolio. Because relative strength is a trend-following methodology, the ETF should perform well when there are definable trends in place, but it will tend to struggle when trends change.

The Claymore/Sabrient Stealth ETF (STH), based on the Sabrient Stealth Index, is intended to comprise "undiscovered" and undervalued stocks. Approximately 150 stocks are selected from a broad universe of U.S.-traded stocks and ADRs (American Depository Receipts) that have little or no Wall Street analyst coverage (no more than two analysts). The objective of the index is to track a group of stocks that are relatively unnoticed by Wall Street analysts but that have displayed robust growth characteristics that give them the potential to outperform, on a risk-adjusted basis, the Russell 2000 Small Cap Index. The components are given a modified equal weight in the portfolio. No more than 25 percent of the stocks in the index may be from any single sector under the S&P Global Industry Classification System.

In June 2007, First Trust launched 16 ETFs based on AlphaDEX, a quantitative index strategy that tries to outperform existing indexes by modifying their methodologies. The stocks in each index are classified into growth, core, and value buckets. The value index looks at price/book return on assets and price/cash flow. The growth is given a score using five metrics: a 3-, 6-, and 12-month price change momentum; 1-year sales growth; and sales-to-price ratio. The value stocks are given a score based on three ratios: book value-to-price, cash flow-to-price, and return on assets. The goal is to create an index that emphasizes the "best" growth stocks and "best" value stocks. Changes are made to the index quarterly. The funds charge 0.70 percent in expenses, among the highest fee for any non-leveraged equity ETF.

PowerShares Intellidex ETFs are based on the Intellidex indexes, which rank securities according to risk factors, momentum, fundamental growth, and stock valuation to identify those with high expected capital appreciation potential. A modified equal-dollar weighting system assigns a higher fixed weighting to the larger stocks and a lower percentage to the smaller stocks. Stocks are selected and reallocated every quarter to match the composition of the indexes.

TAKE NOTE: ACTIVELY MANAGED ETFS DO NOT FOLLOW BUY-AND-HOLD STRATEGIES

These "actively managed" ETFs can be held in a buy-and-hold portfolio, but they are not following a buy-and-hold strategy. PowerShares' annual turnover is more than 100 percent, meaning that it holds stocks on average for less than a year. (Turnover for the S&P 500 index is about 5 percent.) The annual expense ratios are much higher than the cheapest S&P 500 ETF.

Because the oldest of these funds is only three or four years old, there is little data available for evaluating their performance. The methods used for selecting stocks in the underlying indexes tend to make them value-biased, even when the objective is to track the performance of growth stocks. Value companies tend to do well during growth periods and not as well when the economy is in a decline. Over time, similar mutual funds have averaged a lower performance than the S&P 500.

SECTOR ROTATION ETFS

A few ETFs track sector rotation indexes, which employ various methodologies to shift assets from one industry sector to another in an effort to capture the best market performance. (See the "Sector Rotation" section in "Chapter 18: Active Investing with ETFs.")

The Claymore/Zacks Sector Rotation ETF (XRO) tracks the Zacks Sector Rotation Index, which strives to outperform, on a risk-adjusted basis, the S&P 500. Zacks pinpoints where the economy is in the business cycle using macroeconomic analysis. Then, they heavily weight cyclical sectors (sectors whose performance is historically linked to economic cycles) prior to anticipated periods of economic expansion and overweight noncyclical sectors (those that tend to perform steadily in all economic conditions) prior to anticipated periods of economic contraction. Exposure for any one sector may range from 0 percent to a maximum of 45 percent of the index.

Within each sector, stocks are selected based on liquidity and are weighted using various factors, including earnings growth, price momentum, and relative market capitalization (size) within the sector. No individual stock may consist of more than 5 percent of the total index.

The PowerShares Value Line Industry Rotation Portfolio Fund (PYH) seeks to follow the Value Line Industry Rotation Index, comprised of 75 stocks chosen based on their Value Line Timeliness rank and their industry timeliness rank. Value Line Timeliness is a measure of the annual performance of a stock relative to the performances of the Dow Jones Industrial Average and the S&P 500. The index first ranks industries by their industry timeliness. The index then selects the highest-ranked stock for timeliness from each of the 50 highest timeliness-rated industries, as well as the second-highest timeliness-ranked stock from each of the 25 highest-rated industries.

The Claymore/Zacks Country Rotation ETF (CRO) uses the Zacks Country Rotation Index, a proprietary quantitative methodology developed by Zacks to determine those countries with potentially superior risk/return profiles and to select a basket of stocks within those countries. The country allocation methodology utilizes a bottom-up approach to determine the weightings of each country based on quantitative macroeconomic factors focusing on the global economic environment and other factors. Exposure for any one country may range from 0 percent to a maximum of 45 percent of the index. Each company within the chosen countries is ranked using a quantitative rules-based multifactor methodology that focuses on company growth, liquidity, relative value, and other factors. The securities selected for each country should provide a reflection of the countries' stock market performance. Individual constituent weightings tend to be determined by market capitalization.

Leveraged and Short ETFs

Leveraged ETFs are designed to produce twice the returns of a market index on a daily basis, although with twice the volatility of the index. Short ETFs are designed to produce returns that are the opposite of the market returns, going down when the market goes up and going up when the market goes down. Leveraged short ETFs produce double the opposite of a daily market index price return.

LEVERAGED ETFS

Leveraged ETFs use financial derivatives, such as options, swaps, and index futures, to achieve higher returns. All these methods are available to an individual investor, but they are complicated and require capital. A leveraged ETF requires less capital investment and does all the work for the investor.

The doubled daily returns promised by these funds do not mean doubled long-term returns. The expected long-term return of these ETFs is less than double the price return, minus fees. Leveraged funds not only double the returns, but they also double the exposure to price volatility. The volatility of daily price returns affects the annual return; more volatility means lower long-term compounded returns.

In order to maintain the target leverage ratio, a leveraged ETF may have to buy or sell millions of dollars worth of shares every day, increasing transaction costs. Whenever the market makes a big move downward, the fund sells shares and reduces its debt level to maintain its target leverage ratio. This makes the losses permanent and reduces the fund's assets, making it much harder to recover gains in the next market upturn.

Leveraged ETFs buy on margin, which requires interest payments, to increase exposure to the stock market. Dividends are often given up to pay for interest and fees, another consideration that lowers their long-term returns.

If an investor buys into a leveraged ETF just before the market takes off, the long-term returns will outperform the market index returns. If the investor is unfortunate and invests at the peak of the market just before it enters a dramatic decline, the returns will be lower than those of a standard, market index ETF. Leveraged ETFs also have high expense ratios compared to other ETFs.

By the end of 2007, there were 174 leveraged ETFs either on the market or filed with the SEC. These include the ProFunds Ultra series, the Rydex 2x Russell 2000 ETF (RRY), the Rydex 2x S&P 500 ETF (RSU), and the Rydex 2x S&P MidCap 400 ETF (RMM).

SHORT ETFS

Short ETFs move in the opposite direction of the indexes they track. The ProShares Short S&P 500 (SH) seeks to return the inverse of the daily performance of the S&P 500 Index. The ProShares Short QQQ (PSQ) seeks to return inverse of the daily performance of the NASDAQ-100 Index. The ProShares Short MSCI Emerging Markets (EUM) seeks the inverse of the daily performance of the MSCI Emerging Markets Index, which measures equity market performance in the global emerging markets.

Broad market and industry-sector leveraged short ETFs seek to double the inverse return of the indexes they follow. The Rydex Inverse 2x S&P 500 ETF (RSW) seeks returns that are twice (200 percent) the inverse (opposite) daily performance of the S&P 500 Index. A combination of individual securities, futures contracts, options, and swap agreements is used to attain the inverse leveraged performance. ProShares offers a series of leveraged short ETFs for specific industry sectors. The ProShares Ultra Industrials (SIJ) seeks 200 percent the inverse of the daily performance of the Dow Jones U.S. Industrials Index.

Leveraged short ETFs allow an investor to hedge market risk with an investment that will bring in increasing returns when the market as a whole is going down. They can be harmful and double losses for an investor who misjudges the market.

TAKE NOTE: UNDERSTAND LEVERAGED ETFS BEFORE YOU BUY THEM

Leveraged and short ETFs are not recommended for inexperienced investors. Before investing, you should understand the mechanics of these ETFs and how they are expected to respond to short- and long-term changes in the market.

> ### TAKE NOTE: LEVERAGED ETFS MAY NOT MEET THEIR OBJECTIVES
>
> There is not enough historical data to provide an accurate picture of the performance of leveraged ETFs over time and in different market conditions. Similarly leveraged mutual funds have experienced difficulty in meeting their objective of doubling the daily return on an index. Part of the cause for this "lag" is the expenses incurred by buying on margin and by the loss of capital assets over time.

Commodity and Currency ETFs

New ETF products are allowing private investors to add several asset classes to their portfolios that were previously accessible only to institutional or professional investors. Some of the newest ETFs include individual commodities, commodity futures, futures indexes, and foreign currencies. Currency and commodity asset classes help to diversify a portfolio because they have low correlation to traditional investments, such as stocks and bonds.

Individual commodities frequently have low correlation to each other. Historically, investors in commodities tried to profit from the price fluctuations of a particular commodity by anticipating market demand and understanding the global conditions that affect supply. For long-term investors who are using commodities to diversify their portfolios, a broader commodities index offers more protection than individual commodity ETFs because falling prices for one commodity can be offset by rising prices for another.

There are disadvantages to including some of these asset classes in a portfolio, including higher expenses, the absence of a real expected long-term return from a commodity investment, and increased tax liabilities. Some financial advisers question whether commodities belong in a long-term portfolio at all, but spiking commodity prices during the 2000s have created a great deal of interest, and ETF providers have responded with new offerings.

In November 2005, State Street's streetTRACKS introduced the first gold

ETF, making it possible for the first time to purchase ownership of a share of gold held by the fund in a bank vault. Since then, ETFs have come on the market offering silver, nickel, and base metals.

Precious Metals

GOLD

Historically, gold has been widely promoted as insurance against inflation and financial disaster. When a currency collapses or the stock market drops, gold is said to retain its value. The debate continues over what actually causes the price of gold to rise or fall; in bad times, investors rushing to protect their assets by buying gold may cause the price to go up. Owning gold may offer some protection against losses in other areas of your portfolio during an economic downturn.

If you purchase a gold ETF today and hold it over time, you will probably realize a profit when you sell it. The underlying security, gold, will not declare bankruptcy and disappear. Nevertheless, gold should not occupy a major position in your portfolio. Gold prices fluctuated widely during the 20th century, and they are affected by many economic factors. The return on your gold investment will be realized when you sell it for a higher price, adjusted for inflation and minus expenses, than you paid for it.

In the past, buying gold involved purchasing shares of gold-mining companies or paying sizeable commissions to buy gold coins or bricks, storing them in a secure vault, and insuring them. The streetTRACKS Gold Trust, PowerShares DB Gold, and iShares COMEX Gold Trust sell shares in the ownership of gold bullion. Each share represents one-tenth of an ounce of gold at current market prices, minus a 0.40 percent expense ratio.

The introduction of gold ETFs contributed to the rise in the price of gold by attracting the interest of private investors. In the first year after their launch, the streetTRACKS Gold Trust and iShares COMEX Gold Trust ETFs combined attracted $10 billion in assets. ETFs sponsored by the World Gold

Council now hold more than 700 tonnes of gold worth nearly $19 billion.

SILVER

Barclays iShares Silver Trust, introduced in April 2006, works in the same way as the gold ETFs. One share represents the ownership of ten ounces of silver. The expense ratio of 0.50 percent is less than the cost of paying commissions to buy silver and then storing it.

To set up iShares Silver Trust, Barclays had to purchase 1.5 million ounces of silver, causing the price of silver to shoot up in anticipation. In May 2006, the price of silver reached a 23-year high of $14.69 an ounce before declining.

The price of silver is volatile, but it has low correlation to other investments. It has had almost no correlation to the price of bonds, little correlation to stocks, and only 0.66 correlation to the price of gold. (See the "Correlation" section of "Chapter 13: Building Your Buy-and-Hold Portfolio.") This characteristic makes it a possible hedge against losses in other areas of a portfolio.

TAKE NOTE: PRECIOUS METAL ETFS ARE TAXED DIFFERENTLY

The U.S. Internal Revenue Service taxes gold and silver as collectibles, not as investments. Capital gains tax on the sale of collectibles is 28 percent rather than the 15 percent rate applied to capital gains from the sale of stocks. Precious metals should be held in a tax-advantaged account, such as an IRA.

TAKE NOTE: MANAGEMENT COSTS GRADUALLY ERODE ASSETS

Gold and silver do not bring in any income; an investor profits by selling them at a higher price than the original purchase price. Over time, the amount of gold represented by each share in a fund will decrease as gold is sold to pay the sponsor's fee and storage expenses (0.40 percent for gold and 0.50 percent for silver). U.S. investors are liable for taxes on the sale of gold or silver by an ETF to pay expenses.

General Commodity Funds

Commodities are products that are required every day, including food, such as livestock, grain, and sugar; and basic materials, such as steel and aluminum. Energy is traded as crude oil, natural gas, and electricity. Commodities are produced, bought, and sold all over the world all the time. When a shortage results in increased demand and higher prices, new producers gradually enter the market, and existing producers increase their output.

Investment in commodities is usually in the form of futures, or forwards. Futures are contracts to buy a commodity in the future at an agreed price. Only a small amount of money is required to secure the contract, with the remainder to be paid when the commodity is delivered.

Spot prices are the prices for which commodities are currently selling. Futures prices are calculated based on the current spot price, with adjustments for interest rates, seasonal changes, and transportation and storage costs. If it is believed that the spot price at the time a commodity is delivered will be much higher than it is today, the futures price will be set at a higher level than the current spot price. When the futures price is higher than the current spot price, it is known as a market in contango. When the spot price of a commodity at the time of delivery is expected to be lower than the current price, a lower futures price is set, and the market is said to be in backwardation.

When commodity futures are in backwardation, instead of purchasing a commodity at the existing high spot price, an investor can profit by purchasing inexpensive futures contracts and placing the remaining cash in short-term Treasury bills until the contracted commodity is due to be delivered. If the market is in contango, it is more profitable to purchase the commodity at the current lower spot price and store it for future delivery.

Academics are still debating whether investing in futures is more profitable than investing in stocks. Commodities futures are not long-term investments; they are short-term trading vehicles that attempt to take advantage of market timing by buying contracts and selling them just before the physical commodity is due to be delivered. ETFs that invest in futures must continually sell contracts as they near their expiration (delivery date) and buy new ones. If the new contracts are less expensive than the old ones, the fund makes a profit. If the new contracts are more expensive, the fund takes a loss.

For many years, the oil market was stuck in backwardation, and investors in energy futures were able to make money. Launched on April 10, 2006, the first crude oil ETF, United States Oil Fund (USO), was technically a commodity pool speculating on the future price of oil. It began trading at $68.25, roughly the price of a barrel of oil in April 2006. After one year, its closing price was $52.01, a decline of 23.8 percent. During the same period, the average price of a barrel of oil had fallen only 6.5 percent. USO lost money when the oil market moved into contango, and rolling over into new contracts produced a negative yield.

OIL

Several ETFs and ETNs track the price of oil.

NAME	INDEX	DESCRIPTION
United States Oil Fund (USO)	Spot price of West Texas Intermediate light, sweet crude oil	Seeks to have its NAV equal the outstanding value of oil futures contracts
iPath S&P GSCI Crude Oil Total Return ETN (OIL)	Goldman Sachs Crude Oil Total Return Index of futures contracts	Debt notes from Barclays PLC, promising to pay the exact return from the underlying index, minus 0.75 percent expense ratio
PowerShares DB Oil Fund (DBO)	Deutsche Bank Liquid Commodity Index - Optimum Yield Energy Excess Return Index	A rules-based index composed of futures contracts on heavily traded energy commodities

NAME	INDEX	DESCRIPTION
Claymore MACROshares Oil Up Tradeable Trust (UCR)	Settlement price of a designated New York Mercantile Exchange (NYMEX) division light sweet crude oil futures contract	UCR takes a long position on oil futures swap contracts, and DCR takes the opposite position. The two funds are supposed to closely track the price of a barrel of oil but have encountered difficulty doing so.
Claymore MACROshares Oil Down Tradeable Trust (DCR)		

GENERAL COMMODITY FUNDS

Commodities ETFs attempt to track commodity total return indexes. These indexes are futures price indexes and do not reflect current commodity spot prices. Total return indexes are designed to reflect the returns on fully collateralized commodity futures. A small amount of money is required to secure the contract, and the remaining amount to be paid when the commodity is delivered, the collateral, is invested in bonds until the contract matures. The total return is the price return on commodity futures, plus the difference in price between the old contracts that are about to be rolled over and the new contracts that will replace them, plus income from the Treasury bills in which the collateral is invested.

Three popular indexes that measure the performance of commodity prices are the S&P GSCI, the Dow Jones-AIG Commodities Index (DJ-AIGCI), and the Deutsche Bank (BD LCI). Each uses a different methodology for weighting the different commodity sectors and follows a different procedure for rebalancing them.

S&P GSCI (GSCI)

Considered the most widely followed commodities index, the GSCI (Goldman Sachs Commodity Index) was created by Goldman Sachs in 1991 and bought by Standard & Poor's in 2007. The index tracks the overall market value of 24 commodities: 6 energy products, 5 industrial metals, 8 agricultural products, 3 livestock products, and 2 precious metals.

The index is world-production-weighted; the quantity of each commodity in the index is decided according to the average value of its production over the past five years. Because the total value of oil produced is much greater than the production value of all other commodities, this index is heavily weighted to energy.

Dow Jones-AIG Commodities Index (DJ-AIGCI)

This popular index was created in 1998 and follows the movements of 20 commodities futures. It is not a market index following the values of the commodities, but it is a custom index. The index weights are rebalanced every January so that no commodity sector (such as energy) makes up more than 33 percent of the index, and no single commodity makes up more than 15 percent of its group or 2 percent of the total index.

Deutsche Bank (BD LCI)

Created in 2003, this index is designed to reflect the performance of the most liquid, globally traded commodities. Commodities in the index are assigned set weights, according to historic levels of world production and stock:

Deutsche Bank Liquid Commodity Index	
crude oil	35 percent
heating oil	20 percent
aluminum	12.5 percent
gold	10 percent
corn	11.25 percent
wheat	11.25 percent

Deutsche Bank assumes that other commodities in the same sectors are closely correlated with these major commodities so that the index reflects the performance of the market as a whole.

Sector and Subsector Indexes

A number of new ETF offerings track sectors and subsectors of the broad-based indexes. BGI offers the iShares GS Commodity Industrial Metals Trust, tracking a production-weighted index comprised of futures in copper, zinc, aluminum, nickel, and lead. iShares GS Commodity Livestock Indexed Trust tracks livestock commodities.

Other indexes attempt to reduce the exposure to energy-correlated commodities. The iShares S&P GS Commodity Light Energy Indexed Trust reduces the weight of energy from 77 percent to 39 percent. iShares S&P GS Commodity Non-Energy Indexed Trust excludes all energy-related commodities.

TAKE NOTE: COMMODITIES DO NOT OFFER LONG-TERM RETURNS

Though commodity ETFs and ETNs help diversify your portfolio and therefore reduce risk, they do not offer long-term returns. A passive investor should seek out other investments with low correlation that do offer long-term gains. Commodities ETFs and ETNs are good investment tools for active investors, who can profit from market timing.

TAKE NOTE: CURRENT PRICES DIFFER FROM FUTURES PRICES

Remember that commodity ETFs are trading in futures contracts and that the current (spot) price of a commodity can differ substantially from its futures price. When you read that the price of particular commodity is skyrocketing, it does not necessarily mean that the value of your commodity ETF is rising with it!

TAKE NOTE: COMMODITY ETFS ARE LESS TAX-EFFICIENT

Commodity ETFs are less tax-efficient than other ETFs. The U.S. Internal Revenue Service requires that all contracts be "marked to market" at the year's end, meaning that they are taxed as if they had been sold. Gains on commodity futures, including those held by ETFs, cannot be delayed. This does not apply to commodity ETNs because they are debt notes rather than direct investments in futures contracts. The capital gains tax on the sale of contracts is a maximum of 23 percent, which is higher than the tax on capital gains tax from the sale of stocks. Interest from Treasury notes held by commodity ETFs is also taxable. Tax laws change often; always consult a tax advisor before making investment decisions that may affect your annual tax return.

Currency ETFs and ETNs

ETFs now make it possible for individual investors to participate in the currency market, which was dominated by institutional investors in the past. In December 2005, Rydex launched the first currency ETF, the Euro Currency Trust, and has since added ETFs benchmarked to other currencies of major U.S. trading partners. Each ETF holds a different foreign currency with an overseas branch of JPMorgan Chase Bank.

The ETFs are intended to reflect the price of the currency in U.S. dollars. If a currency appreciates (increases in value) relative to the U.S. dollar, an investor can sell shares of the fund at a profit. If the value of the currency depreciates (decreases in value) relative to the U.S. dollar, the shareholder will incur a loss when shares of the ETF are sold. A small interest rate is paid on the money held in trust.

Rydex Foreign Currency ETFs

Each fund tracks the value of its underlying currency relative to the U.S. dollar, based on the Federal Reserve Noon Buying Rate.

PowerShares DB U.S. Dollar Bullish and Bearish

The PowerShares DB U.S. Dollar Bullish Fund (UUP) and the PowerShares DB U.S. Dollar Bearish Fund (UDN) track the Deutsche Bank U.S. Dollar Index (USDX). The index compares the value of the dollar to a GDP-weighted portfolio of six global currencies:

CURRENCIES	
Euro	57.6 percent
Japanese yen	13.6 percent
British pound	11.9 percent
Canadian dollar	9.1 percent
Swedish krona	4.2 percent
Swiss franc	3.6 percent

The two funds are intended to replicate the performance of futures contracts that are long (bullish) or short (bearish) and the U.S. dollar against those currencies. Deposits are placed on contracts to buy or sell U.S. dollars on a future date at a specified exchange rate. The remaining collateral is invested in Treasury notes, which guarantee interest, until the contracts near their execution dates.

Barclays Bank ETNs

In May 2007, Barclays Bank launched three ETNs to track the value of the U.S. dollar relative to the Euro, British pound, and Japanese yen:

- iPath EUR/USD (symbol: ERO)

- iPath GBP/USD (symbol: GBB)

- iPath JPY/USD (symbol: JYN)

These ETNs represent loans and earn interest based on the prevailing rates in their respective countries, minus a 0.40 percent fee; however, the interest is reinvested, and the value of the note continues to increase over time. The investor profits when shares of the note are sold.

Barclays has received an opinion from the Internal Revenue Service that its currency ETNs can be treated as prepaid contracts, and, therefore, owners of ETN shares are not liable for taxes on the interest. Investors in ETNs do not pay any taxes until they sell or redeem their shares, and any profit is taxed as long-term capital gains at 15 percent.

CurrencyShares (www.currencyshares.com). Rydex CurrencyShares pays out interest monthly; it is taxable as ordinary income at 35 percent.

PowerShares DB G10 Currency Harvest Fund (DBV). This ETF follows the Deutsche Bank G10 Currency Harvest Index, which is composed of long futures contracts on the three G10 currencies associated with high interest rates and short futures contracts on the three G10 currencies associated with the lowest interest rates. Collateral is invested in U.S. government securities. Returns from the index are expected to be less volatile because both long and short positions are taken.

Uses of Currency ETFs and ETNs

Currency ETFs and ETNs provide protection against downturns in the value of the U.S. dollar and exposure to foreign financial markets. Adding currency ETFs to a portfolio increases diversity because they have low correlation to other investments. ETFs for a foreign currency can hedge against loss if you have a business that buys imports from that country or invest in a company that conducts transactions in that currency.

If you plan to take an expensive vacation or to make a large purchase, such as real estate, art, or a luxury car, in a foreign country, you can purchase an ETF for the same amount of that country's currency now, to ensure that changes in the value of the U.S. dollar do not unbalance your budget. If the U.S. dollar is strong at the time when you realize your purchase, keep the ETF and sell it later when the dollar weakens.

Currency ETFs and ETNs also make it possible to participate in active currency trading without opening overseas bank accounts.

TAKE NOTE: ABOUT CURRENCY TRADING

Remember that shares of a foreign currency ETF or ETN are different from shares of an ETF tracking the ups and downs of various business sectors. Many factors affect the value of another country's currency relative to the U.S. dollar. Money is made simply by buying low and selling high, not through earnings or growth. With the exception of the ETNs, which invest at foreign interest rates and accumulate value, foreign currency investments do not belong in an average passive portfolio. Active traders can profit by watching the market closely.

TAKE NOTE: CONSIDER TAXES

Remember that profit from the sale of ETFs holding foreign currency is taxed as income rather than as capital gains and that the interest earned is also taxable.

Real Estate Investment Trusts (REITs)

Characteristics of REITs

Real estate investment trusts (REITs) are companies that hold portfolios of properties, such as office buildings, shopping malls, hotels, and timberland; or assets related to real estate, such as commercial mortgages. They use shareholders' investments to purchase, build, and maintain properties; manage tenants; collect rents; and return the profit to investors as dividends. There are approximately 200 publicly held REITs in the United States, and their stocks trade on the stock market. Because REITs make up only a small segment of the economy, the best way to gain exposure to them is to purchase a REIT fund. A number of mutual funds have ownership of groups of REITs, and several ETFs have followed suit. Several characteristics make REITs good candidates for a long-term portfolio.

LIMITED CORRELATION TO BROAD MARKET INVESTMENTS

Investment analysts Callan Associates claim that the FTSE/NAREIT Equity Index, an index of REITs, has had a correlation of 0.43 with the S&P 500 over the past 20 years, meaning that it moved opposite the S&P 500 more than half of the time. (See "Correlation" in "Chapter 13: Building Your Buy-and-Hold Portfolio.") The index has almost no correlation with bonds. REITs help to lower the volatility of a portfolio and ensure steady returns.

HIGH DIVIDENDS

The annual dividend rate of a typical REIT is between 5 percent and 7 percent, two to three times higher than the highest dividends paid by non-REIT stocks. Many stocks do not pay dividends at all. Whether the share price of an REIT rises or falls, dividends continue to be paid as long as the REIT is bringing in money. REITs are required by law to pay out 90 percent of their income as dividends to shareholders.

REITS REPRESENT TANGIBLE PROPERTY

Shares of a REIT ETF represent ownership of actual property.

TAKE NOTE: DIVIDENDS FROM REITS ARE TAXED AS REGULAR INCOME

REITs have a special tax status and do not pay income taxes. Therefore, dividends from REITs are taxed as regular income according to your income bracket and not at the 15 percent tax rate for dividends from stocks.

REIT ETFs

ISHARES COHEN & STEERS REALTY MAJORS INDEX FUND (ICF)

Based on the Cohen & Steers Realty Majors Index, this fund represents the largest REITs, making it less volatile. An investment committee selects 30 REITs for the index, based on each one's management, portfolio quality, geographic diversification, and real estate sector. The securities are weighted according to the value of their shares available on the market (free-float), and no single security can occupy more than 8 percent of the total index. The expenses are 0.35 percent, and the long-term return is probably slightly less than more specialized ETFs.

ISHARES DOW JONES U.S. REAL ESTATE INDEX FUND (IYR)

This ETF is benchmarked to the Dow Jones U.S. Real Estate Index, which contains approximately 93 companies. Some of these are real estate operating companies (REOCs), which have a different tax status and are not required to distribute 90 percent of their earnings to investors; instead, they are able to reinvest earnings in more projects. The expense ratio is 0.60 percent.

STREETTRACKS WILSHIRE REIT INDEX FUND (RWR)

This ETF tracks the Dow Jones Wilshire REIT Index, which attempts to measure the performance of publicly traded REITS rather than real estate companies. It has 85 components and does not hold healthcare REITs or REOCs. The expense ratio is 0.25 percent.

VANGUARD REIT ETF (VNQ)

This ETF is indexed to the Morgan Stanley U.S. REIT Index, which represents 105 REITs, about half of all publicly traded REITs and two-thirds of the value of the whole REIT market. This ETF has the lowest expense ratio and covers a broad market segment.

BGI ISHARES REIT SECTOR ETFS

In 2006, BGI launched three separate ETFs to allow investors to allocate resources to different real estate sectors and increase diversity. The indexes are taken from the broader, capitalization-weighted FTSE NAREIT Composite Index. The three subsectors are residential (apartments), industrial/office space, and retail.

WISDOMTREE INTERNATIONAL REAL ESTATE SECTOR FUND (DRW)

This ETF selects and weights real estate stocks according to the cash value of dividends paid. The index is dominated by Australia, Hong Kong, and Japan, and one-third is allocated to European countries.

REITS IN YOUR PORTFOLIO

Most financial advisors classify REITs as a separate asset class and include them in their clients' portfolios. The main benefit of holding REIT ETFs is the diversity they offer and their potential for growth. REIT ETFs give every investor the opportunity to buy into a broad group of real estate holdings.

Chapter 10

o o o o o

International Investing Global Equity ETFs

International investments are essential to any diversified portfolio. Today, more than two-thirds of the world stock market is outside the United States. Historically, American investors have been underinvested in foreign assets, but during the past few years, they have been hurrying to correct the imbalance. During 2005, 70 percent of money invested by U.S. citizens went to funds that invest overseas. In July 2007, State Street Global Advisors announced that the total assets of international ETFs rose 61 percent year-over-year through June 2007, from $80.8 billion to $129.8 billion. During the first six months of 2007, more than $25 billion flowed into international-stock ETFs, almost double the $13 billion invested in U.S.-stock offerings. Concerns about the U.S. economy during the mid-2000s, a weakening U.S. dollar, and a growing awareness of the globalization of business have fueled investor interest and created a market for more foreign ETF offerings.

Experts differ over what percentage of the equity in a portfolio should be devoted to foreign investments, ranging from a conservative estimate of 15 to 25 percent to an aggressive 50 percent. In the past, investing in foreign countries meant opening a foreign brokerage account, paying sizable commissions, and assuming substantial currency risk. International ETFs have now made international investing as easy as a few clicks on an online brokerage Web site. ETFs are a good tool for adding foreign investments to a portfolio for the same reasons that make them attractive domestic investments: They give instant access to a broad range of stocks and allow you to move your investment capital easily from one style or market sector to another.

Why Should You Include International ETFs in Your Portfolio?

Diversification

Adding foreign ETFs to your portfolio increases the number of securities in which you are investing and gives you exposure to more companies and industry sectors that may potentially expand and grow.

Returns from foreign investments are in foreign currencies. At times when the U.S. dollar weakens, their relative value increases for investors living in the United States. This may help to compensate for declines in the returns from domestic securities.

Lower Correlation

The prices of stocks in different markets tend to go up and down at different times. Since 1975, dominance of the world stock market has regularly alternated between U.S. stocks and non-U.S. stocks. When these fluctuations occur, a globally diversified portfolio naturally hedges one market against another. In the past, regularly rebalancing a portfolio between U.S. and international stocks has lowered overall risk and slightly increased returns.

Greater Returns

Economists and financial analysts are grappling with a rapidly changing global economy and with market trends that may turn out to be irreversible. New economic developments over the last two decades, such as the rapid industrialization of China and India, the establishment of the European

Union and success of the Euro, the movement of U.S. manufacturing overseas, and innovations in telecommunications, may have permanently altered the landscape of the investing world. It is possible that historical patterns will no longer repeat themselves.

Over the past few years, returns from foreign stocks have been greater than returns from U.S. stocks. According to Etfguide.com performance data, as of March 31, 2008, the five-year annualized return for the SPDR 500 (SPY), an ETF that tracks the S&P 500 Index, was 11.49 percent; and the iShares Dow Jones U.S. Total Market (IYY) was 12.37 percent. The annualized five-year return for the iShares S&P Europe 350 (IEV) was 21.71 percent; for iShares MSCI Japan Index (EWJ), it was 14.24 percent; for iShares MSCI Pacific ex-Japan Index Fund, it was 27.68 percent; and for the iShares MSCI Brazil Index Fund (EWZ), it was 65.15 percent. There is no way to predict exactly when the performance of U.S. stocks will improve relative to foreign stocks, but it is clear that these foreign ETFs would have been wise investments during the U.S. downturn of the mid-2000s.

TAKE NOTE: HISTORICAL CYCLES

Foreign stocks have been dominant for about three years, and historically, U.S. and foreign stocks have tended to dominate each other in three-year cycles. If the historical pattern continues, we may be close to a reversal in which U.S. stocks will again dominate.

Disadvantages of International ETFs
Tax Treatment of Dividends

When a company in a foreign country issues dividends to foreign investors, that country often removes taxes before the cash is paid out overseas. U.S. investors with taxable accounts can claim a tax credit for the amount of foreign tax withheld. However, if the investments are held in a nontaxable account, such as an Individual Retirement Account (IRA), the investor cannot claim a foreign tax credit.

Price Discovery

Most of the world's stock markets are closed when the U.S. stock market is actively trading international ETFs because of time differences. The NAV (actual value of the underlying securities in an index), calculated when the home market closed, quickly becomes stale, especially if the market is volatile or currency is fluctuating, and the ETF price on the U.S. market may vary widely from the NAV. Many U.S. investors think the U.S. market price for an international ETF is incorrect because of this, but it is more likely that the price on the U.S. stock market reflects the true value of the underlying securities more accurately than the NAV at that particular moment. If the markets were open in the home countries, the real-time NAV of the securities underlying the ETF would resemble the ETF pricing. Global market participants are able to use ETF prices to "discover" what the prices of the underlying stocks will be during the next trading day.

Increased Volatility Because of Currency Exchange Rates

International-equity ETFs quote prices in U.S. dollars, but the underlying stocks may be valued in another currency, such as Japanese yen. The Japanese price of a stock may not change, but its value in U.S. dollars will change if the value of the dollar goes up or down. ETFs tracking Japanese market indexes such as the Nikkei can experience considerable price movements on the U.S. stock exchange, even when the stock price remains stable in Japan, because the stock markets are closed for the night. If the U.S. dollar falls in value relative to the yen, U.S. investors holding Japanese stock are hedged against the fall; the reverse is also true.

Expenses

Domestic ETFs tend to be less expensive than foreign ETFs. Expense ratios for domestic broad market ETFs range from 0.08 percent to 0.38 percent, while the expense ratio for iShares S&P Europe 350 (IEV) is 0.60 percent, and for PowerShares FTSE RAFI Developed Markets ex-US (PXF), it is 0.75

percent. Expense ratios for international ETFs average 0.53 percent and are as high as 1.32 percent for Claymore/Robeco Developed International Equity (EEN).

Liquidity

The trading volume of the stocks underlying international ETFs may not be large enough to allow rapid creation or redemption of ETF shares if the market demand suddenly increases or decreases. There is increased risk that an international ETF will continue to sell at a price above or below its NAV for extended periods.

TAKE NOTE: VOLATILITY IS COMPOUNDED BY CURRENCY FLUCTUATIONS

Foreign ETFs are more volatile than the markets they represent because they are denominated in foreign currency, such as Euros, yen, or British pounds. Rises and falls in stock prices may be compounded if the exchange rates rise or fall on the same day. If stock prices rise on a day that the exchange rate for the U.S. dollar falls, the value of your ETF will rise dramatically. The reverse is also true; if stock prices and the U.S. dollar exchange rate fall on the same day, the losses will be compounded.

TAKE NOTE: DO NOT PUT ALL YOUR EGGS IN A FOREIGN BASKET

An American investor is living within the economy of the United States. The stock market tends to follow the economy, doing best in a robust economy, which is also accompanied by inflation. Because the value of stocks rises along with inflation, investors are usually able to maintain equilibrium. If the U.S. economy heats up, but your investments are all in Europe or another area of the world where the economy is flat, you will be living with inflation and higher prices, but the value of your stocks will not increase.

What You Should Know About International ETFs

Today, there are more than 140 global and foreign ETFs, offering everything from exposure to the whole world, to investments in specific countries and narrow market sectors. Many of the global ETFs launched during 2007 represented forays into foreign small-cap stocks, pharmaceuticals, real estate, and energy, reflecting increasing investor awareness of economic growth overseas.

Before investing in them, you should become familiar with several ways in which foreign ETFs differ from domestic ones. Foreign ETFs are investing in assets that are regulated by different laws and affected by economic factors different from those that affect business in the United States. Although you can purchase foreign ETFs with U.S. dollars from American providers, the underlying securities are, for the most part, outside the U.S.

Terminology

Global ETFs, also called world mutual funds, may hold U.S. stocks along with the international stocks. International ETFs, also called foreign, overseas, or ex-U.S. securities, hold only non-U.S. stocks. The prospectus of each ETF describes its methodology for selecting stocks.

Developed markets are economically and socially advanced countries with a GDP (Gross Domestic Product) per capita of $20,000 or more. The developed markets include the U.S., Japan, Western Europe, Canada, New Zealand, and Australia, and account for more than 80 percent of the market capitalization in the global equity market.

Emerging markets are developing countries that have maintained sustained economic growth over several years and exhibit good economic potential. They may not have a mature economy, stable securities market, or advanced banking system, and have a GDP lower than $20,000 per capita. Examples of emerging markets are China, India, Mexico, Brazil, Chile, much of Southeast Asia, South Asia, countries in Eastern Europe, the Middle East, parts of Africa, and Latin America. More than 150 economies meet at least some of the criteria for emerging markets; over 100 of them have stock exchanges.

The MSCI Emerging Markets Index, an index created by Morgan Stanley Capital International (MSCI) to measure stock market performance in global emerging markets, included 26 countries (as of May 2005): Argentina, Brazil, Chile, China, Colombia, Czech Republic, Egypt, Hungary, India, Indonesia, Israel, Jordan, Korea, Malaysia, Mexico, Morocco, Pakistan, Peru, Philippines, Poland, Russia, South Africa, Taiwan, Thailand, Turkey, and Venezuela. MSCI evaluates companies according to GDP, local government regulations, foreign ownership limits, capital controls, and perceived investment risk. The index is market capitalization– and free-float–weighted. As of March 2008, the top five countries in the MSCI Emerging Markets Index were Brazil, China, Korea, Taiwan, and Russia, accounting for more than 60 percent of total weight in the benchmark.

The S&P Emerging Markets Indexes and their underlying database, which S&P purchased from International Finance Corporation (IFC) in 2000, now cover more than 2,000 companies in established markets.

Index providers may differ in the way they make the distinction between an emerging market and a developed market. Countries such as South Korea, Taiwan, Israel, and Czech Republic, which have now developed beyond the emerging market phase, may be kept in an index to maintain continuity. Small countries may be excluded from an index because their market liquidity is limited and substituted with a larger neighbor in the same region.

Emerging markets carry additional political, economic, and currency risks. Nevertheless, they often exhibit low correlation with developed markets and can be used to lower the overall risk of a portfolio.

BRIC is an acronym for Brazil, Russia, India, and China. In 2003, Goldman Sachs published a paper arguing that the rapidly developing economies of these four countries would be wealthier than most of the current major economic powers by 2050. The BRIC theory suggests that China and India will become the world's dominant suppliers of manufactured goods and services, respectively, while Brazil and Russia will become dominant as suppliers of raw materials.

TAKE NOTE: THE BRIC COUNTRIES ARE NOT ALL ALIKE

The four BRIC countries should not be regarded as a single economic entity. Each one offers unique possibilities for economic growth and has unique strengths and weaknesses.

Country Risk Factors

In addition to the market risk factors affecting domestic investments, there are special risks associated with investing in specific foreign countries.

Currency risk is the risk that the value of a foreign currency will rise relative to the U.S. dollar, causing the investment to lose value in U.S. dollars, even though the price of the stock remains the same. The reverse is also true; if the value of a foreign currency falls against the U.S. dollar, the value of an investment will increase.

Sovereign risk is the risk that a foreign government will default on its bonds. The U.S. government guarantees repayment of its bond obligations based on its authority to tax the people of the United States. Other governments may not have the same authority, or their economies may become so constrained that they do not have the resources to meet their obligations.

Political risk is the risk that political developments such as civil strife, war, a change of government, or a coup d'etat will weaken an economy or undermine contractual agreements. Examples include the destruction of infrastructure by war, nationalization of private companies by a government, and corruption.

Banking risk is the risk associated with foreign banks. It includes the possibility that banks in other countries may fail because of bad management or poor fiscal policy, or that the banks in a foreign country may not have enough liquidity in U.S. dollars to make payments to American investors.

Economic structure risk is the risk that the economic structure of a country will jeopardize the development of its economy, or that changes in economic structure will affect business. For example, as the economy grows in a developing country with low-wage manufacturing, salaries begin to increase until eventually the manufacturing industry is no longer able to compete with other low-wage economies.

Adding International ETFs to Your Portfolio

Choose international ETFs for your portfolio using the same principles you followed for your domestic investments: Seek diversity and minimize costs. The purpose of investing internationally is to expose your portfolio to new avenues of potential growth and to reduce overall risk with investments that will compensate for downturns in other areas of the market. A single global ETF can meet diversity requirements, but investing in individual market sectors or regions offers greater potential returns. If a portfolio is large enough, it should divide international investments by style as well as market.

To minimize the risks inherent in international investing, research each ETF carefully. Information about international ETFs and their holdings is readily available through their prospectuses and the Web sites of ETF providers, stock exchanges, and brokers. News media and articles by financial advisors provide valuable insight into the political and economic circumstances of each geographical region.

Evaluating International ETFs

There are a number of questions to ask when you are evaluating international ETFs:

What is the correlation between the stock market of a foreign country and the U.S. stock market?

The economies of some countries, such as Canada, closely follow the United States. The economies of Japan, which has the second largest stock market, and the BRIC countries offer the lowest correlation. A high correlation with the U.S. economy does not necessarily mean that you should not invest in that country or region, because other factors, such as the value of the U.S. dollar relative to the currency of that country, may still offer protection when the U.S. economy experiences a decline.

How large is the home stock market of the country?

Most countries do not have large stock markets; the number of securities held by an ETF for a country with a small stock market will be restricted. If the stock market of a country is small, it is better to invest in the region of which that country is a part.

How is the valuation of the country's stock market as a whole?

High prices may mean that a sector or region has already attracted a considerable amount of investment and that stocks may be overvalued. The best time to enter a foreign stock market is when prices are low, but there are signs that the economy is recovering and political problems are coming to an end.

How is the overall political and economic stability of a country?

Examine the political and corporate governance, attitude towards corruption and the process of law, and fiscal discipline of a country or region. Developed markets are characterized by advanced banking structures, mature legal and political systems, and the existence of good working relationships with other countries and regions. They often have safeguards in place to protect the assets of private investors. Emerging markets are considered much more volatile, entailing greater risk but promising the possibility of rapid growth and expansion into new markets. Could impending political unrest disrupt the financial markets in the region? What is the possibility of a bank failure or a change of government that could dramatically alter the economic structure of a country?

What is the price-to-earnings (P/E) ratio of the ETF?

A lower P/E ratio is an indicator of promising returns. A higher P/E ratio is an indication that increasing investor interest has already raised the prices of the underlying securities.

What are the assets and the countries represented by each ETF?

Adding international ETFs to your portfolio does not automatically ensure diversity. Large multinational corporations that are active in the U.S. will be subject to the same economic fluctuations as American companies. An international ETF may be weighted towards an industry sector in which your domestic portfolio is already heavily invested. Look at the ETF prospectus to see what its top ten securities are and how they are weighted. The top ten provides a useful snapshot of the ETF as a whole.

Many international ETFs have more than half of their total assets concentrated in the top five or six companies, increasing exposure to company-specific risk. International ETFs may also contain a large proportion of small-cap companies.

Look closely at the index tracked by an international ETF to get a clear understanding of the markets in which it is investing. For example, several broad market ETFs track the MSCI Europe, Australia, and Far East Index (EAFE), which contains 21 developed countries. The index weights the stock markets of each country by their market value so that 50 percent of its weight goes to just two countries: Japan and the United Kingdom. Smaller countries, such as Singapore, Ireland, and Indonesia, which have potential for rapid growth, make up only a small percentage of the index weight.

Strategies for Global Investing with ETFs

CREATE YOUR OWN INTERNATIONAL PORTFOLIO

International broad market indexes use weighting that tends to concentrate heavily on the countries with the largest stock markets: Japan and the United Kingdom. Simply purchasing one or two international broad market ETFs to fulfill the international allocation of your portfolio does not offer exposure to some of the most promising opportunities for growth in the international market. The establishment of the European Union has stimulated economic growth of smaller European countries. The government of Singapore is investing heavily in research, with a goal of becoming a center for life sciences and financial services. India's middle class has quadrupled in four decades. Diversify the international portion of your portfolio by adding ETFs for specific countries or regions that have the potential to bring in higher returns than the broad market.

Keep track of your international portfolio by creating a simple chart. Make a list of all the countries included in your international broad market ETFs. Multiply the percentage of the broad market index devoted to each country by the amount you have invested in that ETF, and write it down. As you add specialized or country-specific ETFs, record the amount you are investing in each country included in those indexes. Japan, the United Kingdom, and other developed markets, as well as lower-risk international investments, should still dominate your total portfolio, but you can increase your exposure to areas with good potential for growth. If one sector or region begins to decline, you can short an ETF for that region to protect your investment. If a region experiences rapid growth, preserve your gains by rebalancing your international portfolio and moving some of them into safer, more stable areas.

DIVERSIFY WITH COMMODITY AND INDUSTRY-SECTOR ETFS

Globalization and economic growth in emerging markets has increased the demand for transportation and for commodities, such as oil, steel, and construction materials. The media is full of stories about world shortages of food and water. Commodity and industry-sector ETFs provide an opportunity to buy into these global trends and to offset losses caused by economic pressures in the domestic economy.

SEPARATE THE BRIC

In his book, *ETF Investing Around the World*, Carl T. Delfeld points out that Russia and Brazil are essentially dependent on commodity prices, while China and India are rapidly developing their manufacturing and service industries. Each of these countries has a very different economic and political structure. India is a democracy with an established stock market and legal protection for property rights; China has a totalitarian government that can quickly enact reforms, but many of China's companies are state-owned and have limited potential for growth. Brazil is the leading economic power in South America. Russia is undergoing a period of political uncertainty, and its stock market prices depend largely on energy prices. Mr. Delfeld suggests investing in country-specific ETFs to take advantage of the different growth opportunities — and risks — they offer.

USE OPTIONS AS PROTECTION

Buy put options to protect investments in risky international markets. If you are buying an ETF in a foreign market that is exhibiting an upward trend but is subject to an uncertain political risk, invest in put options, which will allow you to limit your loss by selling your ETF at a prearranged price if its value drops. The option will expire unexercised if the upward trend continues, and its cost will have to be subtracted from your earnings, but you are protected against major losses if things go wrong.

TAKE NOTE: INTERNATIONAL INVESTMENTS ARE ASSOCIATED WITH ADDITIONAL RISKS

Make sure you understand the additional risks involved in international investing. International investments may duplicate some of the investments already held by your portfolio, causing it to deviate from your target asset allocation and increasing portfolio risk.

CASE STUDY: MITSUNORI NAKAGAWA

Mitsunori Nakagawa is a private investor living in Hiroshima, Japan. Nakagawa offers the following insights regarding international investing:

I include exchange traded funds in my portfolio because I expect them to bring good returns. I would strongly recommend ETFs to a novice investor because the risk is low compared to other investments. My portfolio includes ETFs from Germany, Switzerland, Spain, and the United States. The ETFs of foreign countries are popular with Japanese investors because interest rates in Japan have become low and foreign investments are much more attractive. Recently, though, Japanese investors have become wary of the U.S. stock market because of the perceived economic downturn.

My biggest investing mistake was attempting to enter the foreign exchange market. When the exchange rate did not move as expected, I incurred losses from which I was not able to recover. My most successful investment has been a European fund. Japanese are cautious about investing in global markets at the moment because of the subprime mortgage crisis, which brings back unpleasant memories of what happened when the Japanese real estate bubble burst. They are interested in India now because the economy there is expanding rapidly and beginning to mature.

Chapter 11

○ ○ ○ ○ ○

Doing the Research

One characteristic that makes ETFs such good vehicles for investment is their transparency. By definition, an ETF is required to make available at all times information about the underlying stocks it holds. Each ETF tracks a rules-based index of some kind and publishes its objectives in its prospectus. The estimated NAV of all ETFs is calculated every 15 seconds and posted on stock exchange Web sites and a number of investment Web sites, including those of the ETF companies, along with price data.

You do not need to do extensive market research before investing in ETFs — the indexes have already done that work for you. Unless you are a day trader, you do not need to check the NAV of an ETF several times a day or even several times a month. In order to allocate assets correctly in a portfolio, you do need to understand the index tracked by each ETF, its investment style, and something about its holdings. The Internet carries a vast quantity of information. With a little perseverance, you should be able to find everything you need to know about an ETF. Never be satisfied until all your questions have been answered and you feel confident that you fully understand how you are investing your capital.

A number of reference books and ETF directories, such as *Morningstar 105*, are available in print, and you can order ETF prospectuses from the fund sponsors. New ETFs are launched almost every week, and developments are occurring so rapidly that you should always double-check printed information against the latest online information. Always look at the publication date of a book or article before jumping to conclusions.

Where to Look for Information

The first place to look for information about an ETF is on the Web site of the exchange on which it is trading. Most ETFs trade on the American Stock Exchange (AMEX) (**www.amex.com**), the New York Stock Exchange (NYSE) (**www.nyse.com**), or NASDAQ (**www.nasdaq.com**). A few of the Barclays Bank ETFs trade on the London Stock Exchange (**www. londonstockexchange.com**). ETF options also trade on the Chicago Board Options Exchange (CBOE) (**www.cboe.com**). ETF futures contracts trade on two futures exchanges: the Chicago Mercantile Exchange (CME) (**www. cme.com**) and OneChicago (**www.onechicago.com**). If you don't know where a particular ETF is trading, you can begin with one of the brokerage or investment information sites, such as Morningstar (**www.morningstar. com**), ETF Guide (**www.etfguide.com**), or Yahoo! Finance (**www.finance. yahoo.com/etf**), where there are complete listings of all ETFs, broken down by style and sector. Still cannot find what you are looking for? Type a few keywords into a search engine, and look for a listing or a relevant article.

The exchange and financial sites contain educational materials, such as tutorials and glossaries, to help you get started. If you are puzzled by the terminology, go to a search engine and find alternative definitions. The first page for an ETF often contains NAV and price data. The ETF profile gives important information, such as its expense ratio, inception date, trading volume, and asset holdings. You will often find an excerpt from the prospectus describing the fund's objectives or a link to the fund sponsor's Web site. You may also find other important information, such as the investment style of the ETF or average data for other ETFs of the same asset class.

After you have studied the official information about an ETF, you will want to know more about the index it is tracking. If this information is not on the fund sponsor's Web site, you can visit the Web site of the index provider. You may want to know what financial analysts or other private investors think about the ETF. Type the ETF symbol or name in a search engine, and you will find blogs and articles related to it. Remember to check the date on which an article was published before reading it. Sites like **www.seekingalpha.com**, **www.indexuniverse.com**, **www.fool.com**, **www.etfconnect.com**, **www.finance.yahoo.com/etf**, **www.indexinvestor. com**, and **www.etfzone.com**, publish commentary and breaking news about ETFs. These articles are written by financial analysts, investment advisers, and individual investors, some of whom may be promoting their own strategies. A review of several articles about an ETF will alert you to potential risks and give you a better understanding of its methodology and the risk it carries.

Finally, if you still have questions about an ETF, pick up the phone and call the sponsor's customer service department, or e-mail your online brokerage.

For official information about the handling of dividends, fund management, and tax issues, visit the Web sites of the IRS (**www.irs.gov**) and the SEC (**www.sec.gov**). The SEC offers detailed information about specific ETFs, ETF sponsors, and brokerages. These sites also feature educational materials.

Understanding the Data

When you look at the financial pages in a newspaper, listings on a stock exchange Web site, or the "ETF screeners" on various online brokerage and financial sites, you will find the same basic information presented in different ways. Many ETF listings allow you to conveniently compare important data for all the ETFs of a particular style or market sector or to select ETFs using different criteria, such as expense ratio or fund group.

Fund Provider:

The fund provider or fund sponsor is the company that has created the ETF.

Ticker or Symbol:

The three-letter (sometimes four-letter) acronym by which the fund is identified in the stock exchange.

Expense Ratio:

The percentage of an ETF's average net assets used to pay its annual expenses. Because these expenses eat into returns over time, a lower expense ratio is more desirable. ETFs following broad market indexes have lower expense ratios than those following custom indexes or specializing in specific asset classes. Higher returns from a more aggressive investment strategy might justify the increased expenses.

Inception Date:

The date on which an ETF was launched. The inception date is important because it tells you how long the fund has been on the market. Many ETFs are so new that there is little data available to evaluate their performance relative to the broad market.

Market Price Return:

The annualized return is the average return of a fund for each year of a multiyear period. If available, annualized returns are shown for one-, three-, five-, and ten-year periods. Annualized return takes into account the reinvestment of dividends and capital gains as well as the change in the price (NAV) of the ETF over a specific period. A consistent return over a long time indicates lower volatility and less risk. Only a few ETFs have been in existence long enough to supply meaningful data. Some ETF providers analyze the past performance of the index on which an ETF is based to make projections about future performance.

The YTD (year to date) return shows how an ETF is performing in the current market. A comparison of the YTD returns of ETFs in different industry sectors provides a snapshot of broad market performance. The NAV YTD of an ETF shows the performance of the underlying stocks in an index and may vary from the performance of the ETF itself.

Price Data:

Price information, including the price of the last trade, price at the close of the previous trading day or week, and price range for the previous trading day, gives you an idea of how much you will pay for shares of an ETF. When you place a buy order, it may not be filled at the exact price listed. Graphs showing daily or weekly price movements may give an indication of the volatility of an ETF and expose an upward or downward trend.

Average Market Capitalization:

The average market capitalization is an indication of the size of the companies included in an ETF. Most brokerage and financial Web sites classify ETFs by style and sector.

Trading Volume, Shares Outstanding, and Total Assets:

Trading volume is the number of shares of an ETF that have been traded over a specific time. Shares outstanding is the number of shares of an ETF that have been created. Total assets is the total amount invested in the ETF.

Larger numbers are an indication of popularity with investors. New shares of an ETF are created whenever investor demand begins to drive the price above the fund's NAV. A relatively new ETF may not have had time to attract large amounts of capital, but one that has been on the market for two or three years and still does not have substantial total assets may be thinly traded. An ETF that is not popular with investors may be difficult to sell.

Risk:

The data on an ETF includes indicators for risk, such as the ETF's beta and Sharpe and Treynor ratios. You can also look at charts showing the ETF's volatility over time and its performance relative to the market or to specific market sectors. Many of the ETFs with the greatest inherent risk are relatively new, and there may not be enough data for an accurate assessment. Some investment Web sites include correlation comparisons that allow you to see how an ETF correlates to other ETFs or to the broad market. The style of an ETF also tells you something about its risk: an emerging market ETF entails more risk than an ETF following a broad market index.

Style:

Most listings classify ETFs by style, and the style of an ETF is usually evident in its name. The description of the index tracked by an ETF will give a clearer picture of its style.

P/E Ratio:

The price-to-earnings ratio is a measure of the price of an ETF relative to its return. A low P/E may be an indicator that an ETF is undervalued and therefore has good potential for growth, but P/E ratios do not have the same significance for ETFs as they do for individual stocks. Each ETF provider calculates the P/E ratio differently. In the case of an ETF, a low P/E ratio may be associated with higher risk, increased volatility, or uncertain foreign markets.

Index and Top Ten Holdings:

This information may be summarized by a brokerage, but detailed information can be found on the ETF provider's Web site. Each prospectus explains the methodology for selecting and weighting securities in the index tracked by the ETF and lists all its holdings. Look at the top ten holdings and how they are weighted in the index. In some indexes, most of the weight may be allocated to two or three companies or countries. It is important to make sure that the ETF holdings are in line with the asset allocations in your portfolio.

ETFGuide.com uses Index Strategy Boxes, developed and pioneered by Richard A. Ferri, CFA of Portfolio Solutions LLC, to provide a quick, graphic representation of the index strategy followed by each ETF.

TAKE NOTE: TAKE IT WITH A GRAIN OF SALT

Always be aware of the source of your information. Literature published by brokerages and investment counselors may paint a rosy or unrealistic picture in an effort to sell a particular investment or financial product. Use other sources to verify the information. Remember that high rates of return entail high risk. Over time, the adjusted return for the stock market as a whole is around 7 percent.

○ ○ ○ ○ ○

Section 2

Investing with ETFs

Chapter 12

o o o o o

Choosing
Your Investment Strategy

What Type of Investor Are You?

The safest, most effective way to profit from ownership of an ETF is simply to buy shares of an ETF based on one of the broad indexes and hold on to them for the long term. Passive investing, a popular strategy implemented by millions of investors, is often called "buy and hold." Passive investing does not involve market timing or predictions about the future of the market. The investor simply holds the ETFs for a time as the underlying shares gradually increase in value. The only trading in a passively managed portfolio is done when it is necessary to rebalance asset classes or when cash is added or withdrawn.

Index Funds plus Active Management

Many passive investors use a strategy in which they combine low-cost, market-index ETFs with a few costlier custom-index ETFs that promise higher yields, or they purchase ETFs from a style or sector that seems about to experience a surge in market value. An investor who has a practical understanding of a particular market sector may invest in an ETF reflecting that market. The hope is that the market-index portion of the portfolio will achieve market returns and that the custom portion will achieve superior returns. Even if the custom portion does poorly, the total portfolio will not be far from market returns.

Another strategy is to have two portfolios: a conservative one to preserve assets and an aggressive one that takes higher risks and aims for rapid growth.

Life-cycle Investing

Life-cycle investing is a form of buy-and-hold strategy in which an investor's portfolio is adjusted as he or she moves through different stages of life. Asset allocations remain constant during each stage, but investment strategies change as the investor moves from youth to middle age to retirement.

Investors pass through four general stages in their financial lives: an aggressive stage during their youth, when they have few financial liabilities and time to make up for financial mistakes; a more conservative stage during middle age, when an investor considers the need to prepare for old age and retirement; retirement, when the investor relies on investment to provide a steady stream of income; and late retirement, when an investor begins to consider the needs of his heirs as well as his own requirements.

Active Trading

Active trading is an attempt to achieve returns greater than those of the financial markets by identifying and buying stocks that are about to increase in value and selling stocks that are about to decline. Active investors use strategies, such as buying on margin, selling short, and purchasing options to increase their returns. An active investor spends time researching the market on a daily basis, looking for opportunities such as price and value discrepancies, studying economic forecasts, and keeping an eye on price momentum. ETFs provide many opportunities for active investors to shift their assets easily and rapidly from one market to another.

Special Strategies

ETFs can be used for special purposes, such as to fill out an asset class that is underrepresented in a portfolio, hedge against a downturn in the price of a particular stock, manage currency risks, or secure certain tax advantages.

TAKE NOTE: HISTORICAL RETURNS OF ACTIVE TRADERS

Statistical research shows that active traders average lower returns than the market over time. The safest, most effective way to profit from ownership of an ETF is to buy shares of an ETF based on one of the broad indexes and to hold on to them for the long term.

Buy and Hold: The Most Successful Investment Strategy

Passive investing, a popular strategy implemented by millions of investors, is often called "buy and hold." The goal of passive management is to achieve the same return as the stock markets. ETFs are ideal for this purpose because even a relatively small investment buys exposure to every area of the financial markets. Broad market ETFs, which are constituted of a mix of shares reflecting one of the major market indexes, will continue to grow in value as the stocks in the index grow, following the fluctuations of the stock market as a whole. The investor holds the ETFs for a time as the underlying shares gradually increase in value. The only trading in a passively managed portfolio is done when it is necessary to rebalance asset classes or when cash is added or withdrawn.

Index mutual funds have been popular with passive investors for a long time because they could invest in the broad market by purchasing shares of just one or two funds. ETFs provide a lower-cost, more tax-efficient alternative to many mutual funds. The transparency of ETFs allows investors to see exactly where their money is invested. Private investors have easy access to ETFs because they are bought and sold on the stock exchanges; theoretically, the minimum investment is the price of one share, and there is no entry fee.

Passive Investing Is Straightforward

Select an assortment of asset classes that fits your long-term investment goals, and decide how much of your portfolio to allocate to each of those asset classes. Most portfolios include fixed-income and growth and value equity assets. Larger portfolios are further diversified with specific market sectors and styles, international equity, and commodity funds.

Buy the correct quantities of low-cost ETFs or mutual funds to represent those asset classes.

Rebalance. Over time, the global financial markets will change, and the portfolio will begin to deviate from its original asset allocation. Periodic rebalancing is needed to maintain the portfolio's original mix of asset classes. From time to time, review your asset allocation to bring your portfolio in line with your financial goals.

Iron Rules for Success

Several rules will optimize the success of a buy-and-hold portfolio of ETFs. Keep these rules in mind when making investment decisions.

SEEK DIVERSITY

A diverse portfolio offers exposure to all sectors of the financial markets so that you can benefit from a sudden upturn in any market sector. It also minimizes risk by offsetting downturns in one sector with gains in another. Make sure your ETFs do not duplicate each other or overlap too much.

BUY LOW-COST ETFS

Most passive investors purchase ETFs that use market indexes because their expense ratio is lower than ETFs following custom indexes, which require some kind of active management and increased trading costs. Over time, an expense ratio that is even a fraction of a percentage point higher can mean a big bite into your returns, especially if the custom index does not perform as expected.

AVOID COMMISSIONS BY TRADING INFREQUENTLY

Each trade incurs a trading fee, which is money that you cannot reinvest. Trading should only be done occasionally to rebalance a portfolio. If you intend to invest small amounts at frequent intervals, such as a portion of your monthly paycheck, save your money in an online savings account until you have accumulated enough capital for a large, one-time purchase.

MINIMIZE CAPITAL GAINS TAXES

Hold on to the ETFs that have increased in value so that you will not have to pay capital gains tax when you sell them. The only exception might be if you are holding the ETFs in a tax-deferred account, such as an IRA, and you will be reinvesting the money immediately. If you need cash, it is better to sell an ETF that has not gained much in value or even to sell at a loss and take a tax credit.

TAKE NOTE: STICK TO YOUR PLAN

At times, when the stock market is going through a difficult period, passive investors are tempted to change their investment strategy, but this inevitably results in lower returns and higher risk. Trading fees for buying and selling shares of stocks or ETFs eat into returns. If the market is depressed, prices will be lower, and the investor will be selling at a loss from which it will be difficult to recover. If an investor buys into market sectors that fare better during difficult times, such as energy and gold, he or she will be buying — at higher prices — the very stocks that will decrease in value as soon as the market improves. In the process, portfolio asset allocations will be changed, making the overall portfolio more volatile.

Chapter 13

o o o o o

Building Your
Buy-and-Hold Portfolio

The key to a successful buy-and-hold portfolio is the selection of a good allocation of asset classes from the beginning. Allocation of assets has been identified as the single most important factor in the growth of a buy-and-hold portfolio. The long-term mix between growth and value stock funds and fixed-income funds will determine the ultimate return and risk of the portfolio. Over the past century, stocks have performed well, but when the stock market falls, bonds retain their value and act as a safety net. On the other hand, if the rate of inflation rises near or above the interest returned by the bonds, a portfolio too heavily invested in fixed income will barely break even.

Time is another important element. The average return of the stock market over time is around 10 percent, 7 percent when adjusted for inflation. Given enough time, the compounded earnings from a modest investment are significant. The passage of time evens out market fluctuations, allowing your investment to grow rapidly when the stock market is doing well and to recover from inevitable downturns. The ideal time to begin a buy-and-hold portfolio is as soon as you become a wage earner, with a long career in front of you. Even if you have only a few years of investment left, a buy-and-hold portfolio can grow significantly if it is carefully maintained.

A third important element is regular investment of capital. The average couple needs to set aside an estimated 15 percent of their annual income to generate a retirement income that will support the lifestyle enjoyed during their working years.

Modern Portfolio Theory

Modern portfolio theory, which quantifies the benefits of diversification, was developed by Harry Markowitz and first presented to the public in an article entitled "Portfolio Selection" in the 1952 *Journal of Finance*. Markowitz suggested that risk should be calculated, not by looking at the risk and return of a single investment, but by evaluating that risk in relation to all the other securities in a diversified portfolio. The risk of owning one investment could be offset by purchasing the stock of companies in other sectors whose risk was not directly related. A portfolio containing a number of high-risk investments could actually carry a moderate risk as a whole if those investments were selected from sectors or styles that historically move up and down under different economic conditions.

Correlation

Correlation is the degree to which two investments move together in the market. The correlation coefficient is a measure of how closely the standard deviations of two stocks or indexes follow each other. A correlation coefficient can range between 1 and -1, with 1 indicating that the standard deviations of the two investments are perfectly synchronized and -1 indicating that they always move in completely opposite directions from each other. Including two investments with a correlation of -1 in your portfolio would constitute ideal diversity and provide optimum protection against risk. Unfortunately, negative correlations between two investments that both bring in positive returns are hard to find.

Efficient Frontier

Using the returns from a specified period, each investment in the portfolio can be assigned an expected value, standard deviation, and correlation. The expected return and volatility of the entire portfolio also can be calculated. Certain portfolios, which optimally balance risk and reward, make up what Markowitz called an efficient frontier. Ideally, an investor should select a portfolio from the efficient frontier.

Managing Risk

What Is Risk?

Risk is the possibility that things will not go as you plan, that something will go wrong and you will experience some kind of detrimental effect because of circumstances beyond your control. You experience some type of risk in every aspect of your life. For example, every time you get into a car to go somewhere, you experience the possibility that you might damage your car, suffer an injury, or even lose your life in an accident. The risk of having an accident does not stop you from using cars as a convenient form of transportation, but you are always aware of it. It may, on occasion, cause you some anxiety. If you stay at home and do not go anywhere, the risk of having an automobile accident is almost negligible. You know that you can decrease the risk of having an accident if you maintain your brakes and tires, obey traffic signals, respect the speed limit, avoid using cell phones while driving, get off the road when you are sleepy, and stay off the road when you have been drinking. Even if you are involved in an accident, you know that you can decrease the risk of serious injury or death if you consistently use seat belts and have air bags in your vehicle. Statistical research confirms that all these factors decrease the risk of driving a car. However, you cannot control the behavior of another impaired driver or the risk of unexpected hazards, such as a cow in the road or a truck skidding on ice. Sometimes a driver, such as a young drag racer or the owner of a new sports car, deliberately increases risk for himself or herself and for other drivers because he or she wants to enjoy a thrill or get somewhere in a hurry.

Investment risk is similar to the risk of driving a car. An investor has a long-term goal, to provide for his or her financial needs or the financial needs of others. That goal can be achieved through investing his or her capital in the stock market, but there is always some risk that the capital will be lost or diminished. An investor can protect his capital and reduce risk by choosing safe investments, such as U.S. Treasury bills, CDs, and Federal Deposit Insurance Corporation (FDIC)-insured savings accounts, which offer lower returns. He or she can do careful research to protect himself or herself against high investment costs, select investments that have a demonstrated rate of return, and maintain a diversified portfolio. He or she can go further and buy some investments in one sector that might compensate for possible losses in another. He or she may choose to take a deliberate risk in hopes of accelerating the rate of return. However, this person cannot control the adverse effects of an economic downturn or a natural disaster.

Two Kinds of Stock Market Risk

Investing in the stock market has two types of risk: systemic and nonsystemic.

Nonsystemic risk is associated with investing all your capital in a single company or market sector. Your investment is tied to the fortunes of that company; if its business fails for some reason or if bad publicity causes the price of its stock to fall, your capital is lost. Exchange traded funds eliminate nonsystemic risk by selling shares in a whole basket of diversified securities. An ETF that is highly concentrated in a particular sector or that contains only a few stocks may be subject to some nonsystemic risk.

Systemic risk is the risk associated with the stock market and the economy as a whole. ETFs do not protect an investor against systemic risk. Systemic risk affects the entire stock market and includes the following:

- **Market fluctuations:** As the stock market rises and falls, the value of most (though not all) stocks will follow.

- **Rising interest rates:** When interest rates increase, the value of bonds and bond ETFs will fall.

- **Inflation:** Rising inflation decreases the value of fixed-income investments and cash.

- **War and political unrest:** If you are holding stocks, bonds, or currency ETFs of a country where political unrest occurs, their value will fall.

Risks Associated with ETFs

Besides risks that affect the stock market as a whole, certain investment risks are common to all ETFs. They include:

- **Asset-class risk:** The possibility that the types of securities in a particular fund will underperform other styles of securities.

- **Concentration risk:** The risk that a narrowly focused index fund will be adversely affected by events that do not affect other sectors of the market.

- **Management risk:** The risk that an ETF will underperform its underlying index because it does not contain all the underlying securities in correct proportions or because administration costs siphon off returns.

Time is an important factor in evaluating the effect of systemic risk on your investments. Interest rates rise and fall, the stock market goes up and down, and political conflicts are eventually resolved. A long-term investment can weather adverse market conditions and eventually come out ahead. A short-term investment may be sharply affected if adverse market conditions exist at the time of its withdrawal. Inflation rarely, if ever, reverses itself. If inflation slows, the value of fixed-income ETFs will remain relatively constant, but if inflation continues to increase rapidly, their value will quickly diminish.

Measuring Risk

STANDARD DEVIATION

The risk of owning a particular security is often measured in terms of standard deviation. Standard deviation shows the degree to which the returns from a security have fluctuated from its mean return over a given period. Standard deviation is a measure of a security's volatility, and it can be used to compare the relative volatility of two or more securities. If an ETF has a three-year standard deviation of six, it would be considered twice as volatile and, therefore, twice as risky as another ETF with a three-year standard deviation of three. The standard deviation for most short-term bond funds, considered to be the most secure investment, is around 0.7, while the standard deviation for most precious metal funds is around 26.0.

> ### TAKE NOTE: ENOUGH DATA MAY NOT BE AVAILABLE
>
> Many ETFs that track custom indexes are relative newcomers to the market, and there may not be enough data available to arrive at a meaningful standard deviation.

BETA

A popular indicator of risk is a statistical measure called beta. Beta measures the volatility of a stock or a fund in relation to the volatility of the market as a whole, represented by the Standard & Poor's 500 Index. The market is assigned a beta of 1.0, and individual stocks are ranked according to how much they deviate from the market. A beta above 1.0 means that a stock has fluctuated more than the market over time. If a stock fluctuates less than the market, the stock's beta is less than 1.0. High-beta stocks are considered riskier, but they provide a potential for higher returns; low-beta stocks pose less risk, but they also promise lower returns.

SHARPE AND TREYNOR RATIOS

It is possible for two investments representing different investment risks, such as pharmaceuticals and ten-year Treasury notes, to produce the same rate of return over time. In 1966, Bill Sharpe, a professor at Stanford, developed a ratio that provides an objective measure of the risk inherent in an investment. The formula for the Sharpe ratio is:

$$\frac{(\text{Average monthly returns of the asset}) - (\text{Risk-free rate of return})}{(\text{Standard deviation of the asset})}$$

The risk-free rate of return is represented by the return on short-term Treasury bills. The average monthly returns are multiplied by 12, and the standard deviation is multiplied by the square root of 12. A variation of the Sharpe ratio, the Sortino ratio, removes the effects of upward price movements on standard deviation and measures only return against downward price volatility.

A good investment is one that offers high returns with a minimum of risk. The higher the Sharpe ratio, the higher the return of the investment in relation to its risk. A stock or an ETF with a high rate of return and a high Sharpe ratio is considered a sound investment. A low Sharpe ratio means that the high returns were achieved by taking excessive risk. Over the past ten years, the Sharpe ratio for the whole cash S&P Index is 0.29; for the New York Stock Exchange, it has ranged between 0.30 and 0.40. An asset or fund with a Sharpe ratio greater than 0.50 would have a better-than-average ratio of reward to risk.

The Sharpe ratio measures the total risk of an investment. Another ratio, created by Jack Treynor in 1965, measures the systemic risk using beta, instead of the standard deviation of the stock, as the denominator. The Treynor ratio can be used to compare the risk of a particular investment to the risk inherent in the stock market as a whole.

Evaluating Performance in Relation to Risk

The performance of an investment can be measured according to nominal return or risk-adjusted return. Most ordinary investors look only at nominal return: If the average return from an investment or a portfolio is higher than the return for the whole U.S. stock market over the same period, it is considered successful. Risk-adjusted return measures the return on an investment relative to the volatility of its price.

An ordinary investor might think that a higher nominal return is better, but it does not necessarily mean more cash in your wallet at the end of the day. A nominal return is arrived at by averaging the daily returns on an investment over time. On the specific day that an investor wants to sell an investment, it will sell for an amount higher or lower than the averaged nominal return. How much higher or lower? The price of a highly volatile stock could be significantly higher or lower than the average. If the price is much higher, the investor can consider himself or herself lucky and pocket a substantial profit. If the price is much lower, the investor will realize lower-than-expected returns and possibly even take a loss, making the investment meaningless and even harmful. A risk-adjusted return incorporates the probability that the investment will realistically achieve the expected return.

Large institutional investors, foundations, trusts, and insurance companies manage their portfolios using risk-adjusted returns.

> **TAKE NOTE: NOMINAL VERSUS RISK-ADJUSTED RETURN**
>
> Brokerages often advertise the expected nominal return of an investment and hope that the investor will not look at the risk-adjusted return. Consider the volatility of an investment when deciding whether to buy it.

Determining Your Asset Allocations

Stocks and Bonds

Historically, bonds have manifested a low correlation to stocks. Most investors allocate between 40 and 50 percent of their portfolios to less volatile bonds and other fixed-income investments, and the remainder to stocks. The following chart shows typical stock/bond allocations for different types of buy-and-hold portfolios:

	Global Equity (Stocks)	Fixed-Income (Bonds)	Expected Long-Term Return
Income-Oriented	20 percent	80 percent	5.8 percent
Conservative	40 percent	60 percent	6.4 percent
Moderate	50 percent	50 percent	6.7 percent
Moderate Growth	60 percent	40 percent	7.0 percent
Aggressive	80 percent	20 percent	7.7 percent

Even though U.S. fixed-income markets (more than $25 trillion in 2007) are much larger than U.S. stock equity markets, there are relatively few bond ETFs compared to the hundreds of stock ETFs. One reason is that it is difficult to realistically track a bond index. (For a detailed explanation of bond indexes and ETFs, see "Fixed-Income ETFs" in "Chapter 9: The ETFs.") However, new bond ETF offerings are appearing on the market in increasing numbers.

Allocating Assets in the Stock Portion of Your Portfolio

STYLES AND SECTORS

Most experts agree that every portfolio should include domestic and international holdings as well as stocks and bonds, though they do not agree on the optimal proportions of each. There is also considerable disagreement over whether the domestic portion of a portfolio should be diversified according to style or market sector.

Style diversification classifies funds according to the market capitalization (size) and characteristics of the companies that make up the indexes on which the funds are based. Companies are classified into market sectors according to the type of industry they represent. There are eleven market sectors representing major industries, and many of them are divided into more specialized subsectors. A portfolio can be diversified by selecting stocks and funds from styles or sectors that perform differently on the stock market.

Diversifying by style or by sector?

The core of a portfolio should be diversified by style. Industry sectors can then be added to accomplish particular investment goals. Buying funds and ETFs of different styles is a more effective way of diversifying a portfolio than dividing it among different market sectors, for a number of reasons:

ETFs devoted to industry sectors are heavily weighted towards large-cap stocks and are evenly divided between value and growth.

Historical data shows that when the performance of one style on the market declines, another tends to rise (low correlation). To optimize the success of a portfolio and keep it growing, you need exposure to mid-cap and small-cap companies that might perform better in times when large-cap stocks are in decline.

Industry-sector ETFs have higher costs than style ETFs.

The expense ratio of industry-sector ETFs tends to be two or three times higher than that of value ETFs. Administration costs and fees eat away at your returns and leave you less money to reinvest.

Diversifying by style requires ownership of fewer funds.

You can diversify by style by purchasing four ETFs: large growth, large value, small growth, and small value. To be fully diversified in industry sectors, you would need to purchase at least 11 ETFs, one for each of the major industry sectors.

How Style Is Defined

Cap size, or market capitalization, measures the size of a company by multiplying the price of a single share of stock times the number of shares outstanding. Growth stocks are those that have been growing rapidly and are expected to continue growing. Value stocks are companies whose size has remained steady but whose stock is considered to be a good value compared to the stock of other, similar companies.

Capitalization:

There is no clear dividing line between large-cap and mid-cap companies. Stocks are classified as large-cap if their market capitalization is over $5 billion, mid-cap if it is between $1 billion and $5 billion, and small-cap if it is between $250 million and $1 billion. Stocks with capitalization of less than $250 million are classified as micro-caps.

Value and growth:

A number of criteria are used to determine whether a stock is a growth stock or a value stock. An important measure is the price-to-earnings (P/E) ratio, sometimes referred to as the multiple. The price of a share of stock is divided by the company's earnings per share. A high price-to-earnings ratio indicates one or both of two things: that the company is investing its capital in expansion and that investors are willing to pay more for the shares because they believe that the company is growing or will grow. A lower price-to-earnings ratio is a sign that investors do not believe the company is going anywhere fast and that the stock can be purchased at a bargain price.

The top-performing funds during any given period tend to resemble each other closely and hold a similar class of assets.

A number of studies have shown that the performance of a portfolio is directly linked to the style of assets it holds. If large-cap growth stocks go up, a portfolio holding large-cap growth ETFs or mutual funds goes up accordingly. Some studies suggest that only between 5 and 10 percent of a fund's performance can be attributed to factors other than its asset class.

Style Boxes

In the 1990s, Morningstar developed Morningstar Style Boxes, sometimes called Morningstar grids, to visually represent the characteristics of fixed-income (bond), domestic equity (stock), and international equity (stock) securities and their respective mutual funds. Style boxes help investors to determine the asset allocation and risk-return structures of their portfolios. A style box for fixed-income investments, such as bonds, organizes investments according to their credit quality and whether they are long-, intermediate-, or short-term.

Fixed-Income Style Box

Short-term high quality	Intermediate-term high quality	Long-term high quality
Short-term medium quality	Intermediate-term medium quality	Long-term medium quality
Short-term low quality	Intermediate-term low quality	Long-term low quality

A style box for an ETF and mutual fund portfolio arranges investments according to their capitalization size and whether they are value or growth.

ETF Equity Style Box

Large-cap value	Large-cap blend	Large-cap growth
Mid-cap value	Mid-cap blend	Mid-cap growth
Small-cap value	Small-cap blend	Small-cap growth

By listing each component of a portfolio in its appropriate box, along with its dollar value and other relevant data, an investor can have a visual snapshot of his or her portfolio and the relative strengths and weaknesses of each component. A style box helps an investor to determine whether his portfolio conforms to his financial strategy and to identify which areas are underrepresented or overinvested.

Most investors would make sure they had some equity in each box of the grid because, historically, large and small companies, as well as value and growth companies, have risen and fallen in value under different economic conditions. When investments in one box of the grid are doing poorly, they will be counteracted by the investments in another box.

Morningstar style grids are often included in listings of ETFs, with the appropriate boxes colored in to indicate the style of each particular ETF.

Diversifying Your Portfolio by Style

Large-cap growth companies receive the most attention in the media, but returns from large-cap value stocks have been historically greater. According to the research of American economists Eugene Fama and Kenneth French, large growth stocks over the last 77 years have had an annualized return rate of about 9.5 percent, while large value stocks during the same period have averaged 11.5 percent. The volatility of both stocks has been relatively equal. Nevertheless, both large-cap growth ETFs and large-cap value ETFs belong in a portfolio because it is impossible to predict the future.

Stocks of large companies should make up between 50 and 80 percent of a total domestic stock portfolio.

Small-cap funds can be added to the extent that the investor can tolerate risk. If a portfolio is large enough, it should hold large growth and large value ETFs separately. This will permit regular rebalancing if value strongly outperforms growth or vice versa. A smaller portfolio may not be able to absorb the trading costs of buying and selling two ETFs without seriously diminishing its returns. In that case, it is better to own a single ETF that has a blend of large growth and value. A small portfolio may be better off holding mutual funds to reduce trading costs, unless it is going to remain untouched for several years.

Diversifying by Investing in Market Sectors

All industry sectors are already represented in a portfolio that holds large, small, value, and growth funds. You can add industry-sector ETFs to optimize your portfolio in several ways. Your goal is diversity, both as protection from declines in one style or sector and to give your portfolio exposure to potential returns if one market sector suddenly begins to blossom.

Add industries that are underrepresented in your other portfolio holdings.

Examine the prospectuses of the ETFs or mutual funds already in your portfolio. You may discover that they hold few technology or healthcare stocks. Adding an ETF in one of these sectors will cover the deficiency.

Add sectors that have low correlation to the rest of the stock market.

Certain asset classes or industry sectors, such as real estate and energy, tend to move out of step with the rest of the market. Adding REIT (real estate investment trust) ETFs or an energy-sector ETF to your portfolio serves as a safety net if the rest of the market declines.

Increase exposure to new or up-and-coming industries.

The structure of the business world is changing rapidly through globalization and the discovery of new technologies. An industry-sector ETF can be used to increase your exposure to a market that, for whatever reason, you feel has good potential for rapid growth.

Increase exposure to foreign industries.

Many industry-sector ETFs include foreign companies, and some are specifically designed for overseas investment in an industry. If you are heavily invested in a U.S. industry that is gaining a strong global presence, buying an ETF that holds foreign investments might be a good idea.

Hedge against loss.

If your portfolio holds a heavy concentration of stock in a particular industry, such as technology, you can short an ETF in the same industry to reduce your exposure. Or you can balance your portfolio by purchasing ETFs for an industry with a low correlation.

Core and Explore

After your basic portfolio is established, you may want to invest some of your capital in areas that are more uncertain but have potential for growth. There are two core-and-explore strategies. One strategy is to purchase ETFs tracking global financial markets that you believe are inefficient (not performing to their full potential) on the assumption that they will grow. The other is market timing: purchasing ETFs tracking industry sectors, styles, or countries that you believe are poised for growth.

Sector Rotation

Sector rotation is an active investment strategy in which the performance of industry sectors is evaluated at regular intervals and part of the portfolio is reinvested in the three or four top-performing sectors.

TAKE NOTE: COSTS AND RISKS OF ETFS CAN VARY SIGNIFICANTLY

Cost, level of risk, and level of diversification can vary significantly, depending on the ETF. Before purchasing an ETF, carefully review the prospectus or product description, and be sure you understand how the ETF is managed and how it derives its value. An ETF's price volatility depends on the volatility of its underlying securities or commodities.

Selecting Your Investments

Learn about the ETFs.

Most ETF companies provide prospectuses to individual investors; those that do not are required to furnish a Product Description, which gives a summary of the ETF's objectives and explains how to obtain its prospectus. Before buying an ETF for your portfolio, you should have a thorough understanding of its investment strategy, holdings, costs, and tax liabilities. (See "Chapter 11: Doing the Research.")

Compare the ETF's stated investment objectives with its historical performance, and see how closely the ETF tracks the index on which it is based. Some specialized ETFs, and those following custom indexes, fall short of the index returns because of costs and issues with the liquidity of the underlying securities.

Determine how an ETF fits in with your investment strategy.

Examine your existing portfolio to see how an ETF complements your other investments. Look at the ETF's holdings for duplications. Some industry-sector ETFs may contain the same companies as your large-cap funds.

Compare similar investments.

Look at other ETFs and mutual funds with similar investment objectives. How do their expense ratios compare? Which ones have the best historical returns? Do they pay dividends?

Consider whether you intend to make a large one-time investment or you plan to make regular additions to your portfolio.

You may decide to invest a substantial portion of your portfolio in one broad market ETF and then build around it later by buying smaller quantities of ETFs that complement it or give you additional exposure to active market sectors.

TAKE NOTE: AVOID BUYING NEW ETFS

Many of the ETFs launched in 2007 and 2008 were benchmarked to specific industry sectors or custom indexes. New ETFs are often launched in response to recent growth in an industry sector and to a spike in investor interest. There is a good chance that the underlying securities of a new ETF are already "selling high," and, therefore, the price of the new ETF will be inflated.

Buy-and-Hold Portfolios

Because every investor has unique economic circumstances, financial goals, and levels of risk tolerance, there is not one single asset allocation formula that is ideal for every buy-and-hold portfolio. One person may be willing to take extra risk to grow his or her savings more rapidly, while another may be primarily concerned with preserving capital. An investor may already hold securities from one or more asset classes in another account. Another factor affecting asset allocation is the investor's need to access cash on short notice.

The following is a sample asset allocation for an ETF portfolio from Steven Schoenfeld's *Active Investing: Maximizing Portfolio Performance and Minimizing Risk Through Global Index Strategies*. In a small, simple portfolio, each major asset class can be represented with a single broad market index ETF. Larger portfolios can be allocated among ETFs from each of the asset subclasses. In the chapters on investing for retirement and for education, you will find other sample asset allocations for ETF portfolios.

ASSET CLASS	CONSERVATIVE PORTFOLIO	MODERATE PORTFOLIO	AGGRESSIVE PORTFOLIO
U.S. Equities	25 percent	45 percent	55 percent
Large-Cap	15 percent	30 percent	35 percent
Mid-/Small-Cap	10 percent	15 percent	20 percent
International Equities	5 percent	10 percent	20 percent
Developed	5 percent	8 percent	15 percent
Emerging	—	2 percent	5 percent
Fixed-Income	55 percent	30 percent	10 percent
Short-Term	15 percent	5 percent	—
Long-Term	15 percent	10 percent	5 percent
High-Yield	10 percent	5 percent	5 percent
TIPS	15 percent	10 percent	—
Alternatives	15 percent	15 percent	15 percent
REITS	10 percent	10 percent	5 percent
Commodities	5 percent	5 percent	5 percent
Hedge Funds	—	—	5 percent

Protecting Your Portfolio

After you have determined your asset allocations and set up your portfolio, there are several things you can do to protect yourself from losses and ensure that your portfolio performs as expected.

Maintain Your Asset Allocations

Almost 90 percent of a portfolio's long-term performance is attributable to asset allocation. Rebalance your portfolio at regular intervals to compensate for excessive gains in any one area, and return it to its target asset allocations. Avoid the temptation to buy into hot market sectors, unless you can do it without overweighting your portfolio in one direction.

Maintain Diversity

Diversity protects your portfolio by compensating for losses in one area with gains in another, and diversity exposes it to every possible opportunity for growth. As economic conditions change, market sectors that once had low correlation may begin to move in tandem, and new market sectors open up. While you are rebalancing your portfolio, check to see that the correlation among different asset classes and ETFs has not changed, and look for new areas with low correlation.

Hedge Against Loss

Diversity provides a natural hedge against market downturns, but if it appears that a particular market sector is headed for a sharp decline, you can compensate for possible losses by selling an ETF for that sector short or by purchasing one of the ETFs that shorts the market.

Set Limits on Loss by Buying Put Options for Risky Investments

If the price of an ETF plunges, you will lose a limited amount, plus the cost of the options, rather than losing your entire investment.

Chapter 14

○ ○ ○ ○ ○

Getting Started:
Choosing a Brokerage

A major objective in getting the best performance from your portfolio is to keep expenses, trading fees, and commissions to a minimum. Discount brokerages charge a flat trading fee for each transaction and offer a variety of services. Their staffs do not receive commissions or solicit sales. You can easily open an account online or by visiting a local branch office. Competition for online customers has motivated these companies to offer increasingly sophisticated investment tools on their Web sites. A technical analysis center at TradeKing uses pattern-recognition technology to look for 60 different patterns in 22,000 publicly traded stocks. TD Ameritrade has a StrategyDesk program that allows investors to test trading strategies without making the trade and to set up programmed trades. Fidelity and Charles Schwab offer online classes to teach customers about investing. Fees now average $7 to $10 per trade and can be as low as $3 for automatic trades on specified days of the week. Some brokerages have special introductory offers, such as free trading for the first month or cash back, which would allow you to put together your initial portfolio without paying any trading fees at all. Shop around to find a brokerage that offers the services you need and a Web site that you find easy to use. You can find reviews and charts comparing all the brokerages on financial Web sites, such as SmartMoney (**www.smartmoney.com**), The Motley Fool (**www.fool.com**), and Stocks and Mutual Funds (**www.stocksandmutualfunds.com**).

Premium Brokers:

E*Trade (**https://us.etrade.com/e/t/home**)

Fidelity (**www.fidelity.com**)

Vanguard (**www.vanguard.com**)

Charles Schwab (**www.schwab.com**)

T. Rowe Price (**www.troweprice.com**)

T. D. Ameritrade (**www.tdameritrade.com**)

Discount Brokers:

TradeKing (**www.tradeking.com**)

Scottrade (**www.scottrade.com**)

Firstrade (**www.firstrade.com**)

OptionsXpress (**www.optionsxpress.com**)

Muriel Siebert (**www.siebertnet.com**)

WallStreet*E (**www.wallstreete.com**)

SogoInvest (**www.sogotrade.com**)

Zecco (**www.zecco.com**)

If you need professional assistance to plan and define your financial objectives, determine your optimum portfolio asset allocations, and select ETFs, consult a fee-only financial planner. A fee-only Certified Financial Planner (CFP) will charge only an hourly or one-time consultation fee and does not receive commissions from the sale of financial products. If you want to check the accreditation and legal status of brokers or financial advisors, look them up on the SEC Web site (**www.sec.gov/investor/brokers.htm**).

CASE STUDY: DAVID JACKSON

David Jackson is the founder of Seeking Alpha (**www.seekingalpha.com**) and author of the online book *The Seeking Alpha ETF Investing Guide*. Mr. Jackson worked for five years as a technology research analyst for Morgan Stanley in New York before leaving in early 2003 to manage money (long/short) and explore new approaches to financial publishing. He has a B.A. from Oxford University and an M.Sc. from The London School of Economics. Seeking Alpha is the leading provider of stock market opinion and analysis from blogs, money managers, and investment newsletters, and it is a provider of its own high-value, complementary financial content.

Excerpt from *The Four Criteria for Picking a Brokerage* by David Jackson:

Now that you've determined your asset allocation and picked a basket of ETFs for your portfolio, you need to find a brokerage to execute the trades and hold your portfolio for you. How do you pick the brokerage? The criteria are relatively straightforward.

1. **Low-cost trades.** You can't control the performance of your portfolio, but you can control the taxes and fees you pay. Keeping trading fees low is a critical element of your investment strategy. Go for an online brokerage firm with per-trade fees below $25.

2. **Easy tax management.** If you are investing in a taxable account, it's crucial to find an online broker that allows you to identify and sell specific tax lots with ease. If the broker also provides a summary of unrealized gains and losses by purchase lot, even better.

3. **Portfolio allocation tools.** It's easy to track your ETF portfolio and asset allocation using a spreadsheet. But it's even easier if your brokerage does that for you. The best online brokerages show you your asset allocation.

4. **Maximum interest on your cash.** Most investors pick their brokerage on the cost of trading alone. Mistake! There are a number of reasons you may be holding cash in your account. The interest you earn on your cash matters and can outweigh the fees you'll pay to buy and sell the ETFs in your portfolio. Here's the problem: Most brokerages sweep the cash in brokerage accounts into money market accounts that pay relatively low interest, and in some instances, they pay no interest at all.

CASE STUDY: DAVID JACKSON

The solution is to keep your cash in a bank account paying higher interest, and you'll also get FDIC insurance. If you can find a brokerage offering high-interest, paying money market accounts linked to brokerage accounts, you'll get the best of both worlds: the convenience of managing your entire portfolio in one place and higher interest.

Now the criteria that don't matter to you:

- **You don't need real-time or streaming quotes.** You can buy ETFs using limit orders, setting the price slightly below where the ETF currently trades. You're not a day trader. You don't need to check your portfolio every day, let alone every second.

- **You don't need stock research.** Because you're not buying individual stocks, you don't care whether your brokerage provides stock research. (It may be fun to read as entertainment, but it shouldn't affect your portfolio.)

- **You don't need a choice of mutual funds.** Why? Because you'll be buying ultra-low-cost, index-tracking ETFs instead.

- **You don't need cheap margin interest.** Your goal is to allocate the assets you have, not to borrow money from your brokerage to buy stock. Because you won't be borrowing, you don't care what your brokerage's margin interest rates are.

Adding ETFs to an Existing Portfolio

You may be satisfied with the performance of your existing portfolio of stocks or mutual funds, but there are a number of ways in which you can use ETFs to enhance your returns, reduce expenses, and protect yourself against loss.

Improving Diversity

Preceding chapters have emphasized the importance of diversity in reducing portfolio risk and increasing exposure to potential areas of growth. Take a close look at the individual stocks and bonds in your portfolio as well as the holdings of your mutual funds. You may find that the majority of your holdings are large U.S. company stocks. You can remedy that disparity by purchasing one or two small-cap ETFs.

Americans are notoriously underinvested in foreign markets, although there has been a sharp increase in foreign investment during the 2000s. Foreign and international ETFs eliminate many of the obstacles to investing overseas, including the need to open accounts with foreign brokerages, currency exchange issues, and tax complications. Shares of foreign ETFs are bought and sold in U.S. dollars, and the fund providers take care of reporting income for tax purposes. International and global ETFs allow you to easily add international diversity to your portfolio. Foreign industry-sector, commodity, currency, and fixed-income ETFs offer instant international exposure to the areas that have been the most active over the last five years.

Minimizing Investment Costs

Look at the expense ratios of the mutual funds already in your portfolio, and compare them to the expense ratios of similar ETFs. You may be able to move a portion of your portfolio into lower-cost ETFs that track the same index or follow a similar investment strategy. Because you are paying a trading fee for each ETF transaction, make those transactions large and infrequent, and continue making small regular payments, such as monthly payroll deductions, into the mutual funds.

Hedging Against Losses

If your portfolio is heavily invested in the stock of one or two companies or in a particular industry, such as technology, purchase an ETF that has low correlation to that industry, or short an ETF in the same industry as insurance against a decline. Use ETFs to build up a balanced portfolio around your existing investments.

Rebalancing Your Portfolio

When one area of your portfolio begins to dominate because of its strong performance, instead of increasing your investment in the other stocks or mutual funds in your portfolio, bring it into balance by purchasing ETFs that track similar indexes or market sectors.

Fixed-Income ETFs

Bonds and notes have to be redeemed when they reach maturity, and the cash reinvested. Fixed-income ETFs do all that work for you, rolling cash over into new bonds and paying out interest. They also reduce risk by spreading your investment over a range of debt, instead of concentrating it all in one place. As fixed-income investments mature, replace them with a fixed-income ETF of a similar type.

Tax-Loss Harvesting

Stocks from an industry sector that has lost value in a particular year can be sold at a loss to reduce the amount of income reported on your tax return. Replace them in your portfolio by buying an ETF for the same industry.

TAKE NOTE: MAINTAIN YOUR TARGET ASSET ALLOCATIONS

When adding ETFs to your existing portfolio, you are responsible for maintaining your target asset allocations. Look carefully at the top ten holdings of any ETF you are considering. Check its expense ratio and whether it pays interest or dividends, which might affect your tax liability. Also, verify that the risk inherent in the ETF is in line with your investment goals. All this information is available on the Internet. If you need assistance, consult an investment advisor.

Chapter 15

o o o o o

Rebalancing Your Portfolio

After your portfolio has been established, it should be rebalanced at regular intervals to maintain diversity. When you first created your portfolio, you decided what percentage of your assets to allocate to each type of investment, based on the amount of risk you could afford. For example, you may have decided to place 30 percent in bonds, 30 percent in U.S. stocks, 28 percent in foreign stocks, and the remainder in commodities and market-neutral funds. As time passes, one area of your portfolio may do well and grow rapidly in value, while the value of another area declines. Even though the overall value of your portfolio has increased, its volatility and risk may also have increased because one type of investment is overtaking the others. Rebalancing is necessary to restore the original percentages of each type of investment.

How Often Should a Portfolio Be Rebalanced?

Most financial professionals agree that a portfolio should be rebalanced once a year. If it is rebalanced at longer intervals, there is a risk that the portfolio will become heavily overbalanced in one direction. If it is rebalanced more frequently, you run the risk of lowering your returns by interrupting rallies (the periods during which prices of a particular stock are on an upswing) too often. Buying and selling ETFs incurs trading fees. More frequent rebalancing results in more trades and, therefore, more expenses.

Is It Necessary to Rebalance a Portfolio Every Year?

If the portion of your assets allocated to a particular type of investment has only dropped 1 or 2 percent, the trading cost to purchase the additional ETF shares to bring it into balance may not be justified. A general rule is that if the trading costs are going to be more than 0.50 percent of your total purchase, it is better to wait another year before rebalancing.

How Do I Rebalance a Portfolio?

Because the division between stocks and bonds has the greatest influence on portfolio risk, it is most important to maintain your fixed-income allocation. If the percentage of your portfolio allocated to bonds has dropped below your original target, increase it by purchasing the necessary additional shares of bond ETFs. Ideally, these bond ETF shares can be purchased using cash from dividends and earnings or from a fresh investment of cash in your portfolio. If necessary, sell some shares of a stock ETF. Remember that you will be paying trading fees for the sale of these shares as well as the purchase of bond ETF shares. You will also be paying capital gains tax on any profit you make by selling shares of an ETF.

TAKE NOTE: WHEN TO BUY AND SELL

The essence of buy-and-hold strategy is to hold investments for the long term and to maintain the balance of those investments in a portfolio while minimizing expenses by avoiding trading fees and capital gains tax. Buying and selling shares of ETFs in your portfolio should be done only when necessary. However, it is common sense to keep an eye on the market as a whole for drastic changes that might signal more than a normal fluctuation in a market sector. For example, technology stocks began to take off late in 1997 and increased rapidly in value until April 2000. By the end of December 2000, they had lost 45 percent; by the end of December 2001, they had last another 30 percent; and by the end of December 2002, they had fallen another 38 percent. From news coverage, it was evident that inexperience, overspending, and ill-conceived business plans had doomed many technology start-ups. A well-read investor would have realized by the end of 2000 that technology stocks should not occupy a large portion of his or her portfolio, but many fund managers held on, hoping for a reversal.

CASE STUDY: MATT HOUGAN

Matt Hougan is editor of Indexuniverse.com (**www.indexuniverse.com**), *ETF Watch*, and *ETFR* (*Exchange-Traded Fund Report*), the oldest, most established ETF newsletter in the world. He supervises a team of writers who provide in-depth analysis, news, columns, research, and features on new ETF launches and the latest developments in the ETF universe.

Mr. Hougan offers the following advice to investors who have decided to invest in ETFs:

You have made a good choice. At their core, ETFs are a better mousetrap; they are inherently low-cost, tax-efficient, and provide focused exposure to different asset classes. They are a good option for many, but not all, investors. ETFs are a good portfolio tool. For instance, if you want a large-cap investment, you could go with one of the many large-cap actively managed mutual funds. But you won't know what the fund is holding or what direction it is taking. With an ETF, you can see exactly what it is holding in real time and what the expenses will be. There are no surprises. Compared to an index fund, they are often more tax-efficient and lower-cost.

They also open up new asset classes. Using ETFs, you can build a portfolio just like the big institutional investors. You can access large-cap, small-cap, commodities, currencies, industry sectors, international markets, and bonds; and you can use them to build a complete, diversified portfolio.

The biggest mistake made by inexperienced investors is performance tracking. Every time there is a new hot category, new ETFs and new mutual funds are launched to take advantage of it. The worst thing you can do is pile all your money into one hot market sector; when that sector starts to cool, you can lose everything. Be careful of the latest hot fund. It's better to buy into more traditional ETFs and hold them for a long time.

Many of the newest launches have been ETNs, which do not hold the assets in the underlying indexes. ETNs are attractive to investors because they provide access to difficult markets, such as Chinese currency and closed-end funds. ETNs are debt notes; the bank guarantees the exact returns of the underlying index.

Why do banks launch them? Partly because they can be good products, and partly because it's easy for the bank to do so. They can charge 75 basis points, and they can make a considerable amount of money. Be aware of the credit risk involved in ETNs; if a bank goes under for any reason, it may default on its obligations.

CASE STUDY: MATT HOUGAN

In the future, everyone will make increasing use of ETFs, from institutional investors to financial advisers and private individuals. Over the last decade, there has been a big shift in the ownership of ETFs from institutional to private investors. But many people still don't know what ETFs are. Everyone should invest steadily in low-cost funds. Every study shows that it gives you the best chance for success.

Today, the average baby boomer has $40,000 saved for retirement — we're going to see a large number of sad elderly people! IRAs and 529s are slowly starting to add ETFs to their investment options. They had some technical issues to work out, but they're getting there. Because the 401(k) market was built by the mutual fund industry, they will be reluctant to make changes.

Chapter 16

o o o o o

Investing for Retirement

Taking Responsibility

Traditional defined-benefit pension plans are quickly disappearing in the U.S. and being replaced with 401(k)s and other defined-contribution plans that make individual Americans responsible for saving for their own retirement. In 1990, these retirement plans held only $385 billion in assets, with about $35 billion of that invested in mutual funds. By the end of 2006, 401(k) plans held total assets of $2.7 trillion, with $1.5 trillion in mutual funds.

Retirement plans often follow a buy-and-hold strategy, reinvesting earnings and depending on the steady growth of the stock market to keep up with inflation. Participants in most retirement plans are offered a selection of investment options or portfolios and, after a brief education, are expected to determine their own allocations and choose the appropriate investments. Participants are also responsible for rebalancing their portfolios periodically to adjust for shifts in the market. Countless financial writers bewail the fact that the majority of investors in 401(k) plans know little about investing, pay exorbitant fees, make poor choices, and are unlikely to meet their goals for retirement. It is essential that ordinary investors take responsibility for setting aside adequate savings and for understanding where their investment dollars are going and how to optimize their returns.

Tax-Free and Tax-Deferred Retirement Savings Accounts

The U.S. government allows two types of tax-advantaged accounts for retirement savings: 401(k) plans and IRA accounts. According to the Investment Company Institute (**www.ici.org**), 71 percent of all U.S. households have retirement plans through work or IRAs.

401(k)s, Solo 401(k)s, and Roth 401(k)s

Company 401(k)s and Solo 401(k)s are tax-deferred plans that allow workers to make pre-tax contributions to an investment account. Income tax is deferred on the investment and earnings until they are withdrawn from the account. Strict restrictions are placed on withdrawals, and funds withdrawn from the account before its owner reaches the age of 59½ are subject to an excise tax equal to 10 percent of the amount distributed. Minimum withdrawals must begin by April 1 of the calendar year after the owner reaches age 70½. Many companies offer matching contributions or profit-sharing incentives to motivate employees to remain with the company longer. A self-employed individual can set up a Solo 401(k) plan. Contributions to a Roth 401(k) plan are made after-tax, and qualified withdrawals are tax-free.

Participants in a 401(k) plan must select from among the investment options offered by the plan provider. Most plans offer mutual funds rather than ETFs, partly because of the cost and recordkeeping involved in trading ETFs when participants are contributing through small, regular payroll deductions. A few providers have introduced 401(k) plans with ETFs, including Invest n Retire (**www.investnretire.com**), BenefitStreet (**www.benefitstreet.com**) teamed with Barclays PLC, and 401K Retirement Solutions (**www.401krs.com**). They keep trading commissions to a minimum by aggregating individual ETF trades into one large daily trade or by negotiating special high-volume trading arrangements with a brokerage. Avatar Associates (**www.avatar-associates.com**) and XTF (**www.xtf.com**) offer actively managed portfolios, called "lifestyle funds," comprised of several ETFs that suit a particular risk level and are matched to participants' individualized risk profiles.

The greatest benefit of 401(k) plans is that many employers match employees' contributions up to a certain percentage of their salaries. This is free money, and you should take full advantage of it by contributing the full amount eligible for matching. If your company's 401(k) does not offer ETFs, choose low-cost mutual funds and rebalance your portfolio regularly. If you leave the company or retire, you will be able to roll the 401(k) over into an IRA, which will give you more flexibility and control over your investment choices.

IRAs and Roth IRAs

Individual retirement accounts (IRAs) were created by the Employee Retirement Income Security Act (ERISA) in 1974 to provide a tax-advantaged savings vehicle for individuals not covered by employer-sponsored retirement plans and to preserve rollover assets from employer-sponsored plans when individuals change jobs or retire. By the end of 2006, Americans were holding an estimated $423 trillion dollars in IRAs.

Contributions to a traditional IRA are tax-deductible, and taxes on the earnings are deferred until the money is withdrawn, allowing all earnings to be reinvested. Strict restrictions are placed on withdrawals, and funds withdrawn from the account before its owner reaches the age of 59½ are subject to an excise tax equal to 10 percent of the amount distributed. Minimum withdrawals must begin by April 1 of the calendar year after the owner reaches age 70½. Anyone can open an IRA, regardless of their income.

Roth IRAs were created by the Taxpayer Relief Act of 1997. Contributions to a Roth IRA are counted as taxable income on your tax return, but all your earnings and principal can be withdrawn tax-free if you follow the rules. Withdrawals of principal can be made at any time without penalty, but any withdrawals of earnings before the account holder reaches the age of 59½ are subject to a 10 percent penalty. (There are exceptions if the money is withdrawn for certain purposes.) There is no mandated withdrawal after the owner reaches a certain age. The tax benefits of a Roth IRA are not realized until the funds are withdrawn, and though a spouse can inherit the Roth IRA without penalty, other heirs will pay income tax on the funds in it. In most cases, the Roth IRA is more advantageous than the traditional IRA, because it allows withdrawals of principal and because taxation rates may rise considerably by the time you begin to make withdrawals. As of 2007, Roth IRAs are available only to single filers making up to $101,000 or married couples making a combined maximum of $159,000 annually.

The maximum allowable contribution to either type of IRA for 2008 is $5,000 for anyone 49 or younger and $6,000 for anyone 50 and older. This limit will be raised in $500 increments depending on the rate of inflation. Contributions must be made by April 15 of the following year.

You can open an IRA or a Roth IRA with a bank or a brokerage and select any of the investments they offer. A brokerage is likely to offer more investment options than a bank. When deciding where to open your IRA, look for:

- A good selection of investment options, including mutual funds and ETFs

- Low commissions and account fees

- The ability to make automated fund transfers from your bank account

- The minimum balance required to open an account or purchase a fund

Low-cost ETFs are good choices for an IRA, but if you are making small, regular contributions, trading fees for purchasing additional ETF shares can be prohibitive. A low-cost mutual fund may be a better choice. You can also put your money aside in a money market account and make one or two larger contributions to the IRA during the year.

Several online brokerages offer IRA accounts with low-fee or no-fee trading that allows you to make regular contributions to an ETF portfolio. For an annual IRA fee of $30, Zecco (**www.zecco.com/trading/zeccoira.aspx**) offers 10 free trades per month as long as a balance of $2,500 is maintained in the account. TradeKing (**www.tradeking.com**) charges no annual fee and a flat $4.95 per trade. ING Direct's Sharebuilder (**www.sharebuilder. com**) offers an IRA account for a $25 annual fee, which is waived if you have another trading account with them. There is no required minimum investment, and a flat trading fee of $4 is charged for their automatic investing program.

Taxable and Tax-Advantaged Accounts

Even after you reach the age of 70, you can let your savings continue to grow in an IRA account without penalties, as long as you withdraw the mandated required minimum distribution (RMD) every year. Unfortunately, limits on the size of contributions restrict the amount of money you can put into a retirement account. You will need to make the most of tax-advantaged accounts while maintaining the rest of your savings in a taxable account. ETFs, which carry out active and passive investment strategies without incurring capital gains taxes and have relatively low expense ratios, are a good choice for a taxable account.

The asset allocations in your portfolio should be spread across both types of accounts, with those generating the most taxable income and those with the most potential for growth in an IRA, and investments with possible tax benefits in the taxable account.

IRAs or Roth IRAs should contain:

- Bond ETFs

- REIT ETFs

- High-dividend ETFs

- Small- and micro-cap ETFs

- Emerging-market ETFs

Taxable accounts should contain:

- Equity ETFs, except for those paying high dividends

- Municipal bonds

- Foreign stock ETFs because the U.S. government will reimburse any taxes these funds paid out to foreign governments

- A cash reserve for emergencies

After Retirement

Traditional life-cycle investing dictates that as a person moves closer to retirement, his or her portfolio becomes increasingly conservative, reducing the allocation to speculative, volatile investments and shifting a larger allocation to bonds and short-term fixed income. Some of these conservative adjustments may not be necessary, depending on how the person will be using his or her savings. At some point close to or just after retirement, it is a good idea to have at least one consultation with a financial advisor to clarify your financial requirements and put them into perspective. There are also a number of Web sites offering advice and retirement calculators.

Will You Be Using Your Savings to Replace Your Paycheck?

Do you have other sources of income, such as pensions, Social Security, royalties, rental properties, and part-time employment, or will you be relying entirely on your savings to support your retirement lifestyle? The purpose of reducing risk in a portfolio is to ensure that cash is available exactly when it is needed, but reduced risk also means lower returns. If you are not relying entirely on your savings, it makes sense to leave some of your portfolio in equity and growth funds that have a greater potential for growth. Are you planning to bequeath some of your savings to your children or to an endowment? If so, they may have a greater tolerance for risk, which should be factored into your own asset allocations.

How Much Will You Need?

How will your lifestyle change after you retire? Will you need more or less than your current income? Are you moving to a smaller house, or to a state like Florida that does not have a state income tax? How much do you need to cover medical expenses and long-term care insurance? Many retirees spend more during their early retirement than in their later years. The American Association of Retired Persons (AARP) Web site has a worksheet to help you estimate your expenses during retirement (**www.aarp.org/money/financial_planning/sessionseven/retirement_**

planning_calculator.html). Vanguard.com and fireseeker.com have calculators that show the expected long-term results from your portfolio.

How Much Can You Safely Withdraw from Your Retirement Savings Each Year?

Experts agree that you can withdraw between 4 and 5 percent of your portfolio annually. This amount can be drawn first from dividends and cash. For the remainder, rebalance your portfolio by selling off the assets that have exceeded your target allocations. Should this withdrawal come out of your tax-advantaged retirement account or your taxable account? Apart from the minimum required distribution from a 401(k) or traditional IRA, the assets in tax-advantaged accounts can continue to accumulate earnings tax-free, but only you and your spouse will benefit from the tax benefits. If you are planning to leave an inheritance to your heirs, it might be more advantageous to draw more from the tax-advantaged accounts and leave the assets in the taxable account.

You are not likely to live long past the age of 100; when you arrive at a certain age, you can safely reduce the size of your portfolio because you will not require an annual income indefinitely.

TAKE NOTE: HISTORICAL PERFORMANCE IS NO GUARANTEE OF THE FUTURE

Historical performance is no guarantee of the future. The global economy is rapidly changing, and new market developments may not repeat the recurring cycles of the past. Always keep an eye on general economic trends. Rapidly increasing inflation may make bonds and fixed-income investments less attractive, and upward trends in the stock market may present growth opportunities for equity funds.

Life-cycle Portfolios

The concept of life-cycle investment is an outgrowth of modern portfolio theory, which suggests that overall risk is reduced when assets with low correlation to each other are combined in a portfolio. A young worker's earning potential is regarded as human capital and considered a fixed, risk-free asset, like insured bonds, with low correlation to the stock market. At the start of his or her career, all the future wages that worker might earn are treated as the "low-risk" allocation of a portfolio, and the remainder is invested in high-risk equity, which has the potential for rapid growth. As the worker ages, potential earnings shrink and are replaced in the portfolio with more bonds and fixed-income investments. When the worker reaches retirement, most of the portfolio will be invested in low-risk, low-return investments.

Some life-cycle allocations use the "100 rule," in which a person's age, subtracted from 100, determines the percentage of his or her portfolio that should be invested in equity. More aggressive allocations use a retirement age of 60 or 65 in place of 100.

The gradual move towards safer, more conservative investments seems to mirror the psychological changes that take place as a person moves through middle age and realizes that there is less time to achieve his or her goals and more to lose if an investment goes bad.

A typical life-cycle portfolio allocation would look something like the following:

	EARLY SAVERS PORT-FOLIO	MID-LIFE ACCUMUL-ATORS PORTFOLIO	NEW RETIREES PORTFOLIO	MATURE RETIREES PORTFOLIO
U.S. Stocks and REITs	45 percent	30 percent	30 percent	30 percent
Real Estate	10 percent	10 percent	5 percent	0 percent
International Stocks	25 percent	20 percent	15 percent	10 percent
Fixed-Income	20 percent	40 percent	45 percent	55 percent
Cash	0 percent	0 percent	5 percent	5 percent

A number of mutual fund companies now offer life-cycle funds designed to carry out portfolio reallocation over time, based on an investor's target retirement year. TD Ameritrade has announced plans to offer a life-cycle ETF. The providers of 401(k)s and IRAs offer suggested investments for each stage of the life cycle.

Some researchers contend that empirical data does not support the life-cycle investment theory (see "Case Study: Dale Kintzel"). Tests using historical data indicate that an S&P index fund would have outperformed life-cycle portfolios as much as two to one over the same time and that equity funds are a much more effective vehicle than fixed-income investments for growing retirement savings at any age. The only advantage of fixed-income investments is the protection they offer for someone who retires when the stock market is in a decline, which occurs only occasionally. Volatility in the labor market means that a young worker can no longer be sure of his or her future earnings.

TAKE NOTE: LIFE-CYCLE FUNDS

The life-cycle funds offered by many mutual fund companies are designed to take over an investor's complete portfolio and offer full diversification. Fund companies have observed that many customers are only investing part of their portfolio in a life-cycle fund and then are buying other investments, which dangerously unbalance their asset allocation and negate the life-cycle investment strategy.

CASE STUDY: DALE KINTZEL

Portfolio Theory, Life-Cycle Investing, and Retirement Income by Dale Kintzel*

Economist
Office of Retirement Policy
Social Security Administration
dale.kintzel@ssa.gov
Policy Brief No. 2007-02
Social Security Administration

October 2007
www.ssa.gov/policy/docs/policybriefs/pb2007-02.html

Portfolio theory suggests life-cycle investing can be optimal in some circumstances. Empirical work has found conflicting results. Life-cycle investing is consistent in many cases with actual portfolio choices individuals make, but some researchers question whether the protection that such funds provide against market downturns is worth the lower average returns produced by shifting assets from stocks to bonds.

Modern portfolio theory originated with the work of Markowitz (1952), who recognized that by combining assets that are not perfectly correlated (for example, assets whose returns do not move in complete unison with each other), an investor could reduce his or her investment risk without reducing expected returns. It is theoretically possible to derive a portfolio of risky assets that returns the smallest amount of risk for a given return. [A collection of all such portfolios would make up an "efficient frontier," which is derived by combining the individual stocks and taking into account the degree of covariation between them. Life-cycle funds can be thought of as moving along the efficient frontier [from the region of highest risk to the region of lowest risk] as one ages.

Several demographic and economic factors provide some rationale for life-cycle funds. The first deals with how the value of human capital varies over time as a fraction of total wealth. A good proxy for measuring the value of human capital is the present value of wages over an individual's remaining working life. This is generally considered much less variable or "stochastic" than equity returns because its determinants are, to some extent, fixed. Therefore, to maintain a constant level of risk exposure over the life-cycle, relatively more of one's total financial assets should beheld in stocks when young and less as one gets older (Bodie, Merton, and Samuelson 1992). To illustrate the constant risk of exposure approach, consider someone who wishes to hold 60 percent of total wealth at any given age in riskless assets (for example, inflation-protected bonds) and 40 percent in risky assets (for example, stocks).

CASE STUDY: DALE KINTZEL

Suppose, further, the person's human capital at a young age is equivalent to a riskless asset valued at $300,000. If the person has $200,000 in financial assets, they should all be held in risky assets (such as stocks) so that the 60/40 balance is achieved. As the person ages, the value of human capital falls (because only a few working years remain), but the financial assets grow. To maintain the 60/40 balance, financial assets must increasingly be shifted out of risky assets.

There is evidence that life-cycle investment strategies reflect people's general preferences. Several researchers have found investment behavior to be broadly consistent with the life-cycle advice. Some researchers, however, have questioned whether life-cycle approaches are appropriate for retirement saving. Several research studies show that these funds still expose investors to significant risk while eliminating most upside potential. Shiller (2005) simulated ending wealth balances of hypothetical life-cycle accounts using historical data for the S&P 500 and bond market returns and found that the life-cycle fund failed to outperform a 3 percent real return in 32 percent of trials, but a 100 percent investment in the S&P 500 would have beaten such a return in 98 percent of trials. Hickman and others (2001) simulated outcomes under Malkiel's approach, the "100 minus age rule," and 100 percent investment in the S&P 500 index fund. Using a 30-year holding period, the two life-cycle approaches (Malkiel and "100 minus age rule") yielded similar outcomes and produced median wealth at retirement that was approximately one-half that associated with the index fund. However, in about 15 percent of the simulations, the life-cycle approaches did outperform the S&P 500, which suggests that occasionally the shift to bonds at later ages will be a correctstrategy. However, the authors question whether protection against this relatively rare outcome warrants the large reduction in expected ending wealth. In a similar fashion, Butler and Domian (1993) simulated ending balances for stocks, bonds, and life-cycle accounts and derived probability distributions for ending wealth. Their conclusion was consistent with Hickman and others in that common stocks are the best vehicle for long-term retirement savings (life-cycle accounts outperformed a portfolio of all stocks in only about 8 percent of their simulations). Ho, Milevsky, and Robinson (1994) also emphasize the importance of stocks, arguing that higher risk/return investments may be necessary to minimize the chances of outliving one's assets in old age.

It is important to emphasize, however, that the literature on the limitations of life-cycle funds is based on historical returns and often uses data from periods when stock returns were strong. While riskless bonds may generally underperform stocks, they also protect against extremely negative outcomes (Bodie 1995). It isquestionable whether the historical period for which data are available is long enough to reflect these extreme outcomes.

CASE STUDY: DALE KINTZEL

Thus, one rationale for life-cycle funds is that they offer protection against extreme outcomes near retirement that occur with a low probability.

Some recent work questions the theoretical and intuitive underpinnings of life-cycle funds. Benzoni, Collin-Dufresne, and Goldstein (2005) argue that changes in labor income tend to be more heavily correlated with stock returns over long horizons. In other words, rather than being "bondlike" in its variability, labor income is "stocklike" over long horizons. In this framework, individuals should diversify by holding less risky assets (such as bonds) when young and riskier assets (such as stocks) at later ages.

References:

Benzoni, Luca, Pierre Collin-Dufresne, and Robert S. Goldstein. 2005. *Portfolio choice over the life-cycle in the presence of "trickle down" labor income.*

Bodie, Zvi. 1995. *On the risk of stocks in the long run.* Financial Analysts Journal 51(3): 18–22.

Bodie, Zvi, Robert C. Merton, and William F. Samuelson. 1992. *Labor supply flexibility and portfolio choice in a life-cycle model.* Journal of Economic Dynamics and Control 16: 427–449.

Butler, Kurt C., and Dale L. Domian. 1993. *Long-run returns on stock and bond portfolios: Implications for retirement planning.* Financial Services Review 2(1): 41–49.

Hickman, Kent, Hugh Hunter, John Byrd, John Beck, and Will Terpening. 2001. *Life-cycle investing, holding periods, and risk.* Journal of Portfolio Management 27(2): 101–111.

Ho, Kwok, Moshe Arye Milevsky, and Chris Robinson. 1994. *Asset allocation, life expectancy, and shortfall.* Financial Services Review 3(2): 109–126.

NBER Working Paper No. 11247, National Bureau of Economic Research, Cambridge, MA.

* "All views and opinions expressed in this book are those of the author and do not necessarily reflect the views and opinions of the Social Security Administration."

Chapter 17

o o o o o

Investing for Education with ETFs

Investing for the future education of a child is different from saving for retirement because you have a maximum of only 18 years to achieve your goal and because the total amount needed will be between $100,000 and $200,000. The funds will then be withdrawn and spent during a period of four to eight years, after which they will no longer be required (for education).

How Much Will an Education Cost?

The total cost of a college education is increasing at twice the rate of inflation. According to the 2007 Annual Survey of Colleges (The College Board, New York, NY), the average cost of tuition and fees for a four-year private college in 2007-2008 was $23,712, the average in-state tuition with fees for a four-year public college was $6,186, and the average out-of-state tuition with fees for a four-year public college was $16,640. In one year, the cost of tuition had increased 6.3 percent for private colleges and 6.6 percent for public colleges. Room and board averaged $7,404 per year at public colleges and $8,595 at private colleges. These figures do not include other expenses, such as medical insurance, the cost of travel, books, supplies, clothing, and other needs. The total cost of an education will be higher if the student does not complete a degree in four years.

You can find helpful college cost calculators and worksheets online at PrincetonReview.com (**www.princetonreview.com/college/finance/tcc**), Savingforcollege.com (**www.savingforcollege.com**), Finaid.org (**www. finaid.org**), and Collegeboard.com (**www.collegeboard.com/parents**).

Understanding Financial Aid

Not all education expenses come out of a parent's pocket. About two-thirds of all full-time undergraduate students receive grant aid. More than $130 billion dollars in financial aid is available to students in the United States. A diligent student or one who excels in athletics may qualify for a merit-based scholarship. When you are designing your college savings plan, it is important to optimize your student's eligibility for financial aid.

According to Finaid.org, your Expected Family Contribution (EFC), the amount of tuition you are expected to pay, is calculated according to this formula:

Parental Income (22 to 47 percent of adjusted gross income from federal income tax return)

+

Parental Assets (3 to 5.6 percent of non-retirement assets, including prepaid tuition plans, 529 Savings Plans, and brokerage/mutual fund accounts)

+

Student Income (50 percent of any student income over $3,000)

+

Student Assets (20 percent of all assets, including Uniform Gifts to Minors Act/Uniform Transfers to Minors Act accounts and other savings).

Assets held in the student's name, such as savings accounts, will be assessed at a much higher percentage than parental assets.

CASE STUDY: JOE HURLEY

Joe Hurley started **www.savingforcollege.com** in 1990 as a way to provide independent, objective information to consumers and professionals about 529 plans. He is the author of *The Best Way to Save for College – A Complete Guide to 529 Plans,* and he is a Certified Public Accountant (CPA) with over 20 years' experience helping families and businesses with tax planning.

Investors who want to begin saving for a child's college education have a number of options: 529 savings plans, 529 prepaid plans, Coverdell education savings accounts, taxable securities in parents' names, taxable securities in child's name, U.S. savings bonds, and IRAs. When choosing a 529, look for:

- An investment option that meets your objectives. For many, the age-based option is the best choice.

- Benefits offered by your state of residence. Often, you will have to use the in-state plan to get these benefits, e.g., state tax deduction for contributions.

- Good-quality underlying investments (funds, ETFs, etc.) at a reasonable price.

- No problematic restrictions. For example, some plans do not permit account owner changes. That can be a problem for some investors, but not for others.

- The Arkansas iShares 529 plan is all ETFs. It is available through registered investment advisors.

"Taxable investments may still be attractive to investors seeking certain high-risk investment strategies generally not found in 529 plans. And, of course, if the 529 plan is ultimately used for something other than college, the tax and penalty cost of a nonqualified distribution dramatically alters the comparison." (Quote from Mr. Hurley's article "7 Reasons Why Mutual Funds Don't Work so Well for College.") An all-ETF portfolio could be appropriate for an investor opting to open a taxable account for college savings if it doesn't throw off much annual income and the investor is buy-and-hold. Of course, most college savers should not be buy-and-hold because their asset allocation targets change as the child gets close to college age. Now that the iShares plan is available, there is less reason to opt for a taxable ETF portfolio, except to avoid plan-level expenses and/or have more choice in particular ETFs.

CASE STUDY: JOE HURLEY

A family would need to invest about $900 per month for a newborn to fully fund four years at an average private college. Few young parents can afford that. Also, because few students end up paying the enter sticker price of the college, some smaller amount would be fine for most.

If a family decides they are able to start saving for education when their child is already 12 or 13 years old, they should start saving whenever they can. Often, the parents of older children want less risky investments, and those are the least tax-efficient — more reason to use a 529 plan.

Scholarship withdrawals are not tax-free, but they are penalty-free. By instructing the plan to make the withdrawal payable to the student, the earnings are reportable by the student. Many students will not pay much, if any, tax, especially if they are able to claim the Hope credit or Lifetime Learning credit and their parents are not able to.

The biggest mistake made by families saving for college is spending all their earnings, thinking that will make their child eligible for financial aid. Income is a bigger determinant than assets. And, if you've spent everything, you have no way to afford college if your income knocks your child out of financial aid, except unsubsidized loans.

Savingforcollege.com offers useful, independent information on its Web site and in its publications. It also offers educational services to financial professionals (seminars, etc.).

The gift tax annual exclusion limit causes some parents and grandparents to limit their contributions to a 529 plan. The five-year election (allowing a one-time contribution of 60,000 to be distributed over five years) provides some help. For many, going above the annual exclusion amount will not cause any gift or estate tax, but it is a hurdle nonetheless.

What Are Your Options?

Tax-Deferred or Tax-Free Education Accounts

The U.S. government allows two types of tax-deferred accounts for education savings: Coverdell Education Savings Accounts and 529 plans.

COVERDELL EDUCATION SAVINGS ACCOUNT (CESA)

An educational savings account (ESA), like a Roth IRA, allows you to make an annual nondeductible contribution to a specially designated investment trust account. Anyone can open an ESA account, and the beneficiary does not have to be a relative or family member. The beneficiary can withdraw funds in any year and use them tax-free for qualified higher education expenses (QHEE) and even for some elementary and secondary school expenses. If the beneficiary withdraws more than the amount of qualified expenses, the earnings portion of that excess is subject to income tax and an additional 10 percent penalty tax.

You can open an ESA account with any bank, mutual fund company, or financial institution that can serve as custodian of traditional IRAs. A parent or guardian of the beneficiary will be made responsible for the account. Your cash contribution can be invested in any qualifying investments, including ETFs, available through the sponsoring institution. You can use an ESA to create a portfolio of ETFs offered by that institution.

Several rules limit the effectiveness of ESAs:

- You cannot make any further contributions to an ESA after the beneficiary's 18th birthday.

- A beneficiary can receive only $2,000 in total contributions per year.

- Joint tax return filers with adjusted gross incomes (AGIs) above $220,000 and single filers with AGIs above $110,000 cannot contribute to an ESA. This requirement can be circumvented by gifting the $2,000 to a child and having the child contribute to the ESA account.

- The ESA must be fully withdrawn by the time the beneficiary reaches age 30. If it is not, the remaining amount will be paid out within 30 days, subject to tax on the earnings and the additional 10 percent penalty tax.

- Unless Congress changes the legislation governing ESAs, certain benefits expire after 2010. K-12 expenses will no longer qualify, and the annual contribution limit will be reduced to $500.

529 PLANS

Under Section 529 of the federal tax code, there are two types of state-sponsored education savings accounts that offer tax benefits: prepaid tuition plans and 529 plans. A prepaid tuition plan locks in the current tuition rates at public state colleges for a future education. Because a prepaid plan guarantees payment upon maturity, it can be considered a safe investment. Prepaid tuition plans are offered by a number of states. You do not have to be a resident of that state to contribute, but the plans have drawbacks. Most of them cover tuition at a public university in their home state; even if they allow you to use the funds at a private or out-of-state school, you will have to make up the difference. Tuition is only part of the cost of a higher education; you will still need a substantial amount of money to cover the student's living expenses. Tuition costs are rising so rapidly that Colorado, Kentucky, Ohio, Texas, and West Virginia plans have begun closing enrollment because they anticipate difficulties in raising enough funds to meet their obligations.

A 529 plan is a state-sponsored college savings plan. Withdrawals are exempt from federal income tax when used for qualified higher education expenses. In most states, withdrawals are also state-tax-free, and some states offer their residents a state-tax deduction or credit on contributions. Over 80 of these state-sponsored 529 plans exist today, each with its own rules, fees, and investment choices. When 529 plans were introduced during the late 1990s, many were unpopular because of the fees charged by the brokers who sold them, their poor selection of investments, and management fees that ate into savings. After congressional hearings in 2004 concerning their high costs and industry concerns over lower-than-expected asset growth, many 529 plans became more competitive, cutting their rates and offering more choices to investors. Many states have dropped and even waived enrollment fees. In 2006, Congress passed the Pension Protection Act, making the tax advantages associated with 529 withdrawals permanent.

You can find detailed information about all the 529 plans on Savingforcollege.com. Morningstar.com compiles an annual list of the best and worst 529s. You do not have to be a resident of a particular state to invest in its 529 plan. Most 529 plans are administered by a financial company that offers a selection of investment choices. In addition to mutual funds, several 529 plans now offer low-cost ETFs. In January 2008, the state of Arkansas, program manager Upromise Investments, and investment manager Barclays Global Investments launched a new ETF-based 529 savings plan investing in iShares ETFs. The investment options include a year-of-enrollment, age-based portfolio; four multi-ETF asset allocations; and nine individual ETFs. Portfolios are subject to program manager and state administration fees of 0.35 to 0.40 percent. It is the first plan to rely solely on registered investment advisors (RIAs) for sales.

The 529 plans offer several advantages that make them attractive:

- Investments are selected and portfolio allocations are decided by experienced fund managers with clear financial objectives.

- Contributions can be made in small increments, such as payroll deductions, without incurring additional trading fees.

- Many 529 plans offer the capability of reallocating assets in the fund free of charge.

- There is no deadline for use of the funds; a beneficiary can use the money from a 529 throughout his or her lifetime.

- Most state plans cap contributions at between $230,000 and $300,000. Any contribution over $12,000 annually may be subject to the gift tax, but a one-time, five-year contribution of $60,000 is allowed, with the gift tax exemption distributed over the ensuing five years. This allows a parent or grandparent to set aside $60,000 in one year to grow, tax-free, in a 529 account.

- The contributor retains control of the 529 and can change the beneficiary to any family member of the original beneficiary, including spouses, children, and cousins.

- Withdrawals for the amount of a student's qualified education expenses are tax-free. The earnings on non-qualified withdrawals are taxable at the student's income tax rate, plus a 10 percent penalty. If a student receives a scholarship, the 10 percent penalty may be waived for a withdrawal equaling the amount of the student's tuition.

- Grandparents can set up a 529 to support the education of a grandchild without affecting that child's eligibility for financial aid. If the child wins a scholarship, any funds left over in the 529 can be transferred to another beneficiary in the family. Some 529 plans allow grandparents to contribute to a parent's account.

529 plans offer several advantages over ESAs: Anyone can contribute

to a 529 plan, regardless of income; contributions are not limited to $2,000 per year; and control of the 529 account remains in the hands of the contributor. Most 529 plans allow the contributor to decide when withdrawals are made and for what purpose. A contributor can even reclaim the funds in a 529 plan at any time; the earnings portion of the "non-qualified" withdrawal will be subject to income tax and an additional 10 percent penalty tax.

TAKE NOTE: RESEARCH YOUR 529 PLAN CAREFULLY

Do your research carefully before investing in a 529 plan. Look closely at the investment options offered by the plan and at the fund's historical returns and volatility. Keep expenses at a minimum; look at the expense ratios of the underlying investments, the plan's management costs, enrollment fees, and any brokerage commissions you may be paying. Some providers, like T. Rowe Price (Alaska) and Fidelity (Delaware, New Hampshire, and Massachusetts), offer no-commission plans. If you enroll through a broker or financial advisor, you may be able to negotiate. Make sure you understand all the details of the plan and what education expenses it will cover.

Funding Higher Education with IRAs and 401(k)s

Some parents and grandparents use IRAs as vehicles for college savings. You can withdraw funds from a traditional or Roth IRA (see "Chapter 16: Investing for Retirement") for qualified education expenses without paying the 10 percent withdrawal penalty. Qualified higher education expenses include tuition, fees, books, supplies, equipment, as well as certain room-and-board expenses if the student is enrolled at least part-time in a degree program. The entire amount of a withdrawal from a traditional IRA is subject to income tax, as is the earnings portion of the withdrawal from a Roth IRA. The entire distribution from a Roth IRA is tax-free if you have reached age 59½ and have held the Roth IRA for at least five years.

You can borrow up to half your vested balance in your 401(k) plan or $50,000, whichever is less, to pay for higher education for yourself, your child, or your spouse. Such loans often charge a percentage point or two above the prime lending rate, and are not taxed as income. The loan must be repaid within five years, and if you leave your employment for any reason, you may be required to make immediate repayment or pay income tax and a 10 percent early withdrawal penalty on the balance. In cases of extreme hardship, you can also withdraw funds from your 401(k) to pay for qualified education expenses, subject to income tax and the early withdrawal penalty if you are younger than 59½.

TAKE NOTE: YOUR IRA IS A LAST RESORT

Unless you already have a retirement income, 401(k)s and IRAs should be used to fund education only as a last resort. The withdrawal will count as untaxed income on next year's Free Application for Federal Student Aid (FAFSA) and will reduce the student's eligibility for need-based financial aid. Money taken from an IRA cannot be replaced, except through limited annual contributions. You will lose not only the amount you withdraw, but also all the earnings it might have brought you, and you will lose many of the benefits of an IRA as a tax shelter. You will be funding your children's education at the risk of becoming a burden to them in your later years. Low-cost federal education loan programs, such as the Stafford loan for students and the Parent Loan for Undergraduate Students (PLUS) loan for parents, offer flexible repayment terms, partial tax deductibility, deferments, and forbearance. There are no federal grants or low-cost loans to fund your retirement. Private student loans can be paid off in the future with any funds left over from your retirement.

Taxable Accounts

According to Financial Research Corporation, an estimated 68 percent of 529 plans are subject to brokerage fees. You may believe that the tax advantages of the 529 plans do not outweigh the brokerage commissions, annual fees, the expense ratios of the underlying investments, and the historical performance of the funds they offer. If you are confident that you can bring in better returns on your own, you may want to create and manage your own portfolio of low-cost ETFs to fund the future education of your child or grandchild. The tax efficiency of ETFs will allow your investment to grow free of capital gains tax until the time comes to pay for college. At that time, a tax advisor may be able to help you offset the capital gains tax through tax-loss harvesting, or you may find you have other resources to pay for education and can keep your investment.

John F. Wasik, author of *The Kitchen-Table Investor*, suggests that you can create an account with mature-growth ETFs that pay dividends, taxable at 15 percent for most taxpayers. As the child approaches college age, gift the assets to the child, who is likely to be in a much lower tax bracket.

Portfolios for Education Savings

Like a life-cycle portfolio, an education portfolio begins with more volatile investments in its early years and then becomes more conservative, aimed at preserving capital and making sure adequate funds are available exactly when the student needs them. When selecting ETFs for an education portfolio, assess your risk tolerance carefully. A volatile fund has greater potential for growth, but what will happen if it is in a decline the year that your student is beginning college? Do you have alternative sources of funding to fall back on? Is the student likely to qualify for a scholarship?

The investments in an education portfolio are reallocated every five years. The following are sample portfolio allocations similar to those used by many 529 plans:

SAMPLE EDUCATION PORTFOLIO ALLOCATIONS						
	AGE	NEW-BORN TO 5 YRS	6-10 YRS	11-15 YRS	16-20 YRS	21 PLUS
Aggressive	Equity Fund	100 %	80 %	60 %	40 %	20 %
	Fixed-Income	0 %	15 %	26 %	36 %	46 %
	Money Market	0 %	0 %	9 %	19 %	29 %
	Real Estate	0 %	5 %	5 %	5 %	5 %

SAMPLE EDUCATION PORTFOLIO ALLOCATIONS					
AGE	NEW-BORN TO 5 YRS	6-10 YRS	11-15 YRS	16-20 YRS	21 PLUS
Growth Equity Fund	80 %	60 %	40 %	20 %	0 %
Fixed-Income	15 %	26 %	36 %	46 %	50 %
Money Market	0 %	9 %	19 %	29 %	50 %
Real Estate	5 %	5 %	5 %	5 %	0 %
Balanced Equity Fund	60 %	40 %	20 %	0 %	0 %
Fixed-Income	26 %	36 %	46 %	50 %	25 %
Money Market	9 %	19 %	29 %	50 %	75 %
Real Estate	5 %	5 %	5 %	0 %	0%
Conserv-ative Equity Fund	40 %	20 %	0 %	0 %	0 %
Fixed-Income	36 %	46 %	50 %	25 %	0 %
Money Market	19 %	29 %	50 %	75 %	100 %
Real Estate	5 %	5 %	0 %	0 %	0 %

TAKE NOTE: WATCH YOUR EDUCATION PORTFOLIO

Always keep a close watch on an education portfolio. The sample portfolio allocations included here are based on historical returns, but you should check that the individual ETFs you selected are performing as expected, and make allowance for market conditions if necessary. Reallocation is normally carried out every five years and should be done thoughtfully because it incurs trading fees for buying and selling ETFs.

Chapter 18

○ ○ ○ ○ ○

Active Investing with ETFs

A well-diversified, buy-and-hold portfolio would be expected, over time, to achieve the same returns as the stock market. Active investing involves using a number of strategies to achieve greater returns by anticipating the market, identifying and buying stocks that are about to increase in value, and selling stocks before their prices decline. ETFs offer many exciting opportunities for active investors because they trade on the stock exchanges, just as individual stocks do, and offer immediate exposure to entire industry or geographic sectors with a single transaction. Assets can be moved quickly from one market to another by buying and selling ETFs. Investors can buy ETFs on margin, sell them short, and purchase options on them.

An investment that will be held for the long term is called a "long position"; a short-term investment is a "short position." Active traders break position times into three categories:

- **Day trade** — A trade in which an investment is bought and sold during the same trading session

- **Swing trade** — An investment is bought and sold again two days to two weeks later

- **Position trade** — Everything else

A passive investor makes an investment and then lets it follow the fluctuations of the market over time. Active investing requires a vision or a theory about the direction that will be taken by the financial markets in the near future.

Access to up-to-the minute information is crucial for the success of active investing. The Internet has transformed the world of active investing, making information that was once restricted to brokers, bankers, and financial "insiders" available to the public. Online brokerage accounts make it possible to execute buy and sell orders in seconds, rather than minutes. Throughout the day, intraday ETF prices are displayed on broker-dealer Web sites and, with slight delays, on the sites of the ETF exchanges. The exchanges recalculate the intraday prices and NAVs (net asset values) of all ETFs approximately every 15 seconds.

Buy and Sell Orders

Active traders execute their trading strategies by placing buy and sell orders with their brokerages. An order has three components:

- **Time** — How long the order stays open. A day order is open for just one day, and is canceled if it is still unfulfilled at the end of the day. Most short-term traders use day orders. GTC (good-till-canceled) orders remain open until they are specifically canceled. GTC orders are risky because they have a tendency to be forgotten; they can have unintended consequences if they are filled unexpectedly when the market situation has changed.

- **Contingency** — Whether the execution of an order is contingent on a particular event

- **Action** — The action to be carried out when the order is received

Market Order

A market order has no contingencies. It is an order to buy or sell a certain number of shares of a particular ETF or stock, and it will be fulfilled at the best bid price available on the market at that moment. The exact price paid for the shares will not be known until the confirmation of the transaction is received.

Example: Buy 50 DIA at the market. (Buy 50 shares of Dow Diamonds at best market price.)

If the shares of that ETF are trading steadily on the market, there is no problem with a market order because it will be filled right away. If an ETF is trading slowly, however, by the time the transaction is executed, there may be a substantial difference, called a spread, between the bid price at which you want to buy the stock and the ask price at which the seller wants to sell it. The ask price is always a little higher than the bid price. The buyer pays the ask price (higher) and the seller receives the bid price (lower) for the stock; the spread, or difference, is kept by the broker/specialist handling the transaction to cover commissions and fees. If time has elapsed between the placing of an order and its fulfillment, the spread may be relatively large, and the order may not be filled as originally expected.

Limit Order

A limit order sets a maximum price that the buyer is willing to pay for shares of an ETF or stock.

Example: Buy 50 DIA at $119.85. (Buy 50 shares of Dow Diamonds at $119.85.)

If DIA is trading at a higher price, such as $120.10, the order will not be activated until the price of DIA drops to a maximum of $119.85. The entire order may not be filled if there are not enough shares available at that price or if the price of DIA quickly rises again. If the order expires without the price of DIA ever dropping to $119.85, the order remains unfilled.

A limit order is triggered when shares of an ETF or stock drops to the specified price, and it allows an active investor to take advantage of market fluctuations to purchase the shares at a price slightly lower than the current average. If the price then rises over the next few days, those shares can be sold at a profit.

Market-if-Touched Order (MIT)

A market-if-touched order is closely related to a limit order. As soon as the specified price is touched, the MIT becomes a market order. Like ordinary market orders, it will be filled completely at the best price available at the time.

Stop Order

Also known as a "stop-loss" order, a stop order is commonly used to limit losses when the price of a stock or ETF begins to drop. When the price of an ETF or stock drops to the specified level, it converts to a market order and is filled immediately.

Example: Sell 50 DIA at $120.90 stop. (Sell 50 shares of Dow Diamonds when the price drops to $120.90.)

If you purchased 50 shares of DIA at $119.85, and the price has now risen to $122, you can protect your gain by using a stop order to sell the 50 shares if the price drops to $120.90. The stop order will only be activated if the price gets down to $120.90. The stop order does not guarantee that all 50 shares will be sold for $120.90. Like any market order, it will be filled at the best available price. If share prices are dropping rapidly, some of your shares could be sold for considerably less than $120.90.

You can control the price at which your shares will be sold by adding a limit to the stop order.

Example: Sell 50 DIA at $120.90 stop, limit $120.40. (Sell 50 shares of Dow Diamonds when the price drops to $120.90; stop selling if the price goes below $120.40.)

When the share prices drop to $120.90 and the stop order is activated, it becomes a limit order. Shares cannot be sold for less than $120.40. In a fast-moving market, there is a risk that the price will fall below $120.40 before all your shares are sold and your order will be only partially filled, leaving you holding some shares that are now worth less than you paid for them.

Selling Short

Selling short is an active trading strategy in which an investor borrows shares of stock from another investor or a brokerage and sells them in the expectation that the price of that stock will go down. This is called establishing a short position. When the price goes down, the investor will buy shares back at the lower price, return them to the lender, and pocket the difference. Shares of ETFs can be sold short in exactly the same way.

To initiate a short sale, an investor borrows shares of an ETF, sells them on the open market, and deposits the proceeds in a special margin account. While the short seller maintains a short position, interest is charged on the value of the shares that have been loaned. Any dividends paid by securities in the ETF during this period must be paid to the lender. To close out the short position, the investor buys shares of the ETF on the open market and returns them to the lender.

If the price of the ETF or stock defies the short seller's expectations and rises instead of falls, he or she will start to accrue losses. An investor who already owns, in another account, the identical number of shares of the same stock or ETF that is being borrowed is covered. As the price rises, the market losses from the short position will be offset by the rising value of the shares still owned by the investor. A covered investor will only lose the opportunity to earn returns by reinvesting that money instead of giving it to the lender. If the investor does not already own the identical stock, he or she is uncovered, and the market risk of selling short is unlimited.

In order to borrow shares of stock or an ETF from a broker, an investor must make a cash deposit, called a margin, in a special margin account. If the investor is covered, the minimum initial margin is 100 percent of the proceeds from the short sale of the shares. The minimum initial margin for an uncovered short sale is 100 percent of the proceeds of the short sale, plus another 50 percent. If market losses lower the investor's equity below a specified level, a margin call will go out requesting an additional maintenance margin to be deposited in the margin account.

Selling Short to Offset Losses

Selling short can be used as a strategy to offset a decline in the price of an ETF. If it seems that the price of an ETF in your portfolio is about to decline, you short it by borrowing and selling shares of the same ETF at the current higher price. If the price declines, those shares can be sold at a profit, which will compensate for the decline in value of the ETF shares in your portfolio.

ETFs that Short the Market

In 2006, ProShares introduced ETFs whose value moves inversely to changes in specific indexes, such as the S&P 500 (ProShares Short S&P 500- SH), Dow Jones Industrial Average (ProShares Short Dow 30 - DOG), NASDAQ

100 (ProShares Short QQQ - PSQ), and the S&P Mid-Cap (PowerShares Short Mid-Cap 400 - MYY). These were followed by funds shorting other indexes, including international markets. By November 2007, ProShares short funds held $9 billion in assets. These funds are intended to hedge against declines in the prices of ETFs tracking major indexes by moving in the opposite direction of the market. When prices rise, the short ETFs fall but continue to pay dividends from the underlying securities. The expense ratio of these ETFs is 0.95 percent annually.

CAUTION: SELLING SHORT IS NOT FOR THE INEXPERIENCED

Selling short is a complicated strategy; there are other, simpler ways for an individual to offset losses or profit from the decline in the price of an ETF. The short ETFs can be included in your portfolio as a safety net, but remember that they decline when the markets rise.

Position Management

The success of active trading depends on efficient position management, or the establishment and maintenance of clear investment parameters. The number one priority in position management is the preservation of your investment capital. The greatest hazard in active trading is that, faced with escalating losses, you will hold on, hoping that the market will reverse itself instead of simply selling, taking a loss, and reinvesting your remaining capital in a more fruitful area. The most successful traders are those who limit their losses. Do not be hesitant to let go of a losing investment when it no longer fits your investment strategy.

You can simply decide the maximum loss you are willing to accept, or you can use technical analysis to identify a logical price level at which you should exit the market. Stop orders can be placed to ensure that your holdings are automatically sold when their price reaches the lowest level you can tolerate. If prices never drop that low, the stop order will never be activated.

After you have developed an investment strategy, stick to it. Do not be swayed by everything you read and hear. If you observe important changes occurring in the markets, you may want to modify your plan, but do it carefully, and do not discard your original analysis. With so much information about the stock markets readily available 24 hours a day, it is easy to lose sight of your original objectives and begin to react to every upturn and downturn. Keep your original objectives in mind.

Capital Leverage
Trading on Margin

ETFs, like many stocks, can be bought on margin. Instead of using your capital to buy shares of an ETF outright, you can open a margin account with a broker and deposit your capital as collateral to borrow up to 50 percent of the purchase price of an ETF. This allows you to double the amount of shares you buy, doubling your returns — and, potentially, your losses.

Buying on margin is more suitable for short-term trading than for long-term trading, because of the interest on the loan. Unless you make regular payments, interest accrued over a long period may offset your returns.

An initial amount of at least $2,000, known as minimum margin, is required to set up a margin account. The securities purchased using the account are held by the broker as collateral. The investor is required to maintain at least 25 percent (some brokerages require up to 40 percent) equity in the margin account. If the price of an ETF drops drastically and the investor's equity falls below the required percentage, the brokerage will issue a margin call, asking the investor to either deposit additional cash or sell shares of the ETF to bring his or her equity back up to the required level. If the investor does not respond to the margin call, the brokerage will sell shares of the ETFs held by the account.

> ### TAKE NOTE: DO NOT BORROW WHAT YOU CANNOT AFFORD TO LOSE
>
> The purpose of buying on margin is to potentially increase your returns by doubling your buying power. You are also potentially doubling your losses; a price drop of more than 50 percent means a 100 percent loss of your capital, plus fees and commissions. Never buy more on margin than you can afford to pay back without hardship.
>
> When prices of an ETF bought on margin drop, the brokerage has the right to sell shares of the ETF to maintain your equity, making your losses permanent.
>
> The brokerage is not required to consult you before selling your securities. If you purchase your ETF with cash, you can hold on to it until the market recovers.

ETF Futures Contracts

A futures contract is a standardized contract to buy or sell shares of a stock or an ETF at a certain date in the future for a specified price. The future date is called the delivery date or final settlement date. The preset price is called the futures price. The price of the underlying asset on the delivery date is called the settlement price. The buyer of a futures contract has a long position, meaning that he or she effectively owns the shares of the underlying ETF and will profit if the price of those shares goes up. The seller of an ETF futures contract takes a short position, meaning that he or she has the obligation to sell the underlying ETF shares on the delivery date for the futures price. If the market price of those shares goes down before the delivery date, the seller will profit.

Futures contracts trade on two futures exchanges: the Chicago Mercantile Exchange and OneChicago. A standard OneChicago Single Stock Futures (SSF) contract is a contract to deliver 100 shares of a specific ETF at a designated date in the future. A trader who holds 10 SSF contracts effectively holds the equivalent of 1,000 shares of the ETF. The price of an ETF futures contract is determined by the market in accordance with a theoretical pricing model that considers the market value of the ETF plus interest, minus any dividends. The price of an ETF futures contract tracks the market price of the underlying ETF closely. A futures contract is priced slightly higher than the price of the ETF to account for interest and other expenses (cost of carry).

All ETF futures contracts mature in March, June, September, or December. Settlement is on the third Friday of those months. Contracts for the next two maturity dates are listed for trading.

The futures exchanges require the buyer and seller to deposit an initial margin, 20 percent of the value of the contract. The margin represents the amount, as determined by historical price changes, that might potentially be lost in a normal day's trading if the price of the ETF changes. A futures account is reconciled with the market daily. If the underlying ETF experiences a large increase or decrease in price and the margin drops below the percentage level required by the exchange listing the futures, a margin call will be issued to bring the account back up to the required level. The futures exchange may reduce or waive margin requirements for investors who have other contracts that offset potential losses or who own shares of the same ETF.

ETF futures currently listed at OneChicago (**http://onechicago.com**) include:

- DIAMONDS

- iShares FTSE/Xinhua China 25 Index

- iShares MSCI Emerging Markets Index

- iShares Russell 2000 Index

- PowerShares QQQ

- SPDR Trust Series 1

- SPDR Selects

ETF futures listed on the Chicago Mercantile Exchange (**www.cme.com**) include:

- CME Futures on Standard & Poor's 500 Depositary Receipts

- CME Futures on PowerShares QQQ

- CME Futures on iShares Russell 2000 Index Fund

Difference Between Owning an ETF and a Futures Contract on an ETF

There are several differences between owning shares of an ETF and owning a futures contract on an ETF:

- The owner of an ETF receives any dividends paid by the underlying stocks. The holder of a futures contract does not receive dividends but is required to pay them to the seller.

- An ETF short seller must borrow actual shares of the ETF to sell; sellers of ETF futures do not.

- An ETF owner can hold a long or short position indefinitely; all futures contracts eventually expire and reach settlement.

The purchase of an ETF futures contract promises greater capital leverage (returns on capital) because the buyer of a futures contract is only required to post a margin of 20 percent of its total value, compared to 50 percent of the total purchase for buying shares of the ETF on margin. For the same amount of capital, the buyer of a futures contract is able to purchase many more shares and increase the potential returns.

A measure of the performance of futures contracts is return on margin (ROM). ROM represents the gain or loss relative to the required margin, which reflects the exchange's perception of risk.

$$ROM = \frac{realized\ return}{initial\ margin}$$

Futures contracts are considered more cost-efficient than buying on margin because the interest rate is built into the price of a futures contract. The interest rate that the investor will pay is locked in when the futures trade is made, and it is determined by a number of participants in a competitive market. When an investor buys on margin, a variable interest rate is determined by the brokerage in a noncompetitive environment. The interest rate can rise significantly under volatile market conditions, incurring unforeseen costs for the investor.

Settlement of ETF Futures

A futures contract is an obligation to buy or sell; this is different from an options contract, which gives the holder the right, but not the obligation, to buy or sell. Unlike an option, a futures contract does not expire worthless; it is settled when it reaches its expiry date. There can be no early settlement of a futures contract. To exit a futures commitment, the buyer of a futures contract must enter into another contract to sell shares of the same ETF; the seller can offset potential losses by purchasing another futures contract for shares of the same ETF. On the settlement date, shares of the ETF are delivered to the buyer.

Futures contracts have several other benefits. If the value of a futures contract rises above its agreed price, the trader can have immediate access to the excess cash, without waiting for the contract to be sold or settled. One hundred shares of the underlying ETF can be moved with a single futures contract. Because the buyer of a futures contract effectively owns the underlying shares, he or she can immediately sell an option on them. Futures can also be used for pairs trading. (See "Pairs Trading and Market-Neutral Strategies" at the end of this chapter).

Speculating with ETF Futures

An ETF futures contract can be used to leverage the returns if the price of an ETF makes a significant move up or down. A trader can sell a futures contract at the ETF's current price and profit when the price goes down significantly before the settlement date. If the trader believes that the price of an ETF will rise over the next few months, he or she can purchase a futures contract at the current price; the underlying shares will be much more valuable when the contract is settled.

Speculators also use futures contracts to establish spread positions. A spread is the difference in price between an asset that is being bought and one that is being sold. A trader buys a futures contract for one ETF and sells an equal futures contract for another, closely related ETF that is expected to underperform it. The prices of the two closely related ETFs tend to go up and down together; as long as the price of the futures that were bought remains higher than the price of those that were sold, the trader will experience a net gain.

A futures ETF can also be sold as a hedge to protect against losses from an ETF already in your portfolio. If you believe the price of your ETF will soon go down, you can sell a futures contract for the same ETF at its current price. The loss from the drop in price of the ETF in your portfolio will be offset by the gain realized on the futures contract.

TAKE NOTE: SPECULATION IS A GAMBLE

Speculation is just that; you are taking your chances that the price of an ETF will rise or fall as expected. If it does not, you lose. Futures contracts allow you to leverage your capital by buying on a margin of 20 percent; they also allow you to compound your losses. Do not speculate with money you cannot afford to lose. The safest way to invest in ETFs is to buy and hold them for the long term.

Forecasting the Markets

Active traders use two approaches to predict how the market will behave. Fundamental analysis looks at a variety of historical and economic factors and attempts to understand how the market is developing, what direction it will take in the near future, and how it will perform in the long run. Technical analysis ignores all these factors and looks at stock price patterns to forecast future price trends.

Fundamental Analysis

TOP-DOWN STRATEGIES

Top-down analysis looks at the entire global economy for macroeconomic trends and tries to determine which countries and industries will benefit the most from those trends. An investor then buys ETFs representing those countries and industry sectors. Because price changes in the stock markets are related to changes in the economy, top-down strategists examine press releases from government agencies and economic firms containing information on tax revenue data, manufacturing trends, monetary policy, supplies of commodities, wholesale prices, and employment.

This type of research reveals macroeconomic developments, which give rise to investing themes. For example, a drop in the price of oil will benefit the transportation and automotive industries and will lower the profits of energy producers. It would benefit countries that import oil and adversely effect countries that export commodities. Political changes affect business and trade in those geographic areas. New technologies have an effect on communications and the way business is carried out. Aging populations have increased healthcare needs; growing economies have a greater demand for materials and construction. Knowledge of these themes might enable an investor to structure his or her portfolio so that it outperforms the market without increasing risk.

Economic Cycle Analysis

Every country experiences cycles of expansion and recession, measurable using its gross domestic product (GDP), or level of business output. Emerging economies are more volatile than mature, diversified economies. The GDP of a country is constantly changing, either expanding or contracting. The GDP cycle is divided into five stages, characterized by changing employment, industrial productivity, and interest rates. Asset price changes are related to the stages of the business cycle. An analysis of business cycles is a means of predicting economic activity and deciding which asset classes to invest in.

Stages of the Business Cycle:

Prosperity (peak):

Employment is high, and there is increasing demand for goods and services, which eventually results in inflation. Inflation escalates as employees demand higher wages, and the rising cost of production causes prices to go even higher.

Contraction:

Interest rates are raised to slow economic growth, and consumer spending slows. Decreased demand causes business growth to slow down and stabilize prices.

Recession:

High interest rates decrease demand to the point where businesses cut back production and lay off workers. Increasing unemployment postpones consumer spending, and national output declines.

Trough:

The trough is the lowest point of the recession just before recovery begins.

Expansion (growth):

Interest rates are lowered, prices become low, demand increases, companies begin hiring, and spending increases.

According to Investopedia ULC (**www.investopedia.com**), "Since World War II, most business cycles have lasted three to five years from peak to peak. The average duration of an .expansion is 44.8 months, and the average duration of a recession is 11 months. As a comparison, the Great Depression, which saw a decline in economic activity from 1929 to 1933, lasted 43 months."

Governments try to control their economies through taxation and spending, and by raising and lowering interest rates. Changes in interest rates affect stock prices. Higher interest rates attract more investors to bonds and simultaneously result in decreased business activity and lower stock prices. Certain times during the business cycle are better than others for investing in stocks, bonds, and commodities. If you are able to determine which stage of a business cycle the economy is about to enter, you can shift the asset allocations in your portfolio to areas that are expected to outperform the market at that stage.

BOTTOM-UP ANALYSIS

Another group of investors carefully researches individual companies, countries, and industries to form value-based opinions. Rather than looking at macroeconomic trends, they focus on the potential of a particular industry or country for growth over the next few years and purchase ETFs for sectors or countries whose potential is undervalued.

Bottom-up analysts look at a number of factors in evaluating an industry.

Price:

Current price-to-sales, price-to-earnings, and price-to-book ratios are compared to the average long-term ratio for that industry. If the stocks for that industry are selling above their historical average, they are avoided; if they are selling below historical average, they are desirable.

Debt:

Bottom-up investors look for industries whose debt relative to their equity is decreasing. This is a sign of good management and proper use of capital.

Cash flow:

Free cash flow in an industry indicates that companies are earning a profit and will be able to pay dividends.

Fundamental analysis can be applied more effectively to market-sector and narrowly based ETFs that track only a small number of stocks. Broad market ETFs follow the trends of the stock market as a whole.

TAKE NOTE: THE PUBLIC DOES NOT ALWAYS UNDERSTAND VALUE

One drawback to fundamental analysis is that it is impossible to know exactly when undervalued industries will start to realize value in the stock market. The stock market is driven largely by public opinion, and prices may continue to rise in a popular, overvalued sector, while an investor may have to wait months or years to see a well-chosen value ETF bring in results.

Technical Analysis

Technical analysts believe that economic cycles, fiscal policies, and all the fundamental factors that affect stock prices are already naturally represented by the price fluctuations of the stock market and that it is unnecessary to look anywhere else to forecast the future behavior of the market. The primary research tool of technical analysts is price charts, graphic representations of price movements over time. Technical analysts look at moving averages, trading volumes, price trends, and market momentum.

MOMENTUM INVESTING

Momentum investing is a price-timing strategy in which an investor jumps into the market when there is an established upward trend in prices, backed by reports of favorable earnings.

Momentum is a measure of the rate at which prices are rising or falling. Relative price momentum can be measured by assigning a price score to each industry, with a baseline of 100 representing the market average. Scores over 100 indicate a higher price momentum than the market, and scores under 100 represent a lower-than-average price momentum.

A widely known measure of price momentum, or momentum oscillator, is the Relative Strength Index (RSI). The RSI measures the strength of a security in relation to its past performance, using a calculation that compares the number of up days and down days over a 14-day period. The result is an index number between 0 and 100. The RSI is recalculated every day to include the previous day's price. RSI values over 50 indicate an upward trend, with values over 70 considered a sign that the market is overextended and the stock price will soon experience a setback. RSI values under 50 indicate a downward trend, with a threshold of 30 as the point where a decline is considered to have run its course. When the RSI of a stock or an ETF begins to move in an opposite direction from its price, it is a warning sign. The RSI for some industries is calculated using more than 14 days if the natural price cycle is considered to be longer than 28 days.

Stock prices of a particular industry tend to rise rapidly for less than a year before their momentum slows, signaling investors to get out of the market. Momentum investing demands constant review of ETF prices and frequent turnover of industry sectors in a portfolio.

An increase in earnings momentum is also seen as an indicator of rising stock prices. The forecasts of financial analysts are used to rank industries from highest to lowest in terms of the rate at which their earnings are growing. When earnings are growing at a faster rate than previously predicted by analysts, it is an indication that prices in that industry will continue on an upward trend.

TAKE NOTE: EVERYONE IS DOING THE SAME THING

Investing according to price momentum is risky because of all the other investors who are doing the same thing. The rush to enter the market when an upward trend is confirmed may drive prices artificially high, and the rush to sell when the trend slows can drive prices rapidly downward.

USING CHARTS TO IDENTIFY TRENDS

Price Trends

Fluctuations in the price of an ETF can be analyzed on a price chart, which graphs the price movements over time. Each day is represented by a thin vertical line, stretching from the lowest to the highest price at which the ETF sold on that day. The closing price for the day is marked with a small dash across the vertical line. A second bar graph, showing daily trading volumes for the same time period, is placed underneath to confirm the trends.

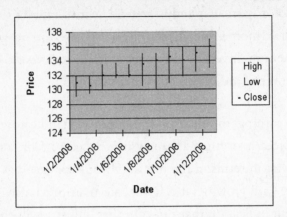

A price trend is the tendency for a series of stock or ETF prices to continue moving in the same direction. When prices have been moving up and down within the same narrow range for an extended period (sideways movement) and then begin to move above or below that range, it could be the beginning of a new price trend. Three price points, the points at which a price reaches a peak or valley and reverses direction, are required to establish an upward or downward trend.

Traders often draw a straight line, called a trend line, across the peaks in a downward trend or the valleys in an upward trend. Each time the price touches the line and then reverses itself, the direction of the trend is confirmed. A trend line serves two purposes. It identifies the high points of a downward trend; each time the price reaches one of these high points is an opportunity to short the ETF (borrow shares and sell them at the high price and then buy them back a few hours or days later when the price drops again and pocket the difference). When the daily price fluctuations penetrate a trend line, it is a sign that the trend has run its course, and the trader should quickly close out any short positions by buying shares (to replace those he borrowed and sold when the price was high) before the price rises.

Trends do not often reverse themselves immediately; instead, the price of a stock or ETF hovers within a narrow range for an extended time. This is called sideways action. When a price finally moves above or below this narrow range, it often initiates a flurry of activity, as millions of traders who have been closely observing price fluctuations rush to buy or sell the shares they have been holding onto.

Price Support and Price Resistance

A support level is the price level at which declines of an ETF or stock price tend to bottom out before the price begins to rise again. Every time the price reaches that level, the decline loses its momentum and reverses direction. A resistance level is the ceiling at which the upward momentum of a particular ETF price tends to stop before entering a decline. Technical analysts identify the support and resistance levels of an ETF price trend and use them as guides. They buy low when the support level is approached, sell high at the resistance level, and place stop-loss orders just below the support level and above the resistance level.

Trading Volume

Daily trading volume is the number of shares of an ETF bought and sold on that day. When trading volume is high, the market is liquid. There are many buyers and sellers, and trades can be executed quickly without affecting the price level too much. A rising price accompanied by a rise in trading volume indicates that investor interest is increasing and that the upward trend is picking up momentum. The same is true for a downward trend.

Moving Averages

Richard Donchian (1905 – 1993), the American futures and commodities trader who pioneered trend following, developed a "weekly rule system" based on moving averages. A moving average is an average of the price of a security or an ETF over the past several days, recalculated every day.

Moving averages are part of almost every trading strategy. A moving average helps to factor out minor daily fluctuations in price and focus attention on major price movements. A downward trend will not emerge in a moving average until prices have been lower for several days, confirming that it is more than a brief fluctuation.

Fewer days in the calculation of a moving average make it more sensitive to new price information. For a volatile ETF, a moving average calculated over a longer period is more useful in identifying a major upward or downward trend. For slower-moving ETFs, the average should be taken over a shorter period so that it reflects a downward trend sooner.

Donchian used 5-day and 20-day moving averages as trading signals to enter and leave the commodities markets. He also charted the moving averages of the highest and lowest daily prices. The area on the chart between these two moving averages, called the "Donchian channel," indicated a safe price range. When prices moved above or below the Donchian channel, it was a signal to act. For ETFs and stocks, 20-day and 200-day moving averages are commonly used.

A simple moving average gives equal importance to each day's price. In the stock market, though, the previous day's price is far more significant than the price 10 or 20 days ago. A weighted moving average accounts for this by multiplying the previous day's price by the number of days in the calculation, the price before that by one less day, and so on. The totals are added up and divided by the total number of "weights." The weighted moving average gives a more accurate portrayal of price behavior. Exponential moving averages take weighting even further by allowing the trader to give most of the total weight in the average to a specified number of the most recent days.

A price chart illustrating the moving average in conjunction with daily price movements is used to determine when to buy and sell shares of an ETF. Charts comparing daily prices with 50-day and 200-day moving averages are also popular indicators.

Point and Figure Charts

Technical analysts also use point and figure charts to generate trading signals. A point and figure chart is done by hand on a daily basis, using a grid with prices marked along the left-hand side. Each box in the grid represents a price increment. One symbol, such as "X," is used for price increases, and another, such as "O," is used for decreases. Each time the price rises one increment, the analyst marks another X in the first column. When the price starts to fall, the analyst moves over to the second column and begins using O's to track the price's downward movement. When the price reverses again, it is tracked with X's in the third column, and so on:

52.75						
52.50						X
52.25			X			X
52.00			X	O	X	X
51.75	X		X	O	X	O
51.50	X	O	X	O	X	
51.25	X	O	X	O	X	
51.00	X	O	X	O		
50.75	X	O	X			
50.50	X	O				
50.25	X					
50.00						

The smaller the price increments, the more sensitive the chart is to price movements.

When an X tops the immediately preceding column of X's, it is a signal to buy. Similarly, when an O drops below the immediately preceding column of O's, it is a signal to sell. Price trends are clearly visible on a point and figure chart.

MARKET BREADTH

Most methods of technical analysis are applied most successfully to single stocks or to ETFs tracking a narrow index or a single market sector. There is one indicator that can be used to identify price trends in the stock market as a whole: market breadth. Market breadth is the ratio of the number of stocks whose price has gone up to the number of stocks whose price has gone down. A ratio near one indicates that the broad market is remaining steady; a ratio lower than one indicates a decline; and a ratio higher than one indicates an upward trend. Market breadth readings can also be visually analyzed on a price chart, and moving averages of market breadth can identify upward and downward trends in the broad market.

Computer Software

There are countless software programs on the market, which carry out all types of technical analysis and promise to beat the market with licensed trading algorithms. Computer software is also used to "backtest" portfolios and investment strategies, compiling data on how these strategies would have performed under past market conditions, and creating projections for the future.

TAKE NOTE: PAST PERFORMANCE DOES NOT GUARANTEE FUTURE RESULTS

Trying to predict the future performance of an ETF or market sector solely on the basis of price patterns is like trying to choose a lottery number by looking at all the past winning numbers. There is absolutely no guarantee that because prices have behaved a certain way in the past, they will continue to do so. Stock prices are based on a constantly evolving economy, which is subject to changing global conditions. Just as we see irreversible political changes occurring, there are economic

TAKE NOTE: PAST PERFORMANCE DOES NOT GUARANTEE FUTURE RESULTS

developments that will never be reversed. Globalization and advances in technology and communications are bringing about change more rapidly. One example is the rapid growth in the number of ETFs on the market. Technical analysis should always be combined with an awareness of the forces active in the global economy.

Sector Rotation

Sector rotation is a strategy in which an investor constantly shifts his or her assets to the best-performing sectors of the market. In *ETF Trading Strategies Revealed* (Marketplace Books, 2006), David Vomund explains several mechanical rotation strategies that can be used to optimize the long-term growth of a portfolio. Mechanical rotation is based on the observation that some asset styles perform better than others at different times. For example, growth stocks excelled from 1994 through 1999. Then, the market environment changed, and returns on the NASDAQ Composite, a good measure of growth stocks, fell by 12 percent annually from 2000 to 2004, while the S&P Value Index gained 0.5 percent annually. The same occurred with large-cap stocks, which did well from 1998 through 1999, only to be superseded by small-cap stocks from 2000 to 2005.

Mechanical rotation strategies identify the ETFs that performed best throughout the previous six-month period and make sure that the portfolio always contains the two top-performing ETFs. The performance of all ETFs is evaluated once a month, and if an ETF in the portfolio is no longer among the top performers, it is sold and replaced with an ETF from among the top three performers.

Most ETFs are relatively new and have little historical data. Vomund ran a "backtest" using historical data from the indexes underlying the current

ETFs and a hypothetical portfolio invested in two ETFs. A portfolio using this rotation strategy substantially outperformed the S&P 500 Index during the years when it was doing well, and during the years when the S&P 500 had negative returns, the portfolio still fared significantly better after trading commissions were accounted for.

Because an ordinary investor would not want to commit for a whole month to a volatile ETF, Vomund developed a model he calls "style index strategy." ETF performance is evaluated every two weeks instead of every month. The six-month period is divided into four equal parts, and the percentage of increase or decrease in returns for each period is calculated, then averaged, with the most recent period being given double weight. (This type of calculation can be done with most market analysis software.) Every two weeks, if either of the two funds in the portfolio is not among the three top-performing ETFs, it is sold and replaced with a top performer. Many times, no replacement is required; over one year, this strategy required an average of ten trades at a cost of $170.

Vomund also tested variations of the rotation strategy, adding a bond fund and adding two international ETFs to his trial portfolio. The international ETFs substantially improved the portfolio's returns.

Options

ETF options offer two kinds of opportunity: control over large numbers of ETF shares with a relatively small investment and the opportunity to make money by selling options on the ETF shares you already own.

Options are the right to buy (call) or to sell (put) an ETF at a certain price before a certain date. These rights are bought and sold on stock exchanges at evolving prices that reflect the value of the underlying ETF and the time left in the contract. The price of an option is its intrinsic value plus a speculative premium.

More than 250 ETF options are traded on the American Stock Exchange (AMEX), Chicago Board Options Exchange (CBOE), and NASDAQ. The AMEX and CBOE also trade options on HOLDRs. Their financial integrity is guaranteed by the exchanges and by third-party option clearinghouses. All ETF options are American style; they can be exercised on any business day before they expire, and they are settled by delivery of shares of the underlying ETF.

Puts and Calls

There are two types of options: put options and call options. A call option gives you the right to purchase shares of an ETF at an agreed price over a specified time. A put option gives you the right to sell shares of an ETF at an agreed price over a specified time. The expiration date is the day the specified time ends. The exercise price of an option is the price at which the underlying ETF is sold if the option is exercised. The premium is the amount of money paid by the buyer of an option to the seller in the opening transaction.

Purchasing a call is speculative because the option may expire worthless and the buyer will have forfeited the premium. If the market price of the ETF rises dramatically and the buyer exercises the call to buy ETF shares at a lower price, the buyer will make a profit; the seller will lose.

To protect a portfolio against loss, an investor can purchase put options for an ETF he or she holds. The put option will allow the investor to sell shares of the ETF if they drop below a specified price (strike price) before the option expires. The seller of the put option is obligated to buy the ETF shares at the agreed price even when the market price is lower. If the put option expires before it is exercised, the seller keeps the premium as profit. Bought or sold by itself, a put option is speculative because there is a chance that it will expire worthless or that the seller will be exposed to a considerable loss if the option is exercised when the underlying ETF drops sharply in value. When it is bought as a hedge to protect against loss from an investment already held in a portfolio, the put becomes a sort of insurance.

> ### TAKE NOTE: SELLING COVERED CALLS CAN RESULT IN LOSS
>
> Some investors regard the sale of covered calls as a source of steady income and may fail to respond appropriately to a severe downturn in the price of their ETFs, losing far more than they ever gained in premiums. If there is a sharp rise in price, covered calls can prevent the seller from taking advantage of windfall profits.

Trading with Options

Open interest in options refers to the number of outstanding options contracts. Puts and calls are tallied separately. Some ETF options have little open interest; the most active options are on the most actively traded ETFs. Changes in open interest are interpreted the same way for options as in futures trading. When open interest and options prices are both on the rise, it is an indication of increased investor interest and an upwards trend; when both are decreasing, there is a downwards trend; when options prices and open interest begin to diverge, it is a sign that the trend is about to reverse itself.

Price

As the price of its underlying ETF increases, a call option becomes more valuable. When the ETF's price reaches a point higher than the price agreed on in the call option (striking price), plus the premium, the call option is said to be "in the money." If the ETF's price is lower than the striking price of the call option, the call is said to be "out of the money." The reverse is true for a put option.

Options have two kinds of value: intrinsic value and time value. Intrinsic value is the difference between the actual price of an ETF and the option's striking price. An option has intrinsic value when it is "in the money." Time value represents what investors are willing to pay for the time remaining on the option. Time value can be found by subtracting intrinsic value from the amount of the premium. Time value diminishes rapidly as an option nears its expiration date. The price of an option is also influenced by the striking price of the option, which affects its intrinsic value, and by the volatility of the underlying ETF because option buyers hope to profit from a dramatic price movement.

An option's exercise price, or striking price, is set by the exchange when the option is first listed for trading, and it is an even dollar amount. Option prices are set at $1 increments above or below the price of the underlying ETF. The option's exercise price does not change. Options contracts are comprised of units of 100 shares of the underlying ETF. Option market prices are determined by bids and offers on the exchange floor, and they are quoted in dollars and cents. Prices of options trading for under $3 are raised or lowered by five-cent increments; options trading at more than $3 are raised and lowered by minimum increments of ten cents.

Trading Strategies with Options

The most straightforward use of options is speculation. Why would a speculator choose to buy and sell options rather than shares of the ETF itself?

Less Risk

Buying and selling options on an ETF in the expectation that the market is about to rise or fall incurs much less risk than buying and selling actual shares of a volatile ETF. If the price makes an unexpected move, the investor's loss will be limited to the price he or she paid for the option. The worst that can happen is that the option will expire worthless and the premium will be lost.

Leverage

The price of an option can register large percentage gains if the price of the underlying ETF makes a big jump. The price of an option is equal to its time value plus its intrinsic value. If the market price of an ETF goes up by only a few percentage points, the intrinsic value (difference between the exercise price of the option and the market price of the underlying ETF) may suddenly double or triple.

Covered Calls

Selling calls, when the investor is covered (owns the underlying ETF), is a conservative way to make a profit. The seller pockets the premium, and if the buyer later exercises the call when the price of the ETF has gone up, the seller only loses the opportunity to sell the ETF at a higher market price. If the price of an ETF drops or fails to climb above the amount of the premium, the buyer of the option is unlikely to exercise it, and the seller has mitigated his or her loss or realized extra income at a time when the market is flat.

The simultaneous purchase of an ETF and sale of a call option on it is considered a single trading strategy. The goal is to keep the ETF shares while earning a profit from the premiums. Research has shown that 80 percent of all options expire without being exercised.

Selling Options Short

Uncovered sales of ETF options, in which the seller does not own the underlying ETF shares, are risky. Most brokerages require the seller to post option margins of 100 percent of the market value of the option, plus 10 percent of the value of the underlying ETF. If the price of the ETF moves in the wrong direction, the seller is subject to margin calls. If the price of the underlying ETF is substantially higher when the buyer exercises the call option, the seller will have to shoulder the loss.

Option Spreads

ETF options can be used to establish spread positions that minimize market risk. A simple spread involves buying and selling two call or put options for the same ETF with the same expiration month but with two different strike prices. If the market price of the ETF is expected to advance, the investor will pay a higher premium to buy a call option with a lower strike price and sell a call option with a higher strike price for a lower premium. The difference between the two premiums constitutes the total market risk of the transaction. When the two options are near their expiration date, if the price of the underlying ETF has risen above the higher strike price, the investor can now realize a profit by selling the call option that was bought earlier at a much higher price and buying back the call option that was sold earlier at only slightly more than the original price.

If the price of the underlying ETF falls, both options will expire "out of the money," and the investor will lose only the difference between the two original premiums. If the call option that was originally sold goes "into the money" and the buyer exercises the call, the spread will be ended, and the investor will exercise the call he or she bought to obtain the necessary shares of the ETF.

TAKE NOTE: TRADING ETF OPTIONS IS COMPLEX

Trading with ETF options is complex, and a number of factors may offset profits. Many ETF options markets are thinly traded and may not be able to respond quickly to buy and sell orders. There can be a considerable difference between the bid price and the ask price of an ETF option. Trading fees can amount to a significant percentage of total spread gains.

CASE STUDY: HIGH LIQUIDITY OF ETFS

The following is taken from "ETF Trading Strategies" on NASDAQ.com, the official Web site of the NASDAQ Stock Market (**www.nasdaq.com/asp/et-ftradingstrategies.asp**):

Covered Call

This popular type of stock option is often considered among the safest positions to take in the world of stock options. A covered call is an attempt to take advantage of a neutral or declining share value of a given stock. The seller writes a call option on the stock while simultaneously holding an equivalent amount of the same stock. If the option expires, the writer keeps the premium. If the holder of the call "exercises" the option, then the seller must deliver the stock, but because the seller is already holding an equivalent amount of the stock, risk is limited (the seller doesn't have to provide the stock at a disadvantageous price and take a loss). ETFs, because of their high liquidity, are more popular for writing covered calls than single-company stocks, which are seen as more likely to lose liquidity in bad market conditions. The top ETFs, such as QQQ, enjoy high trading volumes, and so investors perceive them as excellent resources for hedging and other risk-mitigating strategies.

Hedge Investments

Highly liquid ETFs are widely used by investors employing hedge strategies and seeking to mitigate the risk of investments. Of all characteristics making a security desirable for hedging an investment, liquidity is perhaps the most important. The ability of a security to find buyers or sellers, regardless of conditions, helps mitigate risk in adverse market situations where a higher-risk security may become difficult to trade.

For long-term hedge strategies, adding a short-term or long-term investment position in a liquid ETF to a portfolio helps to diversify overall holdings by exposing the portfolio to the industries and economic sectors represented in the underlying index. Added diversification spreads a portfolio's investment risk across a broader range of industries and economic sectors, mitigating the potential impact of adverse price movement in any single industry or sector. Diversification itself, from this point of view, is a "hedge strategy," though it may lack the dollar-for-dollar correspondence of a classical hedge investment.

For long-term hedge strategies, adding a short-term or long-term investment position in a liquid ETF to a portfolio helps to diversify overall holdings by exposing the portfolio to the industries and economic sectors represented in the underlying index.

> ## CASE STUDY: HIGH LIQUIDITY OF ETFS
>
> Added diversification spreads a portfolio's investment risk across a broader range of industries and economic sectors, mitigating the potential impact of adverse price movement in any single industry or sector. Diversification itself, from this point of view, is a "hedge strategy," though it may lack the dollar-for-dollar correspondence of a classical hedge investment.
>
> Short selling is one short-term hedge strategy many ETFs are well adapted for. A portfolio with holdings in industries and sectors similar to those in (an ETF's) underlying index can use the ETF to offset risk in those categories in a much more direct way. Specifically, a drop in portfolio value is offset by a short position in the ETF as the ETF's price drops. If you, as an investor, anticipate market weakness in the sectors represented by an index, taking a short position on the ETF can reduce or eliminate the exposure of your portfolio to those sectors. As the market rebounds, the short position can be closed out to take full advantage of growth in those sectors. Highly liquid ETFs facilitate this type of strategy.
>
> Some ETFs have derivatives tied to them, offering more opportunities for mitigating risk with hedge investments. For example, buying put options on an ETF provides investors with protection against adverse price movements by "locking in" a current sell price in anticipation that prices will fall. Alternatively, selling futures contracts

Hedging with Options

ETF options can be used to hedge against possible declines in the market price of an ETF. For this strategy to be successful, the ETF option must be "in the money" so that the option premium follows the fluctuations of the ETF price. Put options to sell the ETF when it drops to a specific price can be purchased. As the ETF price drops below that level, the value of the put options will increase, offsetting at least some of the unrealized losses in the ETF price.

Pairs Trading and Market-Neutral Strategies

Pairs trading involves buying an ETF from one industry category and selling short an equal amount of another ETF from a different category in order to profit from a divergence in their total returns. For example, when the economy enters a decline, healthcare stocks often perform better than energy stocks. In pairs trading, an investor would purchase a healthcare ETF and sell short the same amount of an energy ETF. As the two ETFs diverge, the profit would be the difference between the returns of the two ETFs.

In a market-neutral strategy, a broad market ETF is sold short and an industry ETF is purchased at a time when it is believed that the industry sector will outperform the broad market. The investor's profit will be the difference between the returns of the broad market ETF and the industry ETF. This situation is called "market neutral" because the stock market risk has been neutralized. When an industry sector is expected to underperform the broad market, the industry ETF is sold short and an equal amount of a broad market ETF is purchased.

TAKE NOTE: TRUTHS ABOUT ACTIVE INVESTING

- An active investment strategy can succeed and bring in greater-than-average returns, or it can fail and incur significant losses.

- Active investing incurs expenses through trading fees and investment in custom-indexed ETFs with higher expense ratios.

- Active investing requires time and expertise to research the market and evaluate the massive amounts of data available to investors every day.

- Active investing takes an emotional toll on the investor, who will inevitably make some mistakes and experience substantial losses from time to time.

- Research indicates that stock market indexes have historically brought in greater returns than active investors.

Chapter 19

○ ○ ○ ○ ○

Special Uses of ETFs

ETFs can be used for special purposes, such as to fill out an asset class that is underrepresented in a portfolio, hedge against a downturn in the price of a particular stock, manage currency risks, or secure certain tax advantages.

Fleshing out a Portfolio

ETFs provide an efficient way of increasing your holdings in a particular asset class. If a review of your portfolio reveals that it is not meeting your target asset allocations, you can purchase shares of an ETF based on an index in that asset class. Lower trading costs and transparency allow you to invest in convenient increments and to analyze whether your portfolio goals are being met by your acquisitions.

Hedging Against Possible Losses

If you are employed by a company that pays you in stock options or invests pension funds in company stock, you need protection against a possible downturn in the price of that stock. Or perhaps the price of a security you are holding has risen drastically in an uncertain market. You do not want to incur capital gains tax by selling it, but you want to protect yourself against loss if the price of that security drops suddenly.

ETFs provide a convenient way of adding to your portfolio by building up other industry sectors so that your initial holdings will represent a comfortable percentage of your total assets. A build-around portfolio balances a concentration in one industry by adding ETFs from other industry sectors in the same proportions as the broad stock market. There are ten basic industry sectors in the U.S. stock market, and each one is represented by several ETFs. (See ETF table in "Appendix B: Where to Find Information.") There are also a number of leveraged and fundamentally weighted industry-sector ETFs that attempt to improve on market returns.

Some providers are also offering broad market ETFs that exclude specific industry sectors, such as the First Trust NASDAQ-100 Ex-Tech Sector (QQXT). A concentration in technology stocks could be balanced by purchasing a proportionate investment in a broad market industry ETF that excludes technology.

An employee compensated with stock options and restricted stock faces the double risk of losing savings and job security if his or her company should encounter financial difficulties. Industry risk can be hedged by shorting an ETF specific to that industry. Shares of an industry ETF can be borrowed and sold; the profit can be made by buying the ETF shares back after the price drops, and returning them to the lender will offset the losses on company stock. You can also purchase an ETF that does the shorting for you; ProShares and Rydex offer several ETFs that short specific industry sectors.

You can also protect your portfolio from declines in a specific industry by purchasing put options on ETFs in that industry. As options expire, they have to be replaced with new ones, incurring a speculative premium and commission each time.

TAKE NOTE: INHERENT COSTS

All these strategies have inherent costs that will eat into returns. Industry-sector ETFs have higher expense ratios than broad market ETFs. An investor who shorts an ETF must pay his lender interest, plus the dividends paid out by the ETF's underlying securities. Options often expire before they are exercised.

Currency Hedging

The ease with which foreign currency ETFs and ETNs can be bought and sold makes them useful in reducing financial risk for small companies trading abroad and for international travelers or Americans who live overseas. Foreign currency ETFs and ETNs pay the prevailing rate of interest for the foreign markets in which they are invested while hedging against a decline in the value of the U.S. dollar. A U.S. citizen who plans to travel abroad in the future or to purchase real estate in another country can purchase an ETF for that region, accumulate interest, and then sell the ETF and withdraw its value in U.S. dollars when they are needed.

Companies that purchase goods or materials from foreign countries can hedge against a decline in the U.S. dollar by maintaining their cash in ETFs or ETNs for that country.

Tax-Loss Harvesting

Tax-loss harvesting is a strategy that reduces capital gains taxes on a taxable portfolio by selling ETFs that have lost money and using those losses to offset the capital gains from profitable sales. If you do not have capital gains, up to $3,000 in losses can be deducted from ordinary taxable income, a boon for high-income investors. The ETFs must be sold before December 31.

The IRS "wash sale rule" will not allow you to take the tax loss if you sell an ETF and then buy it or a "substantially identical" investment back within 30 days of the sale. That means your portfolio could remain unbalanced for a month out of every year. Historically, January is a good month to purchase investments, but you would not be able to take advantage of this opportunity to replace the fund you sold in December. The wide variety of ETFs on the market offers a means of skirting the "wash sale" rule. Two ETFs that track similar indexes offer the same market exposure but are not considered "substantially identical." A stock or an ETF that has been sold at a loss to take advantage of tax breaks can be temporarily replaced with another ETF representing the same style or industry sector.

TAKE NOTE: CONSULT A PROFESSIONAL

Tax laws change every year. Consult a tax professional before attempting tax-loss harvesting.

TAKE NOTE: ARE THE TRADING FEES WORTH IT?

Tax-loss harvesting incurs trading fees. Make sure the loss on the sale of your ETF will be large enough to make the process worthwhile.

Chapter 20

o o o o o

What Does the Future Hold for ETFs?

The popularity of ETFs continues to grow rapidly as they receive increasing publicity. According to the Investment Company Institute, as of November 3, 2007, ETF assets made up more than $572 billion of the more than $1 trillion invested in stock index funds. As private investors take advantage of the trading opportunities available through the Internet, the convenience and transparency of ETFs are likely to make that amount grow rapidly. The administrators of retirement and educations savings plans are adding lower-cost ETFs to their investment offerings.

Growing interest from private investors has stimulated the creation of hundreds of new ETFs, ETF companies, and ETF derivatives. Many of the newest ETFs offer exposure to industry and geographic sectors of the international market, reflecting an increasing desire to profit from economic development taking place overseas and uncertainty about the future strength of the U.S. economy. New ETFs also track a variety of customized indexes in traditional markets, intended to increase returns by using special methodologies, such as fundamental weighting and sector rotation. New ETFs allowed investors to benefit from the rising prices of Brazilian steel and oil in 2007. Highly specialized ETFs allow certain institutional investors to hedge against losses by investing in specific industry sectors; for example, HealthShares Patient Care Services allows health insurers to invest in the companies that are profiting from payouts of health insurance claims.

New ETFs are also proliferating on overseas stock exchanges, and are regarded as a means of promoting growth by attracting more investors. Early in 2007, the first ETF tracking an Islamic-compliant index, EasyETF DJ Islamic Market Titans 100, launched on the SWX Swiss exchange.

ETFs now cover all areas of fixed-income investments, including municipal bonds and, most recently, foreign bonds. The first U.S.-based global international Treasury Inflation-Protected Securities ETF (WIP) launched in March 2008, opening exposure for investors to TIPS in 18 different countries and 15 different currencies, with 70 percent in developed and 30 percent in emerging markets. In May 2008, ProShares launched the first two inverse-bond ETFs, ProShares UltraShort Lehman 7-10 Year Treasury ETF (PST) and the ProShares UltraShort Lehman 20+ Year Treasury ETF (TBT), designed to deliver twice the inverse of the daily performance of their underlying index.

In March 2008, Barclays Global Investors launched the first truly global ETF available in the U.S., ACWI, holding 2,884 different stocks from developed and emerging markets in every investable market in the world.

PowerShares launched the first series of four actively managed ETFs, which will trade on the stock exchange like traditional ETFs, in April, 2008. Rather than passively following an index, these funds will be actively managed by fund managers in an effort to outperform the indexes on which the funds are based. The holdings of each fund will be listed daily on the PowerShares Web site. State Street Global Advisors has also filed an application with the SEC for a series of actively managed target-date ETFs investing in a diversified sampling of equity and fixed-income securities.

In February 2008, Claymore Securities, Inc., announced the liquidation of 11 of its ETFs because they had not attracted enough investment. These ETFs tracked highly specialized indexes, such as a Clear Global Vaccine Index and the KLB Sudan Free Large-Cap Core, and their closure is a sign that investors are more interested in broad exposure and in traditional market sectors.

As more individuals take on the responsibility of saving for retirement, ETFs will empower them to take control of their portfolios and invest successfully, without spending hours on research and management. ETFs will also have a positive impact on the mutual fund industry, which will have to lower costs and offer more transparency to compete.

Frequently Asked Questions

What is an exchange traded fund?

An ETF is a fund containing a basket of assets that tracks the performance of a particular index or commodity in the stock market. Just like shares of stock, shares of an ETF can be bought and sold throughout the day on the stock market. Some ETFs track broad market indexes; others follow specialized market sectors or customized indexes designed to implement investment strategies.

What is an index?

An index is a measure of stock market performance. A group of representative stocks, commodities, bonds, or other financial instruments is selected, and data about their collective earnings and price behavior is analyzed to create a benchmark against which the performance of individual investments of a similar type can be judged. Indexes are also used to compare the performances of different market sectors.

How is an ETF different from an index mutual fund?

A mutual fund is sold by a mutual fund company, which often charges a "load fee" or an "exit fee" and may require a minimum investment. The price of a mutual fund is calculated once a day, after the close of trading, at which time all transactions are settled. Mutual funds are managed by fund managers, who are paid out of the fund's earnings. When investors "cash out" of a mutual fund, the manager may incur capital gains tax by selling some of the fund's assets to pay them.

ETF shares are traded on the stock market throughout the day and can be purchased through any brokerage. ETFs are passively managed, following the index with a minimum of manipulation, so that their expenses are lower.

How does the performance of an exchange traded fund compare with the performance of its underlying index?

Exchange traded funds are designed to produce a similar price and yield performance to their underlying benchmarks. In the secondary market, a mechanism called arbitrage helps to keep an ETF trading on the exchange at a price close to the value of its underlying portfolio. There may be times when forces of supply and demand and other market factors cause shares of an exchange traded fund to trade at a premium or discount to its underlying portfolio value.

What are the benefits of owning ETFs?

ETFs offer immediate exposure to a broad market or sector with a single purchase. Their expense ratios are relatively low, and the underlying assets they hold can be viewed at any time. ETFs do not incur any capital gains tax until they are sold. ETFs are available for every market sector and investment style and can be used to build an entire portfolio or to diversify an existing portfolio.

How can I buy ETFs?

You can open an account at any brokerage, preferably a discount brokerage or an online brokerage that charges low trading fees. ETFs are also offered by some 529 and 401(k) plans.

Can I create my whole portfolio with ETFs?

Yes, there are ETFs for every asset class, including bonds, commodities, industry sectors, currencies, international markets, and real estate. You can create a core portfolio using several broad market ETFs and diversify by adding other asset classes.

Should I own ETFs instead of mutual funds?

It depends on how much you plan to invest and how often. If you are regularly investing small amounts, a low-cost mutual fund may be a better choice. For larger investments at less frequent intervals, lower-cost ETFs will bring in better long-term returns.

How safe are ETFs?

Owning an ETF is safer than owning individual stocks because it offers diversity. If one company does poorly, losses will be offset by the gains of another company. Fixed-income ETFs are subject to risks similar to those of bonds. An investor's shares, when redeemed or sold, may be worth more or less than when they were purchased. An ETF is expected to produce the same returns as the index it is tracking. There is a risk that an ETF may have difficulty tracking its index accurately because of expenses and liquidity issues. ETFs cannot protect against a stock market slump or a decline in an entire market sector.

How do I select ETFs for my portfolio?

After determining your portfolio asset allocations, select one or more ETFs from each of the asset classes. Read the ETF product descriptions and prospectuses, look at their holdings, and compare expense ratios and performance histories. When two ETFs are similar, choose the one with the lowest expenses. Make sure your ETFs do not duplicate each others' holdings.

Do ETFs pay dividends or interest?

ETFs pay the dividends or interest associated with their underlying stocks and bonds. Read the prospectus of each ETF to see how it is structured, what dividends or interest it pays, and how often distributions are made. Some ETFs offer reinvestment of dividends.

What is the settlement period for an ETF transaction?

ETF transactions are settled three days after a purchase or sale. Cash from the sale of an ETF will not be immediately available for reinvestment.

What is an ETN?

An exchange traded note is a debt instrument offered by a bank, which promises to pay you a return equal to the return on a particular market index. ETNs trade on the stock market just like ETFs.

How can I invest in foreign currency or foreign stocks with ETFs?

Through your brokerage, you can purchase an ETF in U.S. dollars, which holds investments in a foreign stock market, foreign debt instruments, or foreign currencies. There are global and regional international ETFs as well as ETFs for specific countries and international industry sectors. You can also purchase an ETN that promises the exact return you would receive if you invested in a specific foreign index fund.

Can I invest in ETFs with my 401(k), IRA, or 529 plan?

You can open an IRA or a Roth IRA with a brokerage and invest in ETFs. Some 529s and a few 401(k)s now offer ETFs as part of their investment menus. After leaving a company's employment, you can roll your 401(k) over into an IRA.

How do ETFs affect my taxes?

The structure of an ETF eliminates almost all capital gains within the fund. You are purchasing ETF shares from a third party and will only pay capital gains taxes when you sell your ETF shares for a profit. Dividends are taxed at a preferred rate, based on how long the fund has held the stocks. (Older ETFs are more likely to have held securities long enough to qualify for preferred rates.) Interest from bond ETFs is taxed at your ordinary income tax level. Profits from the sale of gold and silver ETFs are taxed at a higher collectible rate of 28 percent. Vanguard ETFs, which are structured as share classes of mutual funds, may incur capital gains tax liabilities. ETFs can be used for tax-loss harvesting strategies.

What happens when an ETF closes?

If an ETF sponsor closes an ETF, you will receive a payout equal to the NAV of the shares that you hold three days after the closing date.

How can I get the highest returns from my ETF investments?

Always try to minimize expenses by choosing low-cost ETFs and trading only when necessary to avoid fees. Buy and hold. Fully diversify your portfolio, and rebalance it regularly so that one asset class does not become dominant. Take advantage of foreign ETFs. Establish a core long-term portfolio, and then invest a small percentage of your savings in higher-risk ETFs with potential for higher returns. Keep an eye on global and domestic economic trends, and review your portfolio for areas in which you might be over- or underinvested.

Top Ten Mistakes Made by Beginners

1. Selling all their mutual funds and buying ETFs

ETFs are wonderful investment tools for the private investor, providing a low-cost means of achieving a broad portfolio. However, low-cost mutual index funds are also good investments. Take a close look at the consequences of selling your existing investments, and compare them to the returns on the ETFs you will be purchasing. The expense ratio of the mutual fund may actually be lower, or the exit fees for selling the mutual fund, plus the trading fees for purchasing shares of an ETF, may cancel out any returns on the ETF for several years. Mutual funds are also appropriate for an investor who wants to invest small amounts at regular intervals.

2. Basing asset allocation on an article in the latest issue of *Kiplinger's* or *Smart Money* magazine

It may be tempting to buy an ETF because you have just read an exciting article about a new market trend or trading strategy or because your son-in-law, a pharmaceutical salesman, is predicting an upsurge in the healthcare sector. However, research demonstrates that time-tested asset allocations bring the greatest returns. Chances are that everyone else has read the article and that prices in that market have already exceeded its actual value, even before the article was written.

3. Trading too frequently

The easy availability of information and the reality that ETF shares trade on the stock exchange all day long may tempt some investors to buy and sell frequently. Brokerage fees will quickly eat up returns. Investing small amounts monthly also incurs trading fees out of proportion to your returns; it is more practical to keep your savings in a savings account or other short-term investment until you can invest a larger amount in a single trade. Frequent trading also reduces your exposure to positive price changes and upward trends.

4. Failing to consider trading fees and expenses

In evaluating whether an ETF is a good investment, factor in brokerage fees, taxes on any dividends paid out by the ETF during the year, and other expenses to the expected rate of return. A slightly higher rate of return might be completely offset by higher expenses, and an ETF with a lower rate of return might leave you with more cash in hand.

5. Trying to beat the market

Research shows that active traders, even experienced active traders, achieve significantly lower returns through market timing than the market as a whole. Their successes are often counteracted by their mistakes and losses, and active trading incurs trading fees and other expenses. Buying and holding an ETF that tracks a broad market index will bring greater returns than attempting to profit from market upswings.

6. Putting too many eggs in one basket

Diversity is a key factor in reducing risk and increasing returns, and one of the attractive features of ETFs is their ownership of a wide variety of securities. However, a number of ETFs follow the same indexes or otherwise resemble each other closely. Inexperienced investors may not realize that though they are buying shares of two or three different ETFs, those ETFs might contain many of the same stocks. Before purchasing shares of an ETF, look at its "top ten" holdings to see how they compare to the "top ten" of the ETFs you already own. If one of your ETFs does extremely well and begins to dominate your portfolio, it is time to rebalance and restore your original asset allocation.

7. Not doing enough research

Not only do some ETFs resemble each other closely, but the indexes that they track may be weighted in such a way that they represent the same asset class even though they appear to be different. For example, ETFs devoted to industry sectors are heavily weighted towards large-cap stocks. You may think you have a diversified portfolio when, on closer inspection, your ETFs hold similar investments. Some of the newer custom-index ETFs are benchmarked to narrow market sectors and may contain only a few stocks. Take some time to understand the ETFs you already hold as well as those you are thinking of adding to your portfolio.

8. Ignoring international and emerging market ETFs

Historically, American investors have not given enough importance to foreign investments. Adding foreign ETFs to your portfolio improves diversity by increasing the number of securities in which you are investing and exposes you to more companies and industry sectors that may potentially expand and grow. Returns in foreign currencies gain value when the U.S. dollar weakens, helping to compensate for declines in the returns from domestic securities. Foreign markets exhibit lower correlation to fluctuations in American securities, providing a natural hedge against losses. The structure of the global economy is changing rapidly, and in recent history, returns for foreign stocks have been greater than returns for U.S. stocks.

9. Not protecting against risk

An important aspect of a successful investment strategy is protection against risk. The best way to accomplish this is to create and maintain a diverse portfolio, containing stocks, bonds, and ETFs of different styles. Do some research on the ETFs you plan to add to your portfolio to make sure that they do not overlap and that your portfolio is not too heavily weighted towards one particular style or sector. If one area of your portfolio takes off and begins to dominate, rebalance it to restore your original asset allocations. Use stop orders during active trading to limit your losses in case of an unexpected downturn.

10. Buying high, selling low

By the time you hear the news of an economic recession and realize that it would be good to own some gold at a time like this or see that a particular market sector is flying high, it is already too late. Everyone else is feeling the same way, and the stock market is driven by consumer demand. Prices will already have risen, and the shares will be selling at a premium, with a strong possibility that the prices are about to drop. You will lose twice if you sell your poorly performing ETFs at a loss to purchase other ETFs representing an overpriced market sector. It is better to hold on to what you have and stick to your original plan. Look for investments that are underpriced. Be wary of new ETFs because they may represent a "hot" sector, and their underlying securities may already be overpriced.

Sample Portfolios

Here are some examples of all-ETF portfolios that follow the asset allocations suggested in the sections on portfolio building. With diversity as the primary goal, your own portfolio should be adjusted to reflect your personal circumstances, taking into account investments you hold in other portfolios, assets such as real estate, or business interests in a foreign country. Does your employer offer stock options or a company pension plan? Do you have special knowledge of a particular industry sector? Do you expect an inheritance that is heavily invested in bonds? Are you in a position to take on additional risk to increase potential earnings?

To get the most out of an ETF portfolio, keep costs down by trading infrequently; buy ETFs and hold them. For a portfolio of less than $30,000, trading costs may offset the first two or three years' returns.

New ETF offerings come on the market almost every month; by the time you read this, there may be additional ETFs that will fill in an asset class or industry sector more effectively than the examples presented here. Always compare the expenses and historical performances of similar funds before selecting one for your portfolio.

The ETFs in these sample portfolios have been selected because their expense ratios are lower than other similar ETFs. Sometimes an ETF with a higher expense ratio may produce higher returns, which more than compensate for the additional cost.

SIMPLE BUY-AND-HOLD ETF PORTFOLIO						
	ETF	Income-Oriented	Conse-rvative	Mode-rate	Moder-ate Growth	Aggr-essive
Fixed-Income	Vanguard Total Bond Market (BND) (0.11 %)	80 %	60 %	50 %	40 %	20 %
U.S. Equity	iShares Dow Jones Total U.S. Stock Market Index (IYY) (0.20 %) or Vanguard Total Stock Market Index (VTI) (0.07 %) or State Street SPDR (SPY) (0.10 %)	15 %	30 %	35 %	32 %	40 %
Intl Equity	iShares MSCI-EAFE Index (EFA) (0.35 %)	5 %	10 %	15 %	28 %	40 %

SIMPLE PORTFOLIO DIVERSIFIED						
	ETF	Income-Oriented	Conse-rvative	Mode-rate	Mode-rate Growth	Aggr-essive
Fixed-Income	Vanguard Total Bond Market (BND) (0.11 %)	48 %	30 %	25 %	20 %	10 %
	iShares Lehman TIPS Bond Fund (TIP) (0.20 %)	16 %	15 %	12.5 %	10 %	5 %
	iShares iBoxx $ Investment Grade Corporate Bond (LQD) (0.15 %)	16 %	15 %	12.5 %	10 %	5 %
U.S. Equity	Vanguard Total Stock Market (VTI) (0.07 percent)	9 %	18 %	22.5 %	27 %	36 %
	iShares S&P SmallCap 600 Value (IJS) (0.25 %)	3 %	6 %	7.5 %	9 %	12 %
Real Estate	Vanguard REIT ETF (VNQ) (0.12 %)	2 %	4 %	5 %	6 %	8 %

SIMPLE PORTFOLIO DIVERSIFIED						
	ETF	**Income-Oriented**	**Conse-rvative**	**Mode-rate**	**Mode-rate Growth**	**Aggr-essive**
Intl Equity	Vanguard MSCI European ETF (VGK) (0.12 %)	2.4 %	4.8 %	6 %	7.2 %	9.6 %
	Vanguard MSCI Pacific ETF (VPL) (0.12 %)	2.4 %	4.8 %	6 %	7.2 %	9.6 %
	Vanguard Emerging Markets ETF (VWO) (0.25 %)	1.2 %	2.4 %	3 %	3.6 %	4.8 %

PORTFOLIO DIVERSIFIED BY STYLE						
	ETF	**Income-Oriented**	**Conser-vative**	**Mode-rate**	**Mode-rate Growth**	**Aggre-ssive**
Fixed-Income	Vanguard Total Bond Market (BND) (0.11 %)	48 %	30 %	25 %	20 %	10 %
	SPDR Lehman International Treasury Bond (BWX) (0.50 %)	16 %	15 %	13 %	10 %	6 %
	iShares Lehman TIPS Bond Fund (TIP) (0.20 %)	8 %	9 %	6 %	5 %	2 %
	SPDR Lehman Municipal Bond ETF (TFI) (0.20 %)	8 %	6 %	6 %	5 %	2 %
U.S. Equity	iShares Morningstar Large Value (JKF) (0.25 %)	4 %	8 %	11 %	13 %	18 %
	iShares Morningstar Large Growth (JKE) (0.25 %)	4 %	7 %	9 %	10 %	14 %

PORTFOLIO DIVERSIFIED BY STYLE					
	ETF	Income-Oriented	Conser-vative	Mode-rate	Mode-rate Growth	Aggre-ssive
	iShares Small Value (IWN) (0.25 %)	2 %	4 %	4 %	5 %	6 %
	Vanguard Small Cap Growth ETF (VBK) (0.11 %)	1 %	3 %	3 %	4 %	5 %
Comm-odities	Dow Jones AIG Total Commodity Index (DJP) (0.75 %)	1 %	2 %	3 %	4 %	5 %
Real Estate	Vanguard REIT ETF (VNQ) (0.12 %)	4 %	8 %	11 %	13 %	18 %
Intl Equity	Vanguard FTSE All-World excl U.S. (VEU) (0.58 %)	2 %	5 %	6 %	7 %	10 %
	WisdomTree International Small Cap Dividend (DLS) (0.25 %)	2 %	5 %	6 %	7 %	10 %
	Vanguard Emerging Markets ETF (VWO) (0.25 %)	1 %	2 %	3 %	4 %	5 %

Appendix A

o o o o o

Exchange Traded Funds

This is a listing of almost all the ETFs on the United States market as of March 2008. Detailed information about each fund, including its price, prospectus, holdings, and performance in relation to the index it is tracking is available on the Internet and in print from the fund providers (Fund Family), the stock exchanges, and many brokerages. Before purchasing a fund, an investor should study the prospectus and be thoroughly familiar with the ETF and its index. For addresses and Web sites of ETF providers, please refer to Appendix B.

BROAD MARKET INDEXES						
Ticker	Symbol	Expense Ratio	Options	Excha-nge	Inception Date	Fund Family
Fidelity NASDAQ Composite Index Trac	ONEQ	0.42	Yes	NAS	9/25/2003	Fidelity Invest-ments
First Trust Multi Cap Growth AlphaDEX Fund	FAD	0.70		AMEX	5/8/2007	First Trust
First Trust Multi Cap Value AlphaDEX Fund	FAB	0.70		AMEX	5/8/2007	First Trust
First Trust NASDAQ-100 Equal Weight	QQEW	0.60	Yes	NAS	4/19/2006	First Trust
First Trust NASDAQ-100 Ex-Tech Sector	QQXT	0.60		NAS	2/8/2007	First Trust

BROAD MARKET INDEXES

Ticker	Symbol	Expense Ratio	Options	Exchange	Inception Date	Fund Family
iShares Dow Jones U.S. Total Market Index	IYY	0.20	Yes	NYSE	6/12/2000	Barclays
iShares NYSE Composite Index	NYC	0.25	Yes	NYSE	3/30/2004	Barclays
iShares Russell 3000	IWV	0.20	Yes	NYSE	5/22/2000	Barclays
iShares Russell 3000 Growth	IWZ	0.25	Yes	NYSE	7/24/2000	Barclays
iShares Russell 3000 Value	IWW	0.25	Yes	NYSE	7/24/2000	Barclays
iShares S&P 1500	ISI	0.20		NYSE	1/20/2004	Barclays
PowerShares Dividend Achievers	PFM	0.60	Yes	AMEX	9/15/2005	PowerShares
PowerShares Dynamic MagniQuant Portfolio	PIQ	0.67	Yes	AMEX	10/12/2006	PowerShares
PowerShares Dynamic Market Portfolio	PWC	0.60	Yes	AMEX	5/1/2003	PowerShares
PowerShares Dynamic OTC Portfolio	PWO	0.60	Yes	AMEX	5/1/2003	PowerShares
PowerShares FTSE RAFI U.S. 1000	PRF	0.76	Yes	NYSE	12/19/2005	PowerShares
PowerShares High Growth Rate Dividend Achievers	PHJ	0.70	Yes	AMEX	9/15/2005	PowerShares
PowerShares High Yield Equity Dividend Achievers	PEY	0.50	Yes	AMEX	12/9/2004	PowerShares
PowerShares QQQ Trust	QQQQ	0.20	Yes	NAS	3/10/1999	NASDAQ-Amex Invst Prod
Rydex S&P Equal Weight	RSP	0.40		AMEX	4/24/2003	Rydex
SPA MarketGrader 100	SIH	0.85		AMEX	10/17/2007	Spa
SPA MarketGrader 200	SNB	0.85		AMEX	10/17/2007	Spa

BROAD MARKET INDEXES

Ticker	Symbol	Expense Ratio	Options	Excha-nge	Inception Date	Fund Family
SPA MarketGrader 40	SFV	0.85		AMEX	10/17/2007	Spa
SPDR DJ Wilshire Total Market ETF	TMW	0.20	Yes	AMEX	10/4/2000	State Street Global Advisors
SPDRS	SPY	0.08		AMEX	1/29/1993	State Street Global Advisors
Vanguard Extended Market ETF	VXF	0.08	Yes	AMEX	12/27/2001	Vanguard
Vanguard Total Stock Market ETF	VTI	0.07	Yes	AMEX	5/24/2001	Vanguard
WisdomTree High-Yield Equity Fund	DHS	0.38	Yes	NYSE	6/16/2006	WisdomTree
WisdomTree Low P/E Fund	EZY	0.38		AMEX	2/23/2007	WisdomTree
WisdomTree Total Dividend Fund	DTD	0.28	Yes	NYSE	6/16/2006	WisdomTree
WisdomTree Total Earnings Fund	EXT	0.28		AMEX	2/23/2007	WisdomTree

LARGE-CAP ETFS

Ticker	Symbol	Expense Ratio	Options	Exchange	Inception Date	Fund Family
Claymore/Great Companies Large-Cap Growth Idx	XGC	1.77	Yes	AMEX	4/2/2007	Claymore Securities
Dow Diamonds	DIA	0.18	Yes	AMEX	1/13/1998	State Street Global Advisors
ELEMENTS DJ High Yield Select 10 Total Return Index	DOD	0.75		NYSE	11/7/2007	Elements
First Trust DB Strategic Value Idx	FDV	0.65	Yes	AMEX	7/6/2006	First Trust

LARGE-CAP ETFS						
Ticker	Symbol	Expense Ratio	Options	Exchange	Inception Date	Fund Family
First Trust Large Cap Core AlphaDEX Fund	FEX	0.70		AMEX	5/8/2007	First Trust
First Trust Large Cap Growth Opportunities AlphaDEX Fund	FTC	0.70		AMEX	5/8/2007	First Trust
First Trust Large Cap Value Opportunities AlphaDEX Fund	FTA	0.70		AMEX	5/8/2007	First Trust
First Trust Morningstar Dividend Leaders Idx	FDL	0.45	Yes	AMEX	3/9/2006	First Trust
First Trust Value Line 100	FVL	0.70	Yes	AMEX	6/12/2003	First Trust
First Trust Value Line Dividend Idx	FVD	0.93	Yes	AMEX	8/19/2003	First Trust
First Trust Value Line Equity Allocation Idx	FVI	0.70		AMEX	12/5/2006	First Trust
iShares Dow Jones Select Dividend Idx	DVY	0.40	Yes	NYSE	11/3/2003	Barclays
iShares KLD 400 Social Idx	DSI	0.50		AMEX	11/14/2006	Barclays
iShares KLD Select Social Idx	KLD	0.50		NYSE	1/24/2005	Barclays
iShares Morningstar Large Core	JKD	0.20		NYSE	6/28/2004	Barclays
iShares Morningstar Large Growth	JKE	0.25		NYSE	6/28/2004	Barclays
iShares Morningstar Large Value	JKF	0.25		NYSE	6/28/2004	Barclays
iShares NYSE 100 Index	NY	0.20	Yes	NYSE	3/29/2004	Barclays

LARGE-CAP ETFS						
Ticker	Symbol	Expense Ratio	Options	Exchange	Inception Date	Fund Family
iShares Russell 1000	IWB	0.15	Yes	NYSE	5/15/2000	Barclays
iShares Russell 1000 Growth	IWF	0.20	Yes	NYSE	5/22/2000	Barclays
iShares Russell 1000 Value	IWD	0.20	Yes	NYSE	5/22/2000	Barclays
iShares S&P 100	OEF	0.20	Yes	AMEX	10/23/2000	Barclays
iShares S&P 500	IVV	0.09	Yes	NYSE	5/15/2000	Barclays
iShares S&P 500 Growth	IVW	0.18		NYSE	5/22/2000	Barclays
iShares S&P 500 Value	IVE	0.18	Yes	NYSE	5/22/2000	Barclays
PowerShares Dynamic Aggressive Growth	PGZ	0.75	Yes	AMEX	12/20/2006	PowerShares
PowerShares Dynamic Deep Value	PVM	0.74	Yes	AMEX	12/20/2006	PowerShares
PowerShares Dynamic Large Cap Growth	PWB	0.63	Yes	AMEX	3/3/2005	PowerShares
PowerShares Dynamic Large Cap Portfolio	PJF	0.74	Yes	AMEX	12/1/2006	PowerShares
PowerShares Dynamic Large Cap Value	PWV	0.63	Yes	AMEX	3/3/2005	PowerShares
PowerShares NASDAQ Next-Q Portfolio	PNXQ	0.70		NASDAQ	4/3/2008	PowerShares
RevenueShares Large Cap Fund	RWL	0.49	n/a	NYSE	2/22/2008	Revenue-Shares IS
Rydex Russell Top 50 Idx	XLG	0.20	Yes	AMEX	5/4/2005	Rydex
Rydex S&P 500 Equal Weight	RSP	0.40	Yes	AMEX	4/24/2003	Rydex
Rydex S&P 500 Pure Growth	RPG	0.35	Yes	AMEX	3/1/2006	Rydex

LARGE-CAP ETFS						
Ticker	Symbol	Expense Ratio	Options	Exchange	Inception Date	Fund Family
Rydex S&P 500 Pure Value	RPV	0.35	Yes	AMEX	3/1/2006	Rydex
SPA MarketGrader Large Cap	SZG	0.85		AMEX	10/17/2007	Spa
SPDR DJ Wilshire Large Cap ETF	ELR	0.20	Yes	AMEX	11/8/2005	State Street Global Advisors
SPDR DJ Wilshire Large Cap Growth ETF	ELG	0.20		AMEX	9/25/2000	State Street Global Advisors
SPDR DJ Wilshire Large Cap Value ETF	ELV	0.20		AMEX	9/25/2000	State Street Global Advisors
SPDR S&P 500 ETF	SPY	0.10	Yes	AMEX	1/29/1993	State Street Global Advisors
SPDR S&P Dividend ETF	SDY	0.35	Yes	AMEX	11/8/2005	State Street Global Advisors
Vanguard Dividend Appreciation ETF	VIG	0.28	Yes	AMEX	4/21/2006	Vanguard

LARGE-CAP ETFS						
Ticker	Symbol	Expense Ratio	Options	Exchange	Inception Date	Fund Family
Claymore/Great Companies Large-Cap Growth Idx	XGC	1.77	Yes	AMEX	4/2/2007	Claymore Securities
Dow Diamonds	DIA	0.18	Yes	AMEX	1/13/1998	State Street Global Advisors
ELEMENTS DJ High Yield Select 10 Total Return Index	DOD	0.75		NYSE	11/7/2007	Elements
First Trust DB Strategic Value Idx	FDV	0.65	Yes	AMEX	7/6/2006	First Trust

LARGE-CAP ETFS						
Ticker	Symbol	Expense Ratio	Options	Exchange	Inception Date	Fund Family
First Trust Large Cap Core AlphaDEX Fund	FEX	0.70		AMEX	5/8/2007	First Trust
First Trust Large Cap Growth Opportunities AlphaDEX Fund	FTC	0.70		AMEX	5/8/2007	First Trust
First Trust Large Cap Value Opportunities AlphaDEX Fund	FTA	0.70		AMEX	5/8/2007	First Trust
First Trust Morningstar Dividend Leaders Idx	FDL	0.45	Yes	AMEX	3/9/2006	First Trust
First Trust Value Line 100	FVL	0.70	Yes	AMEX	6/12/2003	First Trust
First Trust Value Line Dividend Idx	FVD	0.93	Yes	AMEX	8/19/2003	First Trust
First Trust Value Line Equity Allocation Idx	FVI	0.70		AMEX	12/5/2006	First Trust
iShares Dow Jones Select Dividend Idx	DVY	0.40	Yes	NYSE	11/3/2003	Barclays
iShares KLD 400 Social Idx	DSI	0.50		AMEX	11/14/2006	Barclays
iShares KLD Select Social Idx	KLD	0.50		NYSE	1/24/2005	Barclays
iShares Morningstar Large Core	JKD	0.20		NYSE	6/28/2004	Barclays
iShares Morningstar Large Growth	JKE	0.25		NYSE	6/28/2004	Barclays
iShares Morningstar Large Value	JKF	0.25		NYSE	6/28/2004	Barclays
iShares NYSE 100 Index	NY	0.20	Yes	NYSE	3/29/2004	Barclays
iShares Russell 1000	IWB	0.15	Yes	NYSE	5/15/2000	Barclays

LARGE-CAP ETFS						
Ticker	Symbol	Expense Ratio	Options	Exchange	Inception Date	Fund Family
iShares Russell 1000 Growth	IWF	0.20	Yes	NYSE	5/22/2000	Barclays
iShares Russell 1000 Value	IWD	0.20	Yes	NYSE	5/22/2000	Barclays
iShares S&P 100	OEF	0.20	Yes	AMEX	10/23/2000	Barclays
iShares S&P 500	IVV	0.09	Yes	NYSE	5/15/2000	Barclays
iShares S&P 500 Growth	IVW	0.18		NYSE	5/22/2000	Barclays
iShares S&P 500 Value	IVE	0.18	Yes	NYSE	5/22/2000	Barclays
PowerShares Dynamic Aggressive Growth	PGZ	0.75	Yes	AMEX	12/20/2006	PowerShares
PowerShares Dynamic Deep Value	PVM	0.74	Yes	AMEX	12/20/2006	PowerShares
PowerShares Dynamic Large Cap Growth	PWB	0.63	Yes	AMEX	3/3/2005	PowerShares
PowerShares Dynamic Large Cap Portfolio	PJF	0.74	Yes	AMEX	12/1/2006	PowerShares
PowerShares Dynamic Large Cap Value	PWV	0.63	Yes	AMEX	3/3/2005	PowerShares
PowerShares NASDAQ Next-Q Portfolio	PNXQ	0.70		NASDAQ	4/3/2008	PowerShares
RevenueShares Large Cap Fund	RWL	0.49	n/a	NYSE	2/22/2008	Revenue-Shares IS
Rydex Russell Top 50 Idx	XLG	0.20	Yes	AMEX	5/4/2005	Rydex
Rydex S&P 500 Equal Weight	RSP	0.40	Yes	AMEX	4/24/2003	Rydex
Rydex S&P 500 Pure Growth	RPG	0.35	Yes	AMEX	3/1/2006	Rydex
Rydex S&P 500 Pure Value	RPV	0.35	Yes	AMEX	3/1/2006	Rydex

LARGE-CAP ETFS

Ticker	Symbol	Expense Ratio	Options	Exchange	Inception Date	Fund Family
SPA MarketGrader Large Cap	SZG	0.85		AMEX	10/17/2007	Spa
SPDR DJ Wilshire Large Cap ETF	ELR	0.20	Yes	AMEX	11/8/2005	State Street Global Advisors
SPDR DJ Wilshire Large Cap Growth ETF	ELG	0.20		AMEX	9/25/2000	State Street Global Advisors
SPDR DJ Wilshire Large Cap Value ETF	ELV	0.20		AMEX	9/25/2000	State Street Global Advisors
SPDR S&P 500 ETF	SPY	0.10	Yes	AMEX	1/29/1993	State Street Global Advisors
SPDR S&P Dividend ETF	SDY	0.35	Yes	AMEX	11/8/2005	State Street Global Advisors
Vanguard Dividend Appreciation ETF	VIG	0.28	Yes	AMEX	4/21/2006	Vanguard

LARGE-CAP ETFS

Ticker	Symbol	Expense Ratio	Options	Exchange	Inception Date	Fund Family
Vanguard Growth ETF	VUG	0.11	Yes	AMEX	1/26/2004	Vanguard
Vanguard High Dividend Yield ETF	VYM	0.25		AMEX	11/10/2006	Vanguard
Vanguard Large Cap ETF	VV	0.07	Yes	AMEX	1/27/2004	Vanguard
Vanguard Mega Cap 300 ETF	MGC	0.13		NYSE	12/17/2007	Vanguard
Vanguard Mega Cap 300 Growth ETF	MGK	0.13		NYSE	12/17/2007	Vanguard

LARGE-CAP ETFS

Ticker	Symbol	Expense Ratio	Options	Exchange	Inception Date	Fund Family
Vanguard Mega Cap 300 Value ETF	MGV	0.13		NYSE	12/17/2007	Vanguard
Vanguard Value ETF	VTV	0.11	Yes	AMEX	1/26/2004	Vanguard
WisdomTree Dividend Top 100 Fund	DTN	0.38	Yes	NYSE	6/16/2006	WisdomTree
WisdomTree Earnings 500 Fund	EPS	0.28		AMEX	2/23/2007	WisdomTree
WisdomTree Earnings Top 100 Fund	EEZ	0.38		AMEX	2/23/2007	WisdomTree
WisdomTree Large Cap Dividend Fund	DLN	0.28	Yes	NYSE	6/16/2006	WisdomTree

MID-CAP ETFS

Ticker	Symbol	Expense Ratio	Options	Exchange	Inception Date	Fund Family
Claymore/Zacks Mid Cap Core	CZA	1.81	Yes	AMEX	4/2/2007	Claymore Securities
First Trust Mid Cap Core AlphaDEX Fund	FNX	0.70		AMEX	5/8/2007	First Trust
iShares Morningstar Mid Core	JKG	0.25		NYSE	6/28/2004	Barclays
iShares Morningstar Mid Growth	JKH	0.30		NYSE	6/28/2004	Barclays
iShares Morningstar Mid Value	JKI	0.30		NYSE	6/28/2004	Barclays
iShares Russell Midcap	IWR	0.20	Yes	NYSE	7/17/2001	Barclays

MID-CAP ETFS						
Ticker	Symbol	Expense Ratio	Options	Exchange	Inception Date	Fund Family
iShares Russell Midcap Growth	IWP	0.25	Yes	NYSE	7/17/2001	Barclays
iShares Russell Midcap Value	IWS	0.25	Yes	NYSE	7/17/2001	Barclays
iShares S&P 400 Growth	IJK	0.25	Yes	AMEX	7/24/2000	Barclays
iShares S&P 400 Value	IJJ	0.20	Yes	AMEX	7/24/2000	Barclays
iShares S&P Mid-Cap 400 Growth Index	IJK	0.25		NYSE	7/24/2000	Barclays
iShares S&P Mid-Cap 400 Index	IJH	0.20	Yes	NYSE	5/22/2000	Barclays
iShares S&P Mid-Cap 400 Value Index	IJJ	0.25		NYSE	7/24/2000	Barclays
MidCap SPDRs	MDY	0.25		AMEX	5/4/1995	PDR SERVICES LLC
PowerShares Dynamic Mid-Cap Growth	PWJ	0.63	Yes	AMEX	3/3/2005	Power-Shares
PowerShares Dynamic Mid-Cap Portfolio	PJG	0.74		AMEX	12/1/2006	Power-Shares
PowerShares Dynamic Mid-Cap Value	PWP	0.63	Yes	AMEX	3/3/2005	Power-Shares
RevenueShares Mid-Cap Fund	RWJ	0.54	n/a	NYSE	2/22/2008	Revenue-Shares Investor Svc
Rydex S&P 400 Mid-Cap Pure Growth	RFG	0.35	Yes	AMEX	3/1/2006	Rydex
Rydex S&P 400 Mid-Cap Pure Value	RFV	0.35	Yes	AMEX	3/1/2006	Rydex
SPA MarketGrader Mid-Cap	SVD	0.85		AMEX	10/17/2007	Spa

MID-CAP ETFS

Ticker	Symbol	Expense Ratio	Options	Exchange	Inception Date	Fund Family
SPDR DJ Wilshire Mid-Cap ETF	EMM	0.25	Yes	AMEX	11/8/2005	State Street Global Advisors
SPDR DJ Wilshire Mid-Cap Growth ETF	EMG	0.25	Yes	AMEX	11/8/2005	State Street Global Advisors
SPDR DJ Wilshire Mid-Cap Value ETF	EMV	0.25	Yes	AMEX	11/8/2005	State Street Global Advisors
SPDR S&P 400	MDY	0.25	Yes	AMEX	5/4/1995	State Street Global Advisors
Vanguard Mid-Cap ETF	VO	0.13	Yes	AMEX	1/26/2004	Vanguard
Vanguard Mid-Cap Growth ETF	VOT	0.13	Yes	AMEX	8/17/2006	Vanguard
Vanguard Mid-Cap Value ETF	VOE	0.13	Yes	AMEX	8/17/2006	Vanguard
WisdomTree Mid-Cap Dividend Fund	DON	0.38	Yes	NYSE	6/16/2006	Wisdom-Tree
WisdomTree Mid-Cap Earnings Fund	EZM	0.38		AMEX	2/23/2007	Wisdom-Tree

SMALL-CAP ETFS

Ticker	Symbol	Expense Ratio	Options	Exchange	Inception Date	Fund Family
Claymore/ Sabrient Stealth	STH	0.84	Yes	AMEX	9/21/2006	Claymore Securities
First Trust Dow Jones Select Microcap	FDM	0.60	Yes	AMEX	9/27/2005	First Trust

SMALL-CAP ETFS						
Ticker	Symbol	Expense Ratio	Options	Exchange	Inception Date	Fund Family
First Trust Small Cap Core AlphaDEX Fund	FYX	0.70		AMEX	5/8/2007	First Trust
iShares Morningstar Small Core	JKJ	0.25		NYSE	6/28/2004	Barclays
iShares Morningstar Small Growth	JKK	0.30		NYSE	6/28/2004	Barclays
iShares Morningstar Small Value	JKL	0.30		NYSE	6/28/2004	Barclays
iShares Russell 2000	IWM	0.20	Yes	NYSE	5/22/2000	Barclays
iShares Russell 2000 Growth	IWO	0.25	Yes	NYSE	7/24/2000	Barclays
iShares Russell 2000 Value	IWN	0.25	Yes	NYSE	7/24/2000	Barclays
iShares Russell Microcap	IWC	0.60	Yes	NYSE	8/12/2005	Barclays
iShares S&P 600 Growth	IJT	0.25	Yes	AMEX	7/24/2000	Barclays
iShares S&P SmallCap 600 Growth	IJT	0.25		NYSE	7/24/2000	Barclays
iShares S&P SmallCap 600 Index	IJR	0.20	Yes	NYSE	5/22/2000	Barclays
iShares S&P SmallCap 600 Value Index	IJS	0.25	Yes	NYSE	7/24/2000	Barclays
PowerShares Dynamic Small Cap Growth	PWT	0.63	Yes	AMEX	3/3/2005	PowerShares
PowerShares Dynamic Small Cap Portfolio	PJM	0.74		AMEX	12/1/2006	PowerShares
PowerShares Dynamic Small Cap Value	PWY	0.63	Yes	AMEX	3/3/2005	PowerShares

SMALL-CAP ETFS						
Ticker	Symbol	Expense Ratio	Options	Exchange	Inception Date	Fund Family
PowerShares FTSE NASDAQ Small Cap Portfolio	PQSC	0.70		NASDAQ	4/3/2008	PowerShares
PowerShares FTSE RAFI US 1500 Small-Mid Portfolio	PRFZ	0.78		NAS	9/20/2006	PowerShares
PowerShares Zacks Microcap	PZI	0.71	Yes	AMEX	8/18/2005	PowerShares
PowerShares Zacks Small Cap Portfolio	PZJ	0.71	Yes	AMEX	2/16/2006	PowerShares
RevenueShares Small Cap Fund	RWK	0.54	n/a	NYSE	2/22/2008	RevenueShares Investor Services
Rydex S&P 600 Small Cap Pure Growth	RZG	0.35	Yes	AMEX	3/1/2006	Rydex
Rydex S&P 600 Small Cap Pure Value	RZV	0.35	Yes	AMEX	3/1/2006	Rydex
SPA MarketGrader Small Cap	SSK	0.85		AMEX	10/17/2007	Spa
SPDR DJ Wilshire Small Cap ETF	DSC	0.25	Yes	AMEX	11/8/2005	State Street Global Advisors
SPDR DJ Wilshire Small Cap Growth ETF	DSG	0.25		AMEX	9/25/2000	State Street Global Advisors
SPDR DJ Wilshire Small Cap Value ETF	DSV	0.25		AMEX	9/25/2000	State Street Global Advisors
SPDR S&P International Small Cap	GWX	0.59		AMEX	4/20/2007	State Street Global Advisors
Vanguard Small Cap ETF	VB	0.10	Yes	AMEX	1/26/2004	Vanguard

SMALL-CAP ETFS

Ticker	Symbol	Expense Ratio	Options	Exchange	Inception Date	Fund Family
Vanguard Small Cap Growth ETF	VBK	0.12	Yes	AMEX	1/26/2004	Vanguard
Vanguard Small Cap Value ETF	VBR	0.12	Yes	AMEX	1/26/2004	Vanguard
WisdomTree SmallCap Dividend Fund	DES	0.38	Yes	NYSE	6/16/2006	WisdomTree
WisdomTree SmallCap Earnings Fund	EES	0.38		AMEX	2/23/2007	WisdomTree

INDUSTRY- AND MARKET-SECTOR ETFS

Ticker	Symbol	Expense Ratio	Options	Exchange	Inception Date	Fund Family
First Trust S&P REIT	FRI			AMEX	5/8/2007	First Trust
FocusShares ISE Homebuilders Index	SAW			NYSE	11/30/2007	FocusShares
FocusShares ISE SINdex	PUF			NYSE	11/30/2007	FocusShares
FocusShares ISE-CCM Homeland Security	MYP			NYSE	11/30/2007	FocusShares
FocusShares ISE-Revere Wal-Mart Supp	WSI			NYSE	11/30/2007	FocusShares
HealthShares Orthopedic Repair	HHP	0.83		NYSE	7/13/2007	HealthShares, Inc.
iShares S&P GSTI Networking	IGN	0.48		NYSE	7/10/2001	Barclays
iShares S&P GSTI Semiconductor	IGW	0.48		NYSE	7/10/2001	Barclays

INDUSTRY- AND MARKET-SECTOR ETFS

Ticker	Symbol	Expense Ratio	Options	Exchange	Inception Date	Fund Family
iShares S&P GSTI Software	IGV	0.48		NYSE	7/10/2001	Barclays
iShares S&P GSTI Technology	IGM	0.48		NYSE	3/13/2001	Barclays
Adelante Shares RE Classic ETF	ACK	0.58		NYSE	9/28/2007	Adelante Funds
Adelante Shares RE Composite ETF	ACB	0.58		NYSE	9/28/2007	Adelante Funds
Adelante Shares RE Growth ETF	AGV	0.58		NYSE	9/28/2007	Adelante Funds
Adelante Shares RE Kings ETF	AKB	0.58		NYSE	9/28/2007	Adelante Funds
Adelante Shares RE Shelter ETF	AQS	0.58		NYSE	9/28/2007	Adelante Funds
Adelante Shares RE Value ETF	AVU	0.58	n/a	NYSE	9/28/2007	Adelante Funds
Adelante Shares RE Yield Plus ETF	ATY	0.58		NYSE	9/28/2007	Adelante Funds
Claymore/ Clear Global Timber Index	CUT	0.65		AMEX	11/9/2007	Claymore Securities
Claymore/ Morningstar Information Super Sector Index ETF	MZN	0.4		NYSE	8/22/2007	Claymore Securities
Claymore/ Morningstar Manufacturing Super Sector Index ETF	MZG	0.4		NYSE	8/22/2007	Claymore Securities

INDUSTRY- AND MARKET-SECTOR ETFS						
Ticker	Symbol	Expense Ratio	Options	Exchange	Inception Date	Fund Family
Claymore/ Morningstar Services Super Sector Index ETF	MZO	0.4		NYSE	8/22/2007	Claymore Securities
Claymore/ Zacks Sector Rotation	XRO	0.72	Yes	AMEX	9/21/2006	Claymore Securities
Consumer Discretionary Select Sector SPDR	XLY	0.23	Yes	AMEX	12/16/1998	State Street Global Advisors
Consumer Staples Select Sector SPDR	XLP	0.23	Yes	AMEX	12/16/1998	State Street Global Advisors
DJ Wilshire REIT ETF	RWR	0.25	Yes	AMEX	4/23/2001	State Street Global Advisors
ELEMENTS SPECTRUM Large Cap U.S. Sector Momentum Index ETN	EEH	0.75		NYSE	8/1/2007	Elements
Energy Select Sector SPDR	XLE	0.23	Yes	AMEX	12/16/1998	State Street Global Advisors
Financial Select Sector SPDR	XLF	0.23	Yes	AMEX	12/16/1998	State Street Global Advisors
First Trust Amex Biotechnology	FBT	0.6	Yes	AMEX	6/19/2006	First Trust
First Trust Consumer Discretionary AlphaDEX Fund	FXD	0.7		AMEX	5/8/2007	First Trust

INDUSTRY- AND MARKET-SECTOR ETFS

Ticker	Symbol	Expense Ratio	Options	Exchange	Inception Date	Fund Family
First Trust Consumer Staples AlphaDEX Fund	FXG	0.7		AMEX	5/8/2007	First Trust
First Trust Dow Jones Internet	FDN	0.6	Yes	AMEX	6/19/2006	First Trust
First Trust Energy AlphaDEX Fund	FXN	0.7		AMEX	5/8/2007	First Trust
First Trust Financials AlphaDEX Fund	FXO	0.7		AMEX	5/8/2007	First Trust
First Trust Health Care AlphaDEX Fund	FXH	0.7		AMEX	5/8/2007	First Trust
First Trust Industrials/ Producer Durables AlphaDEX Fund	FXR	0.7		AMEX	5/8/2007	First Trust
First Trust ISE Revere Natural Gas	FCG	0.7		NYSE	5/8/2007	First Trust
First Trust ISE Water	FIW	0.65		NYSE	5/8/2007	First Trust
First Trust Materials AlphaDEX Fund	FXZ	0.7		AMEX	5/8/2007	First Trust
First Trust Nasdaq Clean Edge U.S. Liquid	QCLN	0.6		NAS	2/8/2007	First Trust
First Trust Nasdaq-100 Technology	QTEC	0.6	Yes	NAS	4/19/2006	First Trust

INDUSTRY- AND MARKET-SECTOR ETFS

Ticker	Symbol	Expense Ratio	Options	Exchange	Inception Date	Fund Family
First Trust Technology AlphaDEX Fund	FXL	0.7		AMEX	5/8/2007	First Trust
First Trust Utilities AlphaDEX Fund	FXU	0.7		AMEX	5/8/2007	First Trust
Healthcare Select Sector SPDR	XLV	0.23	Yes	AMEX	12/16/1998	State Street Global Advisors

INDUSTRY- AND MARKET-SECTOR ETFS

Ticker	Symbol	Expense Ratio	Options	Exchange	Inception Date	Fund Family
HealthShares Autoimmune-Inflammation	HHA	0.79		NYSE	3/12/2007	HealthShares, Inc.
HealthShares Cancer	HHK	0.78		NYSE	3/12/2007	HealthShares, Inc.
HealthShares Cardio Devices	HHE	0.76		NYSE	1/23/2007	HealthShares, Inc.
HealthShares Cardiology	HRD	0.79		NYSE	3/12/2007	HealthShares, Inc.
HealthShares Composite	HHQ	0.79		NYSE	3/12/2007	HealthShares, Inc.
HealthShares Dermatology/ Wound Care	HRW	0.79		NYSE	4/18/2007	HealthShares, Inc.
HealthShares Diagnostics	HHD	0.76		NYSE	1/23/2007	HealthShares, Inc.
HealthShares Emerging Cancer	HHJ	0.76	Yes	NYSE	1/23/2007	HealthShares, Inc.
HealthShares Enabling Technologies	HHV	0.76		NYSE	1/23/2007	HealthShares, Inc.
HealthShares GI/ Gender Health	HHU	0.79		NYSE	3/12/2007	HealthShares, Inc.
HealthShares Infectious Disease	HHG	0.79		NYSE	4/3/2007	HealthShares, Inc.

INDUSTRY- AND MARKET-SECTOR ETFS

Ticker	Symbol	Expense Ratio	Options	Exchange	Inception Date	Fund Family
HealthShares Metabolic-Endocrine Disorders	HHM	0.79		NYSE	3/12/2007	HealthShares, Inc.
HealthShares Neuroscience	HHN	0.79		NYSE	3/12/2007	HealthShares, Inc.
HealthShares Ophthalmology	HHZ	0.79		NYSE	3/12/2007	HealthShares, Inc.
HealthShares Patient Care Services	HHB	0.76		NYSE	1/23/2007	HealthShares, Inc.
HealthShares Respiratory/ Pulmonary	HHR	0.79		NYSE	3/12/2007	HealthShares, Inc.
Industrial Select Sector SPDR	XLI	0.23	Yes	AMEX	12/16/1998	State Street Global Advisors
iShares Cohen & Steers Realty Majors	ICF	0.35	Yes	NYSE	1/29/2001	Barclays
iShares Dow Jones U.S. Aerospace & Defense	ITA	0.48		NYSE	5/1/2006	Barclays
iShares Dow Jones U.S. Basic Materials	IYM	0.48	Yes	NYSE	6/12/2000	Barclays
iShares Dow Jones U.S. Broker/ Dealers	IAI	0.48	Yes	NYSE	5/1/2006	Barclays
iShares Dow Jones U.S. Consumer Goods	IYK	0.48	Yes	NYSE	6/12/2000	Barclays
iShares Dow Jones U.S. Consumer Service	IYC	0.48	Yes	NYSE	6/12/2000	Barclays
iShares Dow Jones U.S. Energy	IYE	0.48	Yes	NYSE	6/12/2000	Barclays

INDUSTRY- AND MARKET-SECTOR ETFS						
Ticker	Symbol	Expense Ratio	Options	Exchange	Inception Date	Fund Family
iShares Dow Jones U.S. Financial	IYF	0.48	Yes	NYSE	5/22/2000	Barclays
iShares Dow Jones U.S. Financial Services	IYG	0.48	Yes	NYSE	6/12/2000	Barclays
iShares Dow Jones U.S. Healthcare	IYH	0.48	Yes	NYSE	6/12/2000	Barclays
iShares Dow Jones U.S. Healthcare Providers	IHF	0.48		NYSE	5/1/2006	Barclays
iShares Dow Jones U.S. Home Construction	ITB	0.48		NYSE	5/1/2006	Barclays
iShares Dow Jones U.S. Industrial	IYJ	0.48	Yes	NYSE	6/12/2000	Barclays
iShares Dow Jones U.S. Insurance	IAK	0.48		NYSE	5/1/2006	Barclays
iShares Dow Jones U.S. Medical Devices	IHI	0.48		NYSE	5/1/2006	Barclays
iShares Dow Jones U.S. Oil & Gas Exploration/ Production	IEO	0.48		NYSE	5/1/2006	Barclays
iShares Dow Jones U.S. Oil Equipment & Services	IEZ	0.48		NYSE	5/1/2006	Barclays
iShares Dow Jones U.S. Pharmaceuticals	IHE	0.48		NYSE	5/1/2006	Barclays
iShares Dow Jones U.S. Real Estate	IYR	0.48	Yes	NYSE	6/12/2000	Barclays

INDUSTRY- AND MARKET-SECTOR ETFS

Ticker	Symbol	Expense Ratio	Options	Exchange	Inception Date	Fund Family
iShares Dow Jones U.S. Regional Banks	IAT	0.48		NYSE	5/1/2006	Barclays
iShares Dow Jones U.S. Technology	IYW	0.48	Yes	NYSE	5/15/2000	Barclays
iShares Dow Jones U.S. Telecommun- ications	IYZ	0.48	Yes	NYSE	5/22/2000	Barclays
iShares Dow Jones U.S. Transportation Ave	IYT	0.48	Yes	NYSE	10/6/2003	Barclays
iShares Dow Jones U.S. Utilities	IDU	0.48	Yes	NYSE	6/12/2000	Barclays
iShares FTSE EPRA/NAREIT Asia Index Fund	IFAS	0.48		NAS	11/12/2007	Barclays

INDUSTRY- AND MARKET- SECTOR ETFS

Ticker	Symbol	Expense Ratio	Options	Exchange	Inception Date	Fund Family
iShares FTSE EPRA/NAREIT Europe Index Fund	IFEU	0.48		NAS	11/12/2007	Barclays
iShares FTSE EPRA/NAREIT Global Real Estate ex-U.S. Index Fund	IFGL	0.48		NAS	11/12/2007	Barclays
iShares FTSE EPRA/NAREIT North America Index Fund	IFNA	0.48		NAS	11/12/2007	Barclays
iShares FTSE NAREIT Industrial/ Office	FIO	0.48		NYSE	5/1/2007	Barclays

INDUSTRY- AND MARKET- SECTOR ETFS						
Ticker	Symbol	Expense Ratio	Options	Exchange	Inception Date	Fund Family
iShares FTSE NAREIT Mortgage REITs	REM	0.48		NYSE	5/1/2007	Barclays
iShares FTSE NAREIT Real Estate 50	FTY	0.48		NYSE	5/1/2007	Barclays
iShares FTSE NAREIT Residential	REZ	0.48		NYSE	5/1/2007	Barclays
iShares FTSE NAREIT Retail	RTL	0.48	n/a	NYSE	5/1/2007	Barclays
iShares Goldman Sachs Multimedia Networking	IGN	0.48	Yes	AMEX	7/10/2001	Barclays
iShares Goldman Sachs Natural Resources	IGE	0.50		AMEX	10/22/2001	Barclays
iShares Goldman Sachs Semiconductor	IGW	0.48	Yes	AMEX	7/10/2001	Barclays
iShares Goldman Sachs Software	IGV	0.48	Yes	AMEX	7/10/2001	Barclays
iShares Goldman Sachs Technology	IGM	0.48	Yes	AMEX	3/13/2001	Barclays
iShares Nasdaq Biotechnology	IBB	0.48	Yes	AMEX	2/5/2001	Barclays
KBW Bank ETF	KBE	0.35	Yes	AMEX	11/8/2005	State Street Global Advisors

INDUSTRY- AND MARKET- SECTOR ETFS						
Ticker	Symbol	Expense Ratio	Options	Exchange	Inception Date	Fund Family
KBW Capital Markets ETF	KCE	0.35	Yes	AMEX	11/8/2005	State Street Global Advisors
KBWInsurance ETF	KIE	0.35	Yes	AMEX	11/8/2005	State Street Global Advisors
KBW Regional Bank ETF	KRE	0.36	Yes	AMEX	6/19/2006	State Street Global Advisors
Market Vectors Coal ETF	KOL	0.65		NYSE	1/10/2008	Market Vectors
Market Vectors Gaming ETF	BJK	0.65		AMEX	1/22/2008	Market Vectors
Materials Select Sector SPDR	XLB	0.23	Yes	AMEX	12/16/1998	State Street Global Advisors
Morgan Stanley Technology ETF	MTK	0.50	Yes	AMEX	9/25/2000	State Street Global Advisors
NYSE Arca Tech 100	NXT	0.50	Yes	NYSE	3/26/2007	Ziegler Capital Management
PowerShares Aerospace & Defense	PPA	0.66	Yes	AMEX	10/26/2005	PowerShares
PowerShares Cleantech	PZD	0.71	Yes	AMEX	10/24/2006	PowerShares
PowerShares Dynamic Banking	PJB	0.76	Yes	AMEX	10/12/2006	PowerShares
PowerShares Dynamic Basic Materials	PYZ	0.71	Yes	AMEX	10/12/2006	PowerShares
PowerShares Dynamic Biotechnology & Genome	PBE	0.63	Yes	AMEX	6/23/2005	PowerShares

INDUSTRY- AND MARKET- SECTOR ETFS						
Ticker	Symbol	Expense Ratio	Options	Exchange	Inception Date	Fund Family
PowerShares Dynamic Building & Construction	PKB	0.63	Yes	AMEX	10/26/2005	PowerShares
PowerShares Dynamic Consumer Discretionary	PEZ	0.72	Yes	AMEX	10/12/2006	PowerShares
PowerShares Dynamic Consumer Staples	PSL	0.73	Yes	AMEX	10/12/2006	PowerShares
PowerShares Dynamic Energy	PXI	0.71	Yes	AMEX	10/12/2006	PowerShares
PowerShares Dynamic Energy & Exploration	PXE	0.63	Yes	AMEX	10/26/2005	PowerShares
PowerShares Dynamic Financial	PFI	0.72	Yes	AMEX	10/12/2006	PowerShares
PowerShares Dynamic Food & Beverage	PBJ	0.64	Yes	AMEX	6/23/2005	PowerShares
PowerShares Dynamic Hardware & Consumer Electronics	PHW	0.72	Yes	AMEX	12/6/2005	PowerShares
PowerShares Dynamic Healthcare	PTH	0.71	Yes	AMEX	10/12/2006	PowerShares
PowerShares Dynamic Healthcare Services	PTJ	0.70	Yes	AMEX	10/12/2006	PowerShares
PowerShares Dynamic Industrials	PRN	0.71	Yes	AMEX	10/12/2006	PowerShares

INDUSTRY- AND MARKET- SECTOR ETFS

Ticker	Symbol	Expense Ratio	Options	Exchange	Inception Date	Fund Family
PowerShares Dynamic Insurance	PIC	0.63	Yes	AMEX	10/26/2005	PowerShares
PowerShares Dynamic Leisure & Entertainment	PEJ	0.64	Yes	AMEX	6/23/2005	PowerShares
PowerShares Dynamic Media	PBS	0.64	Yes	AMEX	6/23/2005	PowerShares
PowerShares Dynamic Networking	PXQ	0.64	Yes	AMEX	6/23/2005	PowerShares

INDUSTRY- AND MARKET-SECTOR ETFS

Ticker	Symbol	Expense Ratio	Options	Exchange	Inception Date	Fund Family
NYSE Arca Tech 100	NXT	0.5	Yes	NYSE	3/26/2007	Ziegler Capital Management
PowerShares Aerospace & Defense	PPA	0.66	Yes	AMEX	10/26/2005	PowerShares
PowerShares Cleantech	PZD	0.71	Yes	AMEX	10/24/2006	PowerShares
PowerShares Dynamic Banking	PJB	0.76	Yes	AMEX	10/12/2006	PowerShares
PowerShares Dynamic Basic Materials	PYZ	0.71	Yes	AMEX	10/12/2006	PowerShares
PowerShares Dynamic Biotechnology & Genome	PBE	0.63	Yes	AMEX	6/23/2005	PowerShares
PowerShares Dynamic Building & Construction	PKB	0.63	Yes	AMEX	10/26/2005	PowerShares
PowerShares Dynamic Consumer Discretionary	PEZ	0.72	Yes	AMEX	10/12/2006	PowerShares

INDUSTRY- AND MARKET-SECTOR ETFS

Ticker	Symbol	Expense Ratio	Options	Exchange	Inception Date	Fund Family
PowerShares Dynamic Consumer Staples	PSL	0.73	Yes	AMEX	10/12/2006	PowerShares
PowerShares Dynamic Energy	PXI	0.71	Yes	AMEX	10/12/2006	PowerShares
PowerShares Dynamic Energy & Exploration	PXE	0.63	Yes	AMEX	10/26/2005	PowerShares
PowerShares Dynamic Financial	PFI	0.72	Yes	AMEX	10/12/2006	PowerShares
PowerShares Dynamic Food & Beverage	PBJ	0.64	Yes	AMEX	6/23/2005	PowerShares
PowerShares Dynamic Hardware & Consumer Electronics	PHW	0.72	Yes	AMEX	12/6/2005	PowerShares
PowerShares Dynamic Healthcare	PTH	0.71	Yes	AMEX	10/12/2006	PowerShares
PowerShares Dynamic Healthcare Services	PTJ	0.7	Yes	AMEX	10/12/2006	PowerShares
PowerShares Dynamic Industrials	PRN	0.71	Yes	AMEX	10/12/2006	PowerShares
PowerShares Dynamic Insurance	PIC	0.63	Yes	AMEX	10/26/2005	PowerShares
PowerShares Dynamic Leisure & Entertainment	PEJ	0.64	Yes	AMEX	6/23/2005	PowerShares
PowerShares Dynamic Media	PBS	0.64	Yes	AMEX	6/23/2005	PowerShares
PowerShares Dynamic Networking	PXQ	0.64	Yes	AMEX	6/23/2005	PowerShares

INDUSTRY- AND MARKET-SECTOR ETFS

Ticker	Symbol	Expense Ratio	Options	Exchange	Inception Date	Fund Family
PowerShares Dynamic Oil & Gas Services	PXJ	0.63	Yes	AMEX	10/26/2005	PowerShares
PowerShares Dynamic Pharmaceuticals	PJP	0.63	Yes	AMEX	6/23/2005	PowerShares
PowerShares Dynamic Retail	PMR	0.64	Yes	AMEX	10/26/2005	PowerShares
PowerShares Dynamic Semiconductor	PSI	0.63	Yes	AMEX	6/23/2005	PowerShares
PowerShares Dynamic Software	PSJ	0.63	Yes	AMEX	6/23/2005	PowerShares
PowerShares Dynamic Technology	PTF	0.71	Yes	AMEX	10/12/2006	PowerShares
PowerShares Dynamic Telecommunications & Wireless	PTE	0.66	Yes	AMEX	12/6/2005	PowerShares
PowerShares Dynamic Utilities	PUI	0.63	Yes	AMEX	10/26/2005	PowerShares
PowerShares FTSE RAFI Basic Materials Sector Portfolio	PRFM	0.76	Yes	NAS	9/20/2006	PowerShares
PowerShares FTSE RAFI Consumer Goods Sector Portfolio	PRFG	0.76	Yes	NAS	9/20/2006	PowerShares
PowerSharesFTSE RAFI Consumer Services Sector Portfolio	PRFS	0.77	Yes	NAS	9/20/2006	PowerShares
PowerShares FTSE RAFI Energy Sector Portfolio	PRFE	0.74	Yes	NAS	9/20/2006	PowerShares
PowerSharesFTSE RAFI Financials Sector Portfolio	PRFF	0.78	Yes	NAS	9/20/2006	PowerShares

INDUSTRY- AND MARKET-SECTOR ETFS

Ticker	Symbol	Expense Ratio	Options	Exchange	Inception Date	Fund Family
PowerSharesFTSE RAFI Health Care Sector Portfolio	PRFH	0.75	Yes	NAS	9/20/2006	PowerShares
PowerSharesFTSE RAFI Industrials Sector Portfolio	PRFN	0.73	Yes	NAS	9/20/2006	PowerShares
PowerSharesFTSE RAFI International Real Estate	PRY	0.75		NYSE	12/28/2007	PowerShares
PowerSharesFTSE RAFI Telecommunications & Technology Portfolio	PRFQ	0.75	Yes	NAS	9/20/2006	PowerShares
PowerShares FTSE RAFI Utilities Sector Portfolio	PRFU	0.75	Yes	NAS	9/20/2006	PowerShares
PowerShares Global Nuclear Energy Portfolio	PKN	0.75		NYSE	4/3/2008	PowerShares
PowerShares LUX Nanotech	PXN	0.71	Yes	AMEX	10/26/2005	PowerShares
PowerShares Water Resources	PHO	0.66	Yes	AMEX	12/6/2005	PowerShares
PowerShares WilderHill Clean Energy	PBW	0.7	Yes	AMEX	3/3/2005	PowerShares

INDUSTRY- AND MARKET-SECTOR ETFS

Ticker	Symbol	Expense Ratio	Options	Exchange	Inception Date	Fund Family
PowerShares WilderHill Progressive Energy	PUW	0.74	Yes	AMEX	10/24/2006	Power-Shares
Rydex S&P Equal Weight Consumer Discretionary	RCD	0.5		AMEX	11/1/2006	Rydex
Rydex S&P Equal Weight Consumer Staples	RHS	0.5		AMEX	11/1/2006	Rydex

INDUSTRY- AND MARKET-SECTOR ETFS

Ticker	Symbol	Expense Ratio	Options	Exchange	Inception Date	Fund Family
Rydex S&P Equal Weight Energy	RYE	0.5		AMEX	11/1/2006	Rydex
Rydex S&P Equal Weight Financial Services	RYF	0.5		AMEX	11/1/2006	Rydex
Rydex S&P Equal Weight Healthcare	RYH	0.5		AMEX	11/1/2006	Rydex
Rydex S&P Equal Weight Industrial	RGI	0.5		AMEX	11/1/2006	Rydex
Rydex S&P Equal Weight Materials	RTM	0.5		AMEX	11/1/2006	Rydex
Rydex S&P Equal Weight Technology	RYT	0.5		AMEX	11/1/2006	Rydex
Rydex S&P Equal Weight Utilities	RYU	0.5		AMEX	11/1/2006	Rydex
SPDR S&P Biotech ETF	XBI	0.35	Yes	AMEX	1/31/2006	State Street Global Advisors
SPDR S&P Homebuilders ETF	XHB	0.35	Yes	AMEX	1/31/2006	State Street Global Advisors
SPDR S&P Metals & Mining ETF	XME	0.35	Yes	AMEX	6/19/2007	State Street Global Advisors
SPDR S&P Oil & Gas Equipment & Services ETF	XES	0.35	Yes	AMEX	6/19/2006	State Street Global Advisors
SPDR S&P Oil & Gas Exploration & Production ETF	XOP	0.35	Yes	AMEX	6/19/2006	State Street Global Advisors
SPDR S&P Pharmaceuticals ETF	XPH	0.35	Yes	AMEX	6/19/2006	State Street Global Advisors
SPDR S&P Retail ETF	XRT	0.35	Yes	AMEX	6/19/2006	State Street Global Advisors
SPDR S&P Semiconductor ETF	XSD	0.35	Yes	AMEX	1/31/2006	State Street Global Advisors

INDUSTRY- AND MARKET-SECTOR ETFS

Ticker	Symbol	Expense Ratio	Options	Exchange	Inception Date	Fund Family
Technology Select Sector SPDR	XLK	0.23	Yes	AMEX	12/16/1998	State Street Global Advisors
Ultra Telecommunications ProShares	LTL	na		AMEX	3/26/2008	ProShares
UltraShort Telecommunications ProShare	TLL	na		AMEX	3/26/2008	ProShares
Utilities Select Sector SPDR	XLU	0.23	Yes	AMEX	12/16/1998	State Street Global Advisors
Vanguard Consumer Discretionary ETF	VCR	0.22	Yes	AMEX	1/26/2004	Vanguard
Vanguard Consumer Staples ETF	VDC	0.22	Yes	AMEX	1/26/2004	Vanguard
Vanguard Energy ETF	VDE	0.22	Yes	AMEX	9/23/2004	Vanguard
Vanguard Financials ETF	VFH	0.22	Yes	AMEX	1/26/2004	Vanguard
Vanguard Health Care ETF	VHT	0.22	Yes	AMEX	1/26/2004	Vanguard
Vanguard Industrials ETF	VIS	0.22	Yes	AMEX	9/23/2004	Vanguard
Vanguard Information Technology ETF	VGT	0.22	Yes	AMEX	1/26/2004	Vanguard
Vanguard Materials ETF	VAW	0.22	Yes	AMEX	1/26/2004	Vanguard
Vanguard REIT ETF	VNQ	0.12	Yes	AMEX	9/23/2004	Vanguard
Vanguard Telecommunications ETF	VOX	0.23	Yes	AMEX	9/23/2004	Vanguard
Vanguard Utilities ETF	VPU	0.22	Yes	AMEX	1/26/2004	Vanguard

FIXED-INCOME ETFS						
Ticker	Symbol	Expense Ratio	Options	Exchange	Inception Date	Fund Family
Ameristock/ Ryan 1 Year Treasury ETF	GKA	0.15		AMEX	6/28/2007	Ameristock Corporation
Ameristock/ Ryan 10 Year Treasury ETF	GKD	0.15		AMEX	6/28/2007	Ameristock Corporation
Ameristock/ Ryan 2 Year Treasury ETF	GKB	0.15		AMEX	6/28/2007	Ameristock Corporation
Ameristock/ Ryan 20 Year Treasury ETF	GKE	0.15		AMEX	6/28/2007	Ameristock Corporation
Ameristock/ Ryan 5 Year Treasury ETF	GKC	0.15		AMEX	6/28/2007	Ameristock Corporation
Bear Stearns Current Yield	YYY	0.35	No	AMEX	3/25/2008	Bear Stearns Asset Management
BearLinx Alerian MLP Select Index ET	BSR			NYSE	7/20/2007	Bear Stearns Asset Management
Claymore CEF Index Linked GS Connected Index-Linked Notes	GCE	0.95		NYSE	12/10/2007	Claymore Securities
Claymore U.S. Capital Markets Bond ETF	UBD	0.27		AMEX	2/12/2008	Claymore Securities
Claymore U.S. Micro-Term Fixed Income ETF	ULQ	0.27		AMEX	2/12/2008	Claymore Securities
iShares 1-3 YR Credit Bond	CSJ	0.2		AMEX	1/5/2007	Barclays
iShares iBoxx $ High Yield Corporate Bond	HYG	0.5	Yes	AMEX	4/4/2007	Barclays

FIXED-INCOME ETFS						
Ticker	Symbol	Expense Ratio	Options	Exchange	Inception Date	Fund Family
iShares iBoxx $ Investment Grade Corporate Bond	LQD	0.15	Yes	NYSE	7/22/2002	Barclays
iShares Lehman 10-20 YR Treasury Bond	TLH	0.15		NYSE	1/5/2007	Barclays
iShares Lehman 1-3 YR Treasury Bond	SHY	0.15	Yes	NYSE	7/22/2002	Barclays
iShares Lehman 20+ YR Treasury Bond	TLT	0.15	Yes	NYSE	7/22/2002	Barclays
iShares Lehman 3-7 YR Treasury Bond	IEI	0.15		AMEX	1/5/2007	Barclays
iShares Lehman 7-10 YR Treasury Bond	IEF	0.15	Yes	NYSE	7/22/2002	Barclays
iShares Lehman Aggregate Bond	AGG	0.2	Yes	NYSE	9/22/2003	Barclays
iShares Lehman Credit Bond	CFT	0.2		NYSE	1/5/2007	Barclays
iShares Lehman Government/ Credit Bond	GBF	0.2		NYSE	1/5/2007	Barclays
iShares Lehman Intermediate Credit Bond	CIU	0.2		NYSE	1/5/2007	Barclays

FIXED-INCOME ETFS						
Ticker	Symbol	Expense Ratio	Options	Exchange	Inception Date	Fund Family
iShares Lehman Intermediate Government/ Credit Bond	GVI	0.2		NYSE	1/5/2007	Barclays
iShares Lehman MBS Fixed Rate Bond	MBB	0.25	Yes	AMEX	3/13/2007	Barclays
iShares Lehman Short Treasury Bond	SHV	0.15		NYSE	1/5/2007	Barclays
iShares Lehman TIPS Bond	TIP	0.2	Yes	NYSE	12/4/2003	Barclays
iShares S&P California Municipal Bond Fund	CMF	0.25		AMEX	10/4/2007	Barclays
iShares S&P National Municipal Bond	MUB	0.25		AMEX	9/7/2007	Barclays
iShares S&P New York Municipal Bond	NYF	0.25		AMEX	10/4/2007	Barclays
iShares S&P US Preferred Stock Index	PFF	0.48		AMEX	3/26/2007	Barclays
Market Vectors Lehman AMT-Free Interm. Municipal	ITM	0.2		AMEX	12/4/2007	Van Eck
Market Vectors Lehman AMT-Free Long Municipal	MLN	0.24		AMEX	1/2/2008	Van Eck

FIXED-INCOME ETFS							
Ticker	Symbol	Expense Ratio	Options	Exchange	Inception Date	Fund Family
PowerShares 1-30 Laddered Treasury	PLW	0.25		AMEX	10/11/2007	PowerShares
PowerShares Emerging Markets Sovereign Debt Portfolio	PCY	0.5		AMEX	10/11/2007	PowerShares
PowerShares Financial Preferred Portfolio	PGF	0.72	Yes	AMEX	12/1/2006	PowerShares
PowerShares High Yield Corporate Bond Portfolio	PHB	0.5		AMEX	11/15/2007	PowerShares
PowerShares Insured California Municipal Bond Portfolio	PWZ	0.28		AMEX	10/11/2007	PowerShares
PowerShares Insured National Municipal Bond Portfolio	PZA	0.28		AMEX	10/11/2007	PowerShares
PowerShares Insured New York Municipal Bond Portfolio	PZT	0.28		AMEX	10/11/2007	PowerShares
PowerShares Preferred Portfolio	PGX	0.5		AMEX	1/31/2008	PowerShares
PowerShares VRDO Tax Free Weekly Portfolio	PVI	0.25		AMEX	11/15/2007	PowerShares
SPDR Barclays TIPS ETF	IPE	0.19	Yes	AMEX	5/25/2007	State Street Global Advisors

FIXED-INCOME ETFS						
Ticker	Symbol	Expense Ratio	Options	Exchange	Inception Date	Fund Family
SPDR DB Intl Govt Infl-Protected Bon	WIP	0.5		AMEX	3/19/2008	State Street Global Advisors
SPDR Lehman 1-3 Month T-Bill ETF	BIL	0.14	Yes	AMEX	5/25/2007	State Street Global Advisors
SPDR Lehman Aggregate Bond ETF	LAG	0.13		AMEX	5/23/2007	State Street Global Advisors
SPDR Lehman California Municipal Bond ETF	CXA	0.2		AMEX	10/10/2007	State Street Global Advisors
SPDR Lehman High Yield Bond ETF	JNK	0.4		AMEX	11/28/2007	State Street Global Advisors
SPDR Lehman Intermediate Term Treasury ETF	ITE	0.14	Yes	AMEX	5/23/2007	State Street Global Advisors
SPDR Lehman International Treasury Bond ETF	BWX	0.5		AMEX	10/2/2007	State Street Global Advisors
SPDR Lehman Long Term Treasury ETF	TLO	0.14	Yes	AMEX	5/23/2007	State Street Global Advisors
SPDR Lehman Municipal Bond ETF	TFI	0.2		AMEX	9/11/2007	State Street Global Advisors
SPDR Lehman New York Municipal Bond ETF	INY	0.2		AMEX	10/11/2007	State Street Global Advisors
SPDR Lehman Short Term Municipal Bond ETF	SHM	0.2		AMEX	10/10/2007	State Street Global Advisors
SPDR S&P International Dividend ETF	DWX	0.45		AMEX	2/12/2008	State Street Global Advisors

FIXED-INCOME ETFS

Ticker	Symbol	Expense Ratio	Options	Exchange	Inception Date	Fund Family
Vanguard Extended Duration	EDV	0.14		AMEX	12/6/2007	Vanguard
Vanguard Intermediate Term Bond ETF	BIV	0.11	Yes	AMEX	4/3/2007	Vanguard
Vanguard Long Term Bond ETF	BLV	0.11	Yes	AMEX	4/3/2007	Vanguard
Vanguard Short Term Bond ETF	BSV	0.11	Yes	AMEX	4/3/2007	Vanguard
Vanguard Total Bond Market ETF	BND	0.11	Yes	AMEX	4/3/2007	Vanguard

COMMODITY ETFS

Ticker	Symbol	Expense Ratio	Options	Exchange	Inception Date	Fund Family
Claymore/Zacks International Yield Hog	HGI			AMEX	7/11/2007	Claymore Securities
Claymore/Zacks Yield Hog	CVY	0.79	Yes	AMEX	9/21/2006	Claymore
DB Gold Double Long ETN	DGP	0.75		NYSE	2/27/2008	Deutsche Bank
DB Gold Double Short ETN	DZZ	0.75		NYSE	2/27/2008	Deutsche Bank
ELEMENTS MLCX Biofuels Index TR ETN	FUE	0.75		NYSE	2/5/2008	Elements
ELEMENTS MLCX Grains Index TR ETN	GRU	0.75		NYSE	2/5/2008	Elements
ELEMENTS Rogers Intl Commodity Idx Agriculture Total Rtn	RJA	0.75		AMEX	10/17/2007	Elements

COMMODITY ETFS						
Ticker	Symbol	Expense Ratio	Options	Exchange	Inception Date	Fund Family
ELEMENTSRogers Intl Commodity Idx Energy Total Rtn	RJN	0.75		AMEX	10/17/2007	Elements
ELEMENTSRogers Intl Commodity Idx Metals Total Rtn	RJZ	0.75		AMEX	10/17/2007	Elements
ELEMENTSRogers Intl Commodity Idx Total ETN	RJI	0.75		AMEX	10/17/2007	Elements
E-TRACS UBS Bloomberg CMCI Agric ETN	UAG	0.65		NYSE	4/2/2008	UBS Investment Bank
E-TRACS UBS Bloomberg CMCI Energy ET	UBN	0.65		NYSE	4/2/2008	UBS Investment Bank
E-TRACS UBS Bloomberg CMCI ETN	UCI	0.65		NYSE	4/2/2008	UBS Investment Bank
E-TRACS UBS Bloomberg CMCI Food ETN	FUD	0.65		NYSE	4/2/2008	UBS Investment Bank
E-TRACS UBS Bloomberg CMCI Gold ETN	UBG	0.65		NYSE	4/2/2008	UBS Investment Bank
E-TRACS UBS Bloomberg CMCI Ind Metal	UBM	0.65		NYSE	4/2/2008	UBS Investment Bank
E-TRACS UBS Bloomberg CMCI Livestock	UBC	0.65		NYSE	4/2/2008	UBS Investment Bank
E-TRACS UBS Bloomberg CMCI Silver ET	USV	0.65		NYSE	4/2/2008	UBS Investment Bank
Greenhaven Continuous Commodity Index Fund	GCC	1.95	Yes	AMEX	1/24/2008	Greenhaven Commodity Svices
GS Connect S&P GSCI Enh Commodity TR	GSC	1.25		NYSE	7/31/2007	Goldman Sachs

COMMODITY ETFS

Ticker	Symbol	Expense Ratio	Options	Exchange	Inception Date	Fund Family
iPath DJ AIG Agriculture TR Sub-Idx	JJA			NYSE	10/23/2007	Barclays
iPath DJ AIG Copper TR Sub-Idx ETN	JJC			NYSE	10/23/2007	Barclays
iPath DJ AIG Energy TR Sub-Idx ETN	JJE			NYSE	10/23/2007	Barclays
iPath DJ AIG Grains TR Sub-Idx ETN	JJG			NYSE	10/23/2007	Barclays
iPath DJ AIG Ind Metals TR Sub-Idx E	JJM			NYSE	10/23/2007	Barclays
iPath DJ AIG Livestock TR Sub-Idx ET	COW			NYSE	10/23/2007	Barclays
iPath DJ AIG Natural Gas TR Sub-Idx	GAZ			NYSE	10/23/2007	Barclays
iPath DJ AIG Nickel TR Sub-Idx ETN	JJN			NYSE	10/23/2007	Barclays
iPath Dow Jones AIG Commodity Idx Total Rtn	DJP	0.75		NYSE	6/6/2006	Barclays
iPath GS Crude Oil Total Return Idx	OIL	0.75		NYSE	8/15/2006	Barclays
iPath GSCI Total Return Idx	GSP	0.75		NTSE	6/6/2006	Barclays
iShares Comex Gold Trust	IAU	0.4		AMEX	1/21/2005	Barclays
iShares S&P GSCI Commodity-Indexed Tr	GSG	0.75	Yes	NYSE	7/10/2006	Barclays
iShares S&P GSSI Natural Resources	IGE	0.48		NYSE	10/22/2001	Barclays
iShares Silver Trust	SLV	0.5		AMEX	4/21/2006	Barclays

COMMODITY ETFS						
Ticker	Symbol	Expense Ratio	Options	Exchange	Inception Date	Fund Family
MACROshares Oil Down Tradeable Share	DCR			AMEX	11/29/2006	MacroMarkets
MACROshares Oil Up Tradeable Shares	UCR			AMEX	11/29/2006	MacroMarkets
Market Vectors Lehman AMT-Free Shrt	SMB	0.16		AMEX	2/28/2008	Market Vectors
Opta Lehman Cmdty Pure Beta Agric TR	EOH	0.85		AMEX	2/20/2008	Lehman Brothers
Opta Lehman Commodity Pure Beta TR E	RAW	0.85		AMEX	2/20/2008	Lehman Brothers
PowerShares DB Agriculture	DBA	0.91	Yes	AMEX	1/5/2007	PowerShares
PowerShares DB Base Metals	DBB	0.78	Yes	AMEX	1/5/2007	PowerShares
PowerShares DB Commodity Idx Tracking	DBC	0.83	Yes	AMEX	2/23/2006	PowerShares
PowerShares DB Energy	DBE	0.78	Yes	AMEX	1/5/2007	PowerShares
PowerShares DB Gold	DGL	0.79	Yes	AMEX	1/5/2007	PowerShares
PowerShares DB Oil	DBO	0.79	Yes	AMEX	1/5/2007	PowerShares
PowerShares DB Precious Metals	DBP	0.79	Yes	AMEX	1/5/2007	PowerShares
PowerShares DB Silver	DBS	0.79	Yes	AMEX	1/5/2007	PowerShares
streetTRACKS Gold Shares	GLD	0.4		NYSE	11/18/2004	World Gold Trust Services, LLC
United States 12 Month Oil	USL	0.6		AMEX	12/6/2007	United States Oil
United States Gasoline	UGA	0.6		AMEX	2/26/2008	Victoria Bay Asset Management

COMMODITY ETFS

Ticker	Symbol	Expense Ratio	Options	Exchange	Inception Date	Fund Family
United States Natural Gas Fund	UNG	0.6	Yes	AMEX	4/18/2007	United States Oil
United States Oil Fund	USO	0.5		AMEX	4/10/2006	United States Oil

CURRENCY ETFS

Ticker	Symbol	Expense Ratio	Options	Exchange	Inception Date	Fund Family
CurrencyShares Australian Dollar Trust	FXA	0.4	Yes	NYSE	6/21/2006	Rydex
CurrencyShares British Pound Sterling Trust	FXB	0.4	Yes	NYSE	6/21/2006	Rydex
CurrencyShares Canadian Dollar Trust	FXC	0.4	Yes	NYSE	6/21/2006	Rydex
CurrencyShares Euro Trust	FXE	0.4	Yes	NYSE	12/9/2005	Rydex
CurrencyShares Japanese Yen	FXY	0.4	Yes	NYSE	2/12/2007	Rydex
CurrencyShares Mexican Peso Trust	FXM	0.4	Yes	NYSE	6/21/2006	Rydex
CurrencyShares Swedish Krona Trust	FXS	0.4	Yes	NYSE	6/21/2006	Rydex
CurrencyShares Swiss Franc Trust	FXF	0.4	Yes	NYSE	6/21/2006	Rydex
ELEMENTS Australian Dollar - AUD/USD	ADE	0.40		NYSE	2/20/2008	Elements
ELEMENTS British Pound - GBP/USD ETN	EGB	0.40		NYSE	2/20/2008	Elements
ELEMENTS Canadian Dollar - CAD/USD E	CUD	0.40		NYSE	2/20/2008	Elements

CURRENCY ETFS						
Ticker	Symbol	Expense Ratio	Options	Exchange	Inception Date	Fund Family
ELEMENTS Euro - EUR/USD ETN	ERE	0.40		NYSE	2/20/2008	Elements
ELEMENTS Swiss Franc - CHF/USD ETN	SZE	0.04		NYSE	2/20/2008	Elements
iPath EUR/USD Exchange Rate ETN	ERO	0.4		NYSE	5/8/2007	Barclays
iPath GBP/USD Exchange Rate ETN	GBB	0.4		NYSE	5/8/2007	Barclays
iPath JPY/USD Exchange Rate ETN	JYN	0.4		NYSE	5/8/2007	Barclays
iPath Optimized Currency Carry ETN	ICI	0.65		NYSE	1/31/2008	Barclays Global Investors
Market Vectors - Chinese Renminbi/USD ETN	CNY	0.55		AMEX	3/17/2008	Market Vectors
Market Vectors - Indian Rupee/ USD ETN	INR	0.55		AMEX	3/17/2008	Market Vectors
PowerShares DB G10 Currency Harvest	DBV	0.83	Yes	AMEX	9/18/2006	PowerShares
PowerShares DB U.S. Dollar Index Bearish Fund	UDN	0.55		AMEX	2/20/2007	PowerShares
PowerShares DB U.S. Dollar Index Bullish Fund	UUP	0.55		AMEX	2/20/2007	PowerShares

EMERGING MARKET ETFS						
Ticker	Symbol	Expense Ratio	Options	Exchange	Inception Date	Fund Family
Claymore/ BNY BRIC	EEB	0.64	Yes	AMEX	9/21/2006	Claymore Securities
First Trust ISE Chindia	FNI	0.60	Yes	NYSE	5/8/2007	First Trust
iPath MSCI India ETN	INP	0.89		NYSE	12/19/2006	Barclays
iShares FTSE/ Xinhua China 25	FXI	0.74	Yes	NYSE	10/5/2004	Barclays
iShares MSCI Brazil	EWZ	0.74	Yes	NYSE	7/10/2000	Barclays
iShares MSCI BRIC	BKF	0.75		NYSE	11/12/2007	Barclays
iShares MSCI Emerging Markets	EEM	0.75	Yes	NYSE	4/7/2003	Barclays
iShares MSCI Malaysia	EWM	0.59	Yes	NYSE	3/12/1996	Barclays
iShares MSCI Mexico	EWW	0.59		NYSE	3/12/1996	Barclays
iShares MSCI South Africa	EZA	0.74	Yes	NYSE	2/3/2003	Barclays
iShares MSCI South Korea	EWY	0.74		NYSE	5/9/2000	Barclays
iShares MSCI Taiwan	EWT	0.77	Yes	NYSE	6/20/2000	Barclays
PowerShares BLDRS Emerging Markets 50 ADR	ADRE	0.30	Yes	NAS	11/13/2002	BLDRS
Russia ETF	RSX	0.69	Yes	NYSE	4/24/2007	Market Vectors
SPDR S&P BRIC 40 ETF	BIK	0.40	Yes	AMEX	6/19/2007	State Street Global Advisors
SPDR S&P China	GXC	0.60	Yes	AMEX	3/19/2007	State Street Global Advisors

EMERGING MARKET ETFS

Ticker	Symbol	Expense Ratio	Options	Exchange	Inception Date	Fund Family
SPDR S&P Emerging Asia Pacific	GMF	0.63	Yes	AMEX	3/19/2007	State Street Global Advisors
SPDR S&P Emerging Europe	GUR	0.60		AMEX	3/19/2007	State Street Global Advisors
SPDR S&P Emerging Latin America	GML	0.60		AMEX	3/19/2007	State Street Global Advisors
SPDR S&P Emerging Markets	GMM	0.60	Yes	AMEX	3/19/2007	State Street Global Advisors
SPDR S&P Emerging Middle East & Africa	GAF	0.60	Yes	AMEX	3/19/2007	State Street Global Advisors
Vanguard Emerging Markets ETF	VWO	0.30	Yes	AMEX	3/4/2005	Vanguard
WisdomTree Emerging Markets High Yielding Index	DEM	0.63		NYSE	7/13/2007	WisdomTree

GLOBAL AND INTERNATIONAL ETFS

Ticker	Symbol	Expense Ratio	Options	Exchange	Inception Date	Fund Family
Market Vectors Global Agribusiness ETF	MOO			AMEX	8/31/2007	Van Eck
Market Vectors Russia ETF	RSX			NYSE	4/24/2007	Van Eck
PowerShares India Portfolio	PIN	0.78		ARCA	3/5/2008	PowerShares
Vanguard European Stock ETF	VGK	0.12		AMEX	3/4/2005	Vanguard

GLOBAL AND INTERNATIONAL ETFS						
Ticker	Symbol	Expense Ratio	Options	Exchange	Inception Date	Fund Family
HealthShares Euro Medical Prod & Dev	HHT	1.01		NYSE	6/1/2007	HealthShares, Inc.
Claymore/ AlphaShares China Real Estate ETF	TAO	0.65		NYSE	12/18/2007	Claymore Securities
Claymore/ AlphaShares China Small Cap Index ETF	HAO	0.70		AMEX	1/30/2008	Claymore Securities
Claymore/ Clear Global Exchanges, Brokers & Asset Mgrs	EXB	0.65		AMEX	6/27/2007	Claymore Securities
Claymore/ Robeco Developed International Equity	EEN	1.32	Yes	AMEX	3/1/2007	Claymore Securities
Claymore/ SWM Canadian Energy Income	ENY	0.65		AMEX	7/3/2007	Claymore Securities
Claymore/ Zacks Country Rotation ETF	CRO	0.65		AMEX	7/11/2007	Claymore Securities
DJ EURO STOXX 50 ETF	FEZ	0.32	Yes	NYSE	10/15/2002	State Street Global Advisors
DJ STOXX 50 ETF	FEU	0.31		NYSE	10/15/2002	State Street Global Advisors
First Trust DJ Global Select Dividend Index Fund	FGD	0.60		AMEX	11/21/2007	First Trust

GLOBAL AND INTERNATIONAL ETFS

Ticker	Symbol	Expense Ratio	Options	Exchange	Inception Date	Fund Family
First Trust DJ STOXX Select Dividend 30 Index Fund	FDD	0.60		AMEX	8/27/2007	First Trust
First Trust FTSE EPRA/ NAREIT Global Real Estate Index Fnd	FFR	0.70		AMEX	8/27/2007	First Trust

GLOBAL AND INTERNATIONAL ETFS

Ticker	Symbol	Expense Ratio	Options	Exchange	Inception Date	Fund Family
HealthShares European Drugs	HRJ	0.99		NYSE	4/3/2007	Health-Shares, Inc.
iShares Dow Jones EPAC Select Dividend	IDV	0.5		NYSE	6/11/2007	Barclays
iShares FTSE Developed Small Cap ex-North America IF	IFSM	0.5		NAS	11/12/2007	Barclays
iShares JPMorgan USD Emerg Markets B	EMB			London Stock Exchange	12/17/2007	Barclays
iShares MSCI Australia	EWA	0.59	Yes	NYSE	3/12/1996	Barclays
iShares MSCI Austria	EWO	0.54		NYSE	3/12/1996	Barclays
iShares MSCI Belgium	EWK	0.54		NYSE	3/12/1996	Barclays
iShares MSCI Canada	EWC	0.59	Yes	NYSE	3/12/1996	Barclays
iShares MSCI Chile	ECH	0.74		NYSE	11/12/2007	Barclays
iShares MSCI EAFE	EFA	0.35	Yes	NYSE	8/14/2001	Barclays

GLOBAL AND INTERNATIONAL ETFS

Ticker	Symbol	Expense Ratio	Options	Exchange	Inception Date	Fund Family
iShares MSCI EAFE Growth Index	EFG	0.4		NYSE	8/1/2005	Barclays
iShares MSCI EAFE Small Cap Index	SCZ			NYSE	12/10/2007	Barclays
iShares MSCI EAFE Value Index	EFV	0.4		NYSE	8/1/2005	Barclays
iShares MSCI EMU	EZU	0.54		NYSE	7/25/2000	Barclays
iShares MSCI France	EWQ	0.54		NYSE	3/12/1996	Barclays
iShares MSCI Germany	EWG	0.54		NYSE	3/12/1996	Barclays
iShares MSCI Hong Kong	EWH	0.59	Yes	NYSE	3/12/1996	Barclays
iShares MSCI Italy	EWI	0.54		NYSE	3/12/1996	Barclays
iShares MSCI Japan	EWJ	0.59	Yes	NYSE	3/12/1996	Barclays
iShares MSCI Japan Small Cap	SCJ			NYSE	12/20/2007	Barclays
iShares MSCI Kokusai Index	TOK			NYSE	12/10/2007	Barclays
iShares MSCI Netherlands	EWN	0.54		NYSE	3/12/1996	Barclays
iShares MSCI Pacific ex-Japan	EPP	0.5		NYSE	10/25/2001	Barclays
iShares MSCI Singapore	EWS	0.59		NYSE	3/12/1996	Barclays
iShares MSCI Spain	EWP	0.54	Yes	NYSE	3/12/1996	Barclays
iShares MSCI Sweden	EWD	0.54	Yes	NYSE	3/12/1996	Barclays
iShares MSCI Switzerland	EWL	0.54		NYSE	3/12/1996	Barclays
iShares MSCI United Kingdom	EWU	0.54	Yes	NYSE	3/12/1996	Barclays

GLOBAL AND INTERNATIONAL ETFS						
Ticker	Symbol	Expense Ratio	Options	Exchange	Inception Date	Fund Family
iShares S&P Asia 50	AIA	0.5		NYSE	11/13/2007	Barclays
iShares S&P Europe 350	IEV	0.6	Yes	NYSE	7/25/2000	Barclays
iShares S&P Global 100	IOO	0.4	Yes	NYSE	12/5/2000	Barclays
iShares S&P Global Consumer Discretionary	RXI	0.48		NYSE	9/12/2006	Barclays
iShares S&P Global Consumer Staples	KXI	0.48		NYSE	9/12/2006	Barclays
iShares S&P Global Energy	IXC	0.49	Yes	NYSE	11/12/2001	Barclays
iShares S&P Global Financials	IXG	0.49	Yes	NYSE	11/12/2001	Barclays
iShares S&P Global Healthcare	IXJ	0.49	Yes	NYSE	11/13/2001	Barclays
iShares S&P Global Industrials	EXI	0.48		NYSE	9/12/2006	Barclays
iShares S&P Global Infrastructure Index	IGF			NYSE	12/10/2007	Barclays
iShares S&P Global Materials	MXI	0.48		NYSE	9/12/2006	Barclays
iShares S&P Global Technology	IXN	0.49	Yes	NYSE	11/12/2001	Barclays
iShares S&P Global Telecommunication	IXP	0.49	Yes	NYSE	11/12/2001	Barclays
iShares S&P Global Utilities	JXI	0.48		NYSE	9/12/2006	Barclays
iShares S&P Latin America 40	ILF	0.5	Yes	NYSE	10/25/2001	Barclays
iShares S&P TOPIX 150 Index	ITF	0.5	Yes	NYSE	10/23/2001	Barclays

GLOBAL AND INTERNATIONAL ETFS

Ticker	Symbol	Expense Ratio	Options	Exchange	Inception Date	Fund Family
iShares S&P World ex-US Property Ind	WPS			NYSE	7/30/2007	Barclays
Market Vectors Agribusiness ETF	MOO	0.65		AMEX	8/31/2007	Market Vectors
Market Vectors Environmental Services ETF	EVX	0.55	Yes	AMEX	10/10/2006	Van Eck
Market Vectors Global Alternative Energy ETF	GEX	0.65		NYSE	5/3/2007	Van Eck
Market Vectors Gold Miners ETF	GDX	0.55	Yes	AMEX	5/16/2006	Van Eck
Market Vectors Nuclear Energy ETF	NLR	0.65		AMEX	8/13/2007	
Market Vectors Steel ETF	SLX	0.55	Yes	AMEX	10/10/2006	Van Eck
PowerShares BLDRs Asia 50 ADR	ADRA	0.30		NAS	11/13/2002	BLDRS
PowerShares BLDRs Developed Markets 100 ADR	ADRD	0.30		NAS	11/13/2002	BLDRS
PowerShares BLDRs Europe 100 ADR	ADRU	0.30		NAS	11/13/2002	BLDRS
PowerShares DWA Developed Markets Technical Leaders	PIZ	0.80		NYSE	12/28/2007	PowerShares
PowerShares DWA Emerging Markets Technical Leaders	PIE	0.90		NYSE	12/28/2007	PowerShares

GLOBAL AND INTERNATIONAL ETFS

Ticker	Symbol	Expense Ratio	Options	Exchange	Inception Date	Fund Family
PowerShares Dynamic Asia Pacific	PUA	0.80	Yes	AMEX	6/13/2007	PowerShares
PowerShares Dynamic Developed International	PFA	0.75	Yes	AMEX	6/13/2007	PowerShares
PowerShares Dynamic Europe	PEH	0.75	Yes	AMEX	6/13/2007	PowerShares
PowerShares FTSE RAFI Asia Pacific ex-Japan	PAF	0.80	Yes	AMEX	9/27/2007	PowerShares
PowerShares FTSE RAFI Asia Pacific ex-Japan Small-Mid	PDQ	0.80	Yes	NYSE	6/25/2007	PowerShares
PowerShares FTSE RAFI Developed Markets ex-U.S. Small-Mid Cap	PDN	0.75	Yes	NYSE	6/25/2007	PowerShares
PowerShares FTSE RAFI Developed Markets ex-U.S.	PXF	0.75	Yes	AMEX	9/27/2007	PowerShares
PowerShares FTSE RAFI Emerging Markets	PXH	0.85	Yes	AMEX	9/27/2007	PowerShares
PowerShares FTSE RAFI Europe	PEF	0.75	Yes	NYSE	6/25/2007	PowerShares
PowerShares FTSE RAFI Europe Small-Mid Cap	PWD	0.75	Yes	AMEX	9/27/2007	PowerShares
PowerShares FTSE RAFI Japan	PJO	0.75	Yes	NYSE	6/25/2007	PowerShares
PowerShares Global Clean Energy	PBD	0.75	Yes	AMEX	6/13/2007	PowerShares

GLOBAL AND INTERNATIONAL ETFS

Ticker	Symbol	Expense Ratio	Options	Exchange	Inception Date	Fund Family
PowerShares Global Water Portfolio Fund	PIO	0.75		AMEX	6/13/2007	PowerShares
PowerShares Golden Dragon Halter USX China	PGJ	0.70	Yes	AMEX	12/9/2004	PowerShares
PowerShares International Dividend Achievers	PID	0.60	Yes	AMEX	9/15/2005	PowerShares
PowerShares International Listed Private Equity	PFP	0.75	Yes	AMEX	9/27/2007	PowerShares
SPDR DJ Global Titans ETF	DGT	0.51	Yes	AMEX	9/25/2000	State Street Global Advisors
SPDR DJ Wilshire International Real Estate ETF	RWX	0.60	Yes	AMEX	12/19/2006	State Street Global Advisors
SPDR FTSE/ Macquarie Global Infrastructure 100 ETF	GII	0.60	Yes	AMEX	1/25/2007	State Street Global Advisors
SPDR International Small Cap ETF	GWX	0.60		AMEX	4/20/2007	State Street Global Advisors
SPDR MSCI ACWI ex-US ETF	CWI	0.35	Yes	AMEX	1/10/2007	State Street Global Advisors
SPDR Russell/ Nomura Prime Japan ETF	JPP	0.51	Yes	AMEX	11/9/2006	State Street Global Advisors
SPDR Russell/ Nomura Small Cap Japan ETF	JSC	0.56	Yes	AMEX	11/9/2006	State Street Global Advisors
SPDR S&P World ex-US ETF	GWL	0.35		AMEX	4/20/2007	State Street Global Advisors

GLOBAL AND INTERNATIONAL ETFS

Ticker	Symbol	Expense Ratio	Options	Exchange	Inception Date	Fund Family
Vanguard FTSE All World ex-US	VEU	0.25	Yes	AMEX	3/2/2007	Vanguard
Vanguard MSCI European ETF	VGK	0.18	Yes	AMEX	3/4/2005	Vanguard
Vanguard MSCI Pacific ETF	VPL	0.18	Yes	AMEX	3/4/2005	Vanguard
Vanguard Europe Pacific ETF	VEA	0.15	Yes	AMEX	7/20/2007	Vanguard
Wisdom Tree India Earnings Fund	EPI	0.88	n/a	NYSE	2/22/2008	Wisdom Tree
WisdomTree DIEFA Fund	DWM	0.48		NYSE	6/16/2006	WisdomTree
WisdomTree DIEFA High Yielding Equity Fund	DTH	0.58		NYSE	6/16/2006	WisdomTree
WisdomTree Emerging Markets Small Cap D	DGS			NYSE	10/30/2007	WisdomTree
WisdomTree Europe High Yielding Equity Fund	DEW	0.58		NYSE	6/16/2006	Wisdom Tree
WisdomTree Europe SmallCap Dividend Fund	DFE	0.58		NYSE	6/16/2006	WisdomTree
WisdomTree Europe Total Dividend Fund	DEB	0.48		NYSE	6/16/2006	WisdomTree
WisdomTree International Basic Materials	DBN	0.58		NYSE	10/13/2006	WisdomTree
WisdomTree International Communications	DGG	0.58		NYSE	10/13/2006	WisdomTree
WisdomTree International Consumer Cyclical	DPC	0.58		NYSE	10/13/2006	WisdomTree

GLOBAL AND INTERNATIONAL ETFS						
Ticker	Symbol	Expense Ratio	Options	Exchange	Inception Date	Fund Family
WisdomTree International Consumer Non-Cyclical	DPN	0.58		NYSE	10/13/2006	Wisdom Tree
WisdomTree International Dividend Top 100 Fund	DOO	0.58		NYSE	6/16/2006	WisdomTree
WisdomTree International Energy	DKA	0.58		NYSE	10/13/2006	WisdomTree
WisdomTree International Financial	DRF	0.58		NYSE	10/13/2006	WisdomTree
WisdomTree International Health Care	DBR	0.58		NYSE	10/13/2006	WisdomTree
WisdomTree International Industrial	DDI	0.58		NYSE	10/13/2006	WisdomTree
WisdomTree International Large Cap Dividend Fund	DOL	0.48		NYSE	6/16/2006	WisdomTree
WisdomTree International Mid Cap Dividend Fund	DIM	0.58		NYSE	6/16/2006	WisdomTree
WisdomTree International Real Estate Fund	DRW	0.58		AMEX	6/5/2007	WisdomTree
WisdomTree International Small Cap Dividend Fund	DLS	0.58		NYSE	6/16/2006	WisdomTree
WisdomTree International Technology	DBT	0.58		NYSE	10/13/2006	WisdomTree
WisdomTree International Utilities	DBU	0.58		NYSE	10/13/2006	WisdomTree

GLOBAL AND INTERNATIONAL ETFS

Ticker	Symbol	Expense Ratio	Options	Exchange	Inception Date	Fund Family
WisdomTree Japan High-Yielding Equity Fund	DNL	0.58		NYSE	6/16/2006	WisdomTree
WisdomTree Japan Small Cap Dividend Fund	DFJ	0.58		NYSE	6/16/2006	WisdomTree
WisdomTree Japan Total Dividend Fund	DXJ	0.48		NYSE	6/16/2006	WisdomTree
WisdomTree Pacific ex-Japan High-Yielding Equity	DNH	0.58		NYSE	6/16/2006	WisdomTree
WisdomTree Pacific ex-Japan Total Dividend	DND	0.48		NYSE	6/16/2006	WisdomTree

SPECIALTY ETFS

Ticker	Symbol	Expense Ratio	Options	Exchange	Inception Date	Fund Family
Claymore MACRO-shares Oil Down Tradeable Trust	DCR	1.60		AMEX	11/29/2006	Claymore Securities
Claymore MACRO-shares Oil Up Tradeable Trust	UCR	1.60		AMEX	11/29/2006	Claymore Securities
Claymore S&P Global Water Index ETF	CGW	0.72		AMEX	5/14/2007	Claymore Securities
Claymore U.S.-1-The Capital Markets Index ETF	UEM	0.37	n/a	AMEX	2/12/2008	Claymore Securities
Claymore/BBD High Income Fund	LVL	0.60		AMEX	6/25/2007	Claymore Securities

SPECIALTY ETFS

Ticker	Symbol	Expense Ratio	Options	Exchange	Inception Date	Fund Family
Claymore/Clear Spin-Off	CSD	0.75	Yes	AMEX	12/15/2006	Claymore Securities
Claymore/Ocean Tomo Growth Index	OTR	2.03	Yes	AMEX	4/2/2007	Claymore Securities
Claymore/Ocean Tomo Patent	OTP	0.91	Yes	AMEX	12/15/2006	Claymore Securities
Claymore/Robb Report Global Luxury	ROB	0.70		NYSE	7/30/2007	Claymore Securities
Claymore/ Sabrient Defender	DEF	0.79	Yes	AMEX	12/15/2006	Claymore Securities
Claymore/ Sabrient Insider	NFO	0.76	Yes	AMEX	9/21/2006	Claymore Securities
Claymore/Zacks Dividend Rotation	IRO	0.60		AMEX	10/24/2007	Claymore Securities
ELEMENTS Morningstar Wide Moat Focus Total Return Idx	WMW	0.75		NYSE	10/17/2007	Elements
First Trust IPOX 100 Index Fund	FPX	0.60	Yes	AMEX	4/12/2006	First Trust
iPath CBOE S&P 500 Buy/Write Index	BWV	0.75		AMEX	5/22/2007	Barclays
Opta S&P Listed Private Equity NR ET	PPE	0.85		AMEX	2/20/2008	Lehman Brothers
PowerShares Buyback Achievers	PKW	0.73	Yes	AMEX	12/20/2006	Power-Shares
PowerShares DWA Technical Leaders Portfolio	PDP	0.72		NYSE	3/1/2007	Power-Shares
PowerShares Listed Private Equity	PSP	0.71	Yes	AMEX	10/24/2006	Power-Shares
PowerShares Value Line Industry Rotation	PYH	0.75	Yes	AMEX	12/1/2006	Power-Shares

SPECIALTY ETFS						
Ticker	Symbol	Expense Ratio	Options	Exchange	Inception Date	Fund Family
PowerShares Value Line Timeliness Selection	PIV	0.70	Yes	AMEX	12/6/2005	Power-Shares
Rydex 2x Russell 2000 ETF	RRY	0.70		AMEX	11/5/2007	Rydex
Rydex 2x S&P 500 ETF	RSU	0.70		AMEX	11/5/2007	Rydex
Rydex 2x S&P MidCap 400 ETF	RMM	0.70		AMEX	11/5/2007	Rydex
Rydex Inverse 2x Russell 2000 ETF	RRZ	0.70		AMEX	11/5/2007	Rydex
Rydex Inverse 2x S&P MidCap 400 ETF	RMS	0.00		AMEX	11/5/2007	Rydex
Rydex Inverse 2x S&P 500 ETF	RSW	0.70		AMEX	11/5/2007	Rydex
Short Dow 30 ProShares	DOG	0.95		AMEX	6/19/2006	ProFunds
Short MidCap S&P 400 ProShares	MYY	0.95		AMEX	6/19/2006	ProFunds
Short MSCI EAFE ProShares	EFZ	0.95		AMEX	10/23/2007	ProFunds
Short MSCI Emerging Markets ProShares	EUM	0.95		AMEX	11/1/2007	ProFunds
Short QQQ ProShares	PSQ	0.95		AMEX	6/19/2006	ProFunds
Short Russell 2000 ProShares	RWM	0.95		AMEX	1/23/2007	ProFunds
Short S&P 500 ProShares	SH	0.95		AMEX	6/19/2006	ProFunds
Short SmallCap 600 ProShares	SBB	0.95		AMEX	1/23/2007	ProFunds
TDAX Independence 2010 ETF	TDD	0.65		NYSE	10/1/2007	XShares

SPECIALTY ETFS							
Ticker	Symbol	Expense Ratio	Options	Exchange	Inception Date	Fund Family	
TDAX Independence 2020 ETF	TDH	0.65		NYSE	10/1/2007	XShares	
TDAX Independence 2030 ETF	TDN	0.65		NYSE	10/1/2007	XShares	
TDAX Independence 2040 ETF	TDV	0.65		NYSE	10/1/2007	XShares	
TDAX Independence In-Target ETF	TDX	0.65		NYSE	10/1/2007	XShares	
Ultra Basic Materials ProShares	UYM	0.95		AMEX	1/30/2007	ProFunds	
Ultra Consumer Goods ProShares	UGE	0.95		AMEX	1/30/2007	ProFunds	
Ultra Consumer Services ProShares	UCC	0.95		AMEX	1/30/2007	ProFunds	
Ultra Dow 30 ProShares	DDM	0.95		AMEX	6/19/2006	ProFunds	
Ultra Financials ProShares	UYG	0.95		AMEX	1/30/2007	ProFunds	
Ultra Health Care ProShares	RXL	0.95		AMEX	1/30/2007	ProFunds	
Ultra Industrials ProShares	UXI	0.95		AMEX	1/30/2007	ProFunds	
Ultra MidCap S&P 400 ProShares	MVV	0.95		AMEX	6/19/2006	ProFunds	
Ultra Oil & Gas ProShares	DIG	0.95		AMEX	1/30/2007	ProFunds	
Ultra QQQ ProShares	QLD	0.95		AMEX	6/19/2006	ProFunds	
Ultra Real Estate ProShares	URE	0.95		AMEX	1/30/2007	ProFunds	

SPECIALTY ETFS						
Ticker	Symbol	Expense Ratio	Options	Exchange	Inception Date	Fund Family
Ultra Russell 1000 Growth ProShares	UKF	0.95		AMEX	2/20/2007	ProFunds
Ultra Russell 1000 Value ProShares	UVG	0.95		AMEX	2/20/2007	ProFunds
Ultra Russell 2000 Growth ProShares	UKK	0.95		AMEX	2/20/2007	ProFunds
Ultra Russell 2000 ProShares	UWM	0.95		AMEX	1/23/2007	ProFunds
Ultra Russell 2000 Value ProShares	UVT	0.95		AMEX	2/20/2007	ProFunds
Ultra Russell MidCap Growth ProShares	UKW	0.95		AMEX	2/20/2007	ProFunds
Ultra Russell MidCap Value ProShares	UVU	0.95		AMEX	2/20/2007	ProFunds
Ultra S&P 500 ProShares	SSO	0.95		AMEX	6/19/2006	ProFunds
Ultra Semiconductors ProShares	USD	0.95		AMEX	1/30/2007	ProFunds
Ultra SmallCap 600 ProShares	SAA	0.95		AMEX	1/23/2007	ProFunds
Ultra Technology ProShares	ROM	0.95		AMEX	1/30/2007	ProFunds
Ultra Utilities ProShares	UPW	0.95		AMEX	1/30/2007	ProFunds
UltraShort Basic Materials ProShares	SMN	0.95		AMEX	1/30/2007	ProFunds
UltraShort Consumer Goods ProShares	SZK	0.95		AMEX	1/30/2007	ProFunds
UltraShort Consumer Services ProShares	SCC	0.95		AMEX	1/30/2007	ProFunds

SPECIALTY ETFS						
Ticker	Symbol	Expense Ratio	Options	Exchange	Inception Date	Fund Family
UltraShort Dow 30 ProShares	DXD	0.95		AMEX	7/11/2006	ProFunds
UltraShort Financials ProShares	SKF	0.95		AMEX	1/30/2007	ProFunds
UltraShort FTSE/ Xinhua China 25 ProShares	FXP	0.95		AMEX	11/8/2007	ProFunds
UltraShort Health Care ProShares	RXD	0.95		AMEX	1/30/2007	ProFunds
UltraShort Industrials ProShares	SIJ	0.95		AMEX	1/30/2007	ProFunds
UltraShort MidCap S&P 400 ProShares	MZZ	0.95		AMEX	7/11/2006	ProFunds
UltraShort MSCI EAFE ProShares	EFU	0.95		AMEX	10/23/2007	ProFunds
UltraShort MSCI Emerging Markets ProShares	EEV	0.95		AMEX	11/1/2007	ProFunds
UltraShort MSCI Japan ProShares	EWV	0.95		AMEX	11/8/2007	ProFunds
UltraShort Oil & Gas ProShares	DUG	0.95		AMEX	1/30/2007	ProFunds
UltraShort QQQ ProShares	QID	0.95		AMEX	7/11/2006	ProFunds
UltraShort Real Estate ProShares	SRS	0.95		AMEX	1/30/2007	ProFunds
UltraShort Russell 1000 Growth ProShares	SFK	0.95		AMEX	2/20/2007	ProFunds
UltraShort Russell 1000 Value ProShares	SJF	0.95		AMEX	2/20/2007	ProFunds

SPECIALTY ETFS						
Ticker	**Symbol**	**Expense Ratio**	**Options**	**Exchange**	**Inception Date**	**Fund Family**
UltraShort Russell 2000 Growth ProShares	SKK	0.95		AMEX	2/20/2007	ProFunds
UltraShort Russell 2000 ProShares	TWM	0.95		AMEX	1/23/2007	ProFunds
UltraShort Russell 2000 Value ProShares	SJH	0.95		AMEX	2/20/2007	ProFunds
UltraShort Russell MidCap Growth ProShares	SDK	0.95		AMEX	2/20/2007	ProFunds
UltraShort Russell MidCap Value ProShares	SJL	0.95		AMEX	2/20/2007	ProFunds
UltraShort S&P 500 ProShares	SDS	0.95		AMEX	7/11/2006	ProFunds
UltraShort Semiconductors ProShares	SSG	0.95		AMEX	1/30/2007	ProFunds
UltraShort SmallCap 600 ProShares	SDD	0.95		AMEX	1/23/2007	ProFunds
UltraShort Technology ProShares	REW	0.95		AMEX	1/30/2007	ProFunds
UltraShort Utilities ProShares	SDP	0.95		AMEX	1/30/2007	ProFunds

Expense ratios from **www.morningstar.com.**

Type classification from **www.theetfguide.com.**

Appendix B

○ ○ ○ ○ ○

Where to Find Information

Index Providers

American Stock Exchange (AMEX)(**www.amex.com**)

Dow Jones and D.J. Wilshire Equity Indexes (**www.djindexes.com**)

Goldman Sachs (**www2.goldmansachs.com**)

Lehman Brothers (**www.lehman.com**)

Morgan Stanley Capital International (**www.morganstanley.com**)

Morningstar Indexes (**www.morningstar.com**)

NASDAQ (**www.nasdaq.com**)

New York Stock Exchange (NYSE) (**www.nyse.com**)

Research Affiliated Fundamental Indexes (RAFI) (**www.ftse.com**)

PowerShares (**www.powershares.com**)

Standard & Poor's (**www.standardandpoors.com/indices**)

ETF Providers

Ameristock Funds (**www.ameristock.com**)

Barclays Global Investors (BGI) (**www.ishares.com**), (**www.ipathetn.com**), (**www.ishares.ca**)

Claymore Securities (**www.claymore.com/etfs**)

Deutsche Bank (**www.dbcfund.db.com**)

Elements (**www.elementsetn.com**)

Fidelity Management & Research Company (**www.nasdaq.com/oneq**)

First Trust (**www.ftportfolios.com**)

FocusShares (**www.focusshares.com**)

HealthShares, Inc. (**www.healthsharesinc.com**)

HOLDRS (Merrill Lynch) (**www.holdrs.com**)

Lehman Brothers (**www.optaetn.com**)

NETS Trust (**www.northerntrust.com**)

Merrill Lynch (**www.totalmerrill.com**)

Invesco PowerShares Capital Management LLC (**www.powershares.com**), (**http://www.adrbnymellon.com/bldrs_overview.jsp**)

ProShares (**www.proshares.com**)

RevenueShares Investor Services (**www.revenuesharesetfs.com**)

Rydex Investments (**www.rydexfunds.com**)

SPA (**www.spa-etf.com**)

Spiders (**www.spdrindex.com**), (**http://amex.com/spy**)

State Street Global Advisors (**www.ssgafunds.com**)

UBS (**www.ubs.com**)

Van Eck Global (**www.vaneck.com**)

Vanguard (**www.vanguard.com**)

WisdomTree (**www.wisdomtree.com**)

XShares (**www.xsharesadvisors.com**)

Victoria Bay Asset Management (**www.unitedstatesoilfund.com**)

Ziegler Capital Management (**www.ziegler.com**)

Brokers

PREMIUM BROKERS (ONLINE TRADING AND REGIONAL OFFICES)

E*Trade (**https://us.etrade.com/e/t/home**)

Fidelity (**www.fidelity.com**)

Vanguard (**www.vanguard.com**)

Charles Schwab (**www.schwab.com**)

T. Rowe Price (**www.troweprice.com**)

T. D. Ameritrade (**www.tdameritrade.com**)

DISCOUNT BROKERS (ONLINE TRADING)

TradeKing (**www.tradeking.com**)

Scottrade (**www.scottrade.com**)

Firstrade (**www.firstrade.com**)

OptionsXpress (**www.optionsxpress.com**)

Muriel Siebert (**www.siebertnet.com**)

WallStreet*E (**www.wallstreete.com**)

SogoInvest (**www.sogotrade.com**)

Zecco (**www.zecco.com**)

Stock Exchanges

American Stock Exchange (**www.amex.com**)

Chicago Mercantile Exchange (**www.cme.com**)

Chicago Board Options Exchange (**www.cboe.com**)

NASDAQ (**www.nasdaq.com**)

New York Stock Exchange (**www.nyse.com**)

OneChicago (**www.onechicago.com**)

Regulatory and Government Agencies

Chartered Financial Analyst Institute (**www.cfainstitute.org**)

Financial Industry Regulatory Authority (**www.finra.org**)

National Futures Association (**www.nfa.futures.org**)

U.S. Commodity Futures Trading Commission (**www.cftc.gov**)

U.S. Federal Reserve Board (**www.federalreserve.gov**)

U.S. Internal Revenue Service (**www.irs.gov**)

U.S. Securities and Exchange Commission (**www.sec.gov**)

U.S. Treasury Department (**www.ustreas.gov**)

ETF Research, News, and Commentary

Business Week (**www.businessweek.com**)

EmergingMarkets (**www.emergingmarkets.org**)

ETF Connect (**www.etfconnect.com**)

Index Universe (**www.indexuniverse.com**)

Market Watch (**www.marketwatch.com**)

Morningstar (**www.morningstar.com**)

Seeking Alpha (**www.seekingalpha.com**)

Smart Money (**www.smartmoney.com**)

Social Investment Forum (**www.socialinvest.org**)

The ETF Guide (**www.etfguide.com**)

TheStreet.com (**www.thestreet.com/life-and-money/etfs/index.html**)

Value Line (**www.valueline.com**)

Wall Street Journal (**www.wsj.com**)

Yahoo Finance (**www.finance.yahoo.com/etf**)

Saving for Retirement and Education

AARP (**www.aarp.com**)

SavingforCollege.com (**www.savingforcollege.com**)

Glossary

40 Act – Investment Company Act of 1940

529 plan – A tax-advantaged college savings account

Active management – Manipulation of asset classes and funds in a portfolio in an attempt to achieve higher returns than the market

Active portfolio strategies – Methods used in the active management of a portfolio

AP – Authorized participant; a third party authorized to create and sell shares of an ETF

Arbitrage – The creation or redemption of shares of an ETF by an authorized provider to bring ETF prices in line with the value of the underlying securities

Ask price – The price at which a seller seeks to sell a share of a stock or an ETF

Asset – Anything that has value, including shares of stock, bonds, notes, commodities, real estate, and cash

Asset class – The style or type of an asset: fixed-income, equity, capitalization, growth, or value

Backtesting – The use of old market data to determine how a new strategy would have worked if it had been in place

Backwardation – When the spot price of a commodity at the time of delivery is expected to be lower than the current price and a lower futures price is set

Basket – The collection of stocks that is exchanged for a creation unit of ETF shares

Beta – A popular indicator of risk that measures the volatility of a stock or a fund in relation to the volatility of the market as a whole, represented by the S&P 500 Index

Bid price – The price that a buyer offers to pay for a stock or an ETF

Bond coupon – The part of a bearer bond that denotes the amount of interest due and on what date and where payment will be made. Physical coupons are no longer issued in the U.S., but the stated interest rate on a registered or book-entry bond is still referred to as the "coupon."

Build-around portfolio – A strategy in which ETFs are added to a portfolio to compensate for a heavy concentration in one particular industry or sector

Broad market index – An index that measures the performance of a securities market as a whole or of a broad subsector

Callable bonds – Bonds that can be called in by the issuer prior to maturity date

Call – A request for payment or redemption

Cap size – Capitalization size; a measure of a company's size, arrived at by multiplying its share price times the number of outstanding shares

Capital leverage – Increasing returns by using capital as collateral to get twice the buying power by buying stocks on margin instead of investing the capital directly

Closed investment trust, closed-end fund – A mutual fund that restricts the number of investors and does not create new shares. Shares can be traded on the stock market.

Collateral – Assets that are offered to secure a loan or other credit. In ETFs trading commodity futures contracts, collateral is the cash set aside for the fulfillment of a contract when it comes due.

Commodities – Products that are required every day, including food, such as livestock, grain, and sugar; and basic materials, such as steel and aluminum

Commodity pool – An arrangement in which multiple investors pool their cash to invest in commodities futures

Commodity total return indexes – Indexes that track the returns on commodity futures contracts, plus interest earned by collateral, minus any expenses

Contango – When the price of a commodity futures contract is higher than the current spot price for that commodity

Corporate actions – The decisions made by a board of directors that affect a company's structure

Correlation – The degree to which two investments move together in the market

Correlation coefficient – A measure of how closely the standard deviations of two stocks follow each other

Creation unit – The block of newly created ETF shares delivered to an ETF manager in exchange for a "basket" of stocks

Currency risk – The risk that the value of a foreign currency will rise relative to the U.S. dollar

Current yield – The ratio of interest to the actual market price of a bond, stated as a percentage

Custom index – A rules-based investment strategy

Day trade – A trade in which an investment is bought and sold during the same trading session

Developed market – An economically and socially advanced country with a GDP per capita of $20,000 or more

Developing market – An emerging market country that is beginning to show some of the characteristics of a developed market

Dividend yield – A financial ratio that shows how much a company pays out in dividends each year relative to its share price

Dow Jones Average – A price-weighted average of the stock prices of 30 companies representing leading U.S. industries

Efficient frontier – Certain portfolios or investment selections that optimally balance risk and reward

Emerging markets – Developing countries with economies that are beginning to expand

Exchange traded fund – A type of mutual fund that tracks an index, a commodity or a basket of assets, but trades like a stock on an exchange.

Exit fee – A one-time fee charged for cashing in an investment in a mutual fund

Expected return – The expected return from an investment after a certain time has passed, calculated using historical data over a given period

Expected value – The expected value of an investment after a certain time has passed, calculated using historical data over a given period

Expense ratio – The percentage of a fund's average net assets used to pay its annual expenses

Fixed income assets – Assets such as bonds that return a fixed amount of interest on a regular basis

Forwards – Contracts to buy a commodity in the future at an agreed price

Free-float – The number of shares of a stock or an ETF available for trading on the market

Futures – Contracts to buy a commodity in the future at an agreed price

Futures contract – A contract to buy or sell shares of an ETF at a certain date in the future at a specified price

Futures price – The price of a commodity futures contract, calculated based on the current spot price, with adjustments for interest rates, seasonal changes, and transportation and storage costs

Gross Domestic Product (GDP) – The total market value of all final goods and services produced within a given country in a given year

Glass-Steagall Act – An act passed by the U.S. Congress in 1933 that separated commercial banking from investment banking and founded the Federal Deposit Insurance Company

Global ETFs – ETFs that may hold U.S. stocks along with international stocks

Growth stocks – Stocks whose value has been growing rapidly and is expected to continue growing

Hedge – An investment strategy used to reduce financial risk or the possibility of loss

Illiquid assets – Assets, such as bonds, that cannot be immediately redeemed for cash

Index – A method used to measure the performance of a financial market

Index fund – A mutual fund or an ETF that tracks the performance of an index

Industry risk – The risk that a particular industry sector will underperform the rest of the stock market

Industry sector – A market sector comprised of all the companies involved in a specific industry

International ETFs – ETFs holding only non-U.S. stocks

Intraday price – The price of a stock or an ETF at any point during a trading day

Investment Company Act of 1940 – An act passed by Congress to regulate the mutual funds industry, under which many ETFs are organized

Investment trust – A company that receives funds for the purpose of investment

Junk bond – A corporate bond that is rated as less than investment grade and has a higher yield because of the increased risk of default

Large-cap – Stocks are generally classified as large-cap if their market capitalization is over $5 billion

Leverage – The use of borrowed capital, such as margin, or of financial instruments, such as futures contracts, to increase the potential return of an investment

Life-cycle investing – An investment strategy in which an investor's portfolio is adjusted as he or she moves through different stages of life

Limit order – An order to buy shares of an ETF or stock that sets a maximum price that the buyer is willing to pay

Load fee – A one-time entry fee charged by some mutual funds

Long position – The holder of a long position owns the security and will profit if the price of the security goes up

Macroeconomic – An approach that examines the performance, structure, and behavior of a national, regional, or global economy as a whole

Margin – A cash deposit made to secure a loan of securities from a broker

Market breadth – The ratio of the number of stocks whose price has gone up to the number of stocks whose price has gone down

Market capitalization – A measure of the size of a company, calculated by multiplying the price of a single share of stock times the number of shares outstanding

Market index – An index that follows the performance of a particular market

Market maker – A third-party company willing to engage in buying or selling stocks on public stock exchanges

Market-if-touched order – An order to sell shares of an ETF or stock the first time that its price drops to a specified level

Market order – An order to buy or sell a certain amount of shares of an ETF on the stock market

Mechanical rotation strategy – A rules-based sector rotation strategy

Micro-cap – Stocks with capitalization of less than $250 million

Mid-cap – Stocks are generally classified as mid-cap if their market capitalization is between $1 billion and $5 billion

Modern portfolio theory (MPT) – A theory that evaluates the overall risk of a portfolio by calculating the risk of each investment in the portfolio in relation to the other investments it holds and that tracks the performance of a portfolio as a whole

Momentum – Measure of the rate at which the price of an ETF is rising or falling

Momentum oscillator – A calculation used to measure momentum

Moving average – The average of the price of a security or an ETF over the past several days, recalculated every day

Multiple – Price-to-earnings ratio

Mutual fund – An investment vehicle that allows investors to pool their capital in order to purchase a broad range of securities

NAV – The Net Asset Value of an ETF or mutual fund that is calculated by adding the current market value of the fund's underlying securities and any cash or other assets it holds, subtracting fund liabilities, and dividing the result by the number of outstanding shares

Nominal return – An unadjusted average of the changes in the price of an investment over time

Nonsystemic risk – The risk associated with investing all your capital in a single company or market sector

Open-end mutual fund – A mutual fund that creates new shares as the demand for them arises

Open interest – The number of futures or options contracts which are outstanding at any given moment

Opportunity cost – The income lost when cash cannot be reinvested to bring in more returns because it is tied up somewhere else

Option – The right to buy or sell a share of a stock or an ETF at a specified price

Passive investing – A strategy in which securities, ETFs, or mutual funds are simply purchased and held in a portfolio over time

Passive management – A style of management in which the portfolio of a mutual fund or an exchange traded fund mirrors a market index, rather than being manipulated by a fund manager

Portfolio – A selection of investments

Portfolio Composition File (PCF) – A file created by an ETF fund manager or trustee each day after the market close to tell authorized participants the securities and share quantities required to compose a creation or redemption unit on the next trading day

Position trade – Any investment that takes longer than two weeks to realize

Preferred stock – A stock issue that pays fixed dividends and gives its owners priority over other shareholders

Price charts – Graphic representations of stock price movements over time

Price-to-book – A ratio used to compare a stock's market value to its book value, calculated by dividing the current closing price of the stock by the latest quarter's book value per share

Price-to-earnings ratio – The price of a share of a company's stock divided by the company's earnings per share

Price-to-sales – A ratio for valuing a stock relative to its own past performance, other companies, or the market itself. It is calculated by dividing a stock's current price by its revenue per share for the trailing 12 months.

Price trend – The tendency for a series of stock or ETF prices to continue moving in the same direction

Principal – The amount of money an investor initially invests in the stock market

Prospectus – The official description of an ETF that describes its holdings and explains its objectives and methodology

Put – An option giving the right to sell an ETF at a specified price within a specified time period

Quadrant – One of four categories used to classify a company relative to other companies in a universe

Qualified dividend income (QDI) – Dividends paid by certain preferred stocks, which are taxable at the lower federal tax rate of 15 percent

Quantitative analysis – A financial analysis technique that seeks to understand behavior by using complex mathematical and statistical modeling, measurement, and research. Quantitative analysts try to replicate reality mathematically by assigning a numerical value to variables.

Real Estate Investment Trusts (REITs) – Companies that hold portfolios of real estate properties or assets related to real estate

Rebalancing – The act of adjusting a portfolio to maintain its target asset allocations

Regulated Investment Company (RIC) – An ETF registered under the Investment Company Act of 1940, which allows it more flexibility

Relative Strength Indicator (RSI) – A measure of the strength of a single stock in relation to its past performance

Required minimum distribution (RMD) – A mandated withdrawal from a tax-advantaged retirement account after the account holder reaches the age of 70

Risk-adjusted return – A concept

in which an investment's return is evaluated by measuring how much risk is involved in producing that return

R-Squared – A statistical measure that represents the percentage of a fund's movements that can be explained by movements in a benchmark index. For fixed income securities, the benchmark is the T-bill; for equities, the benchmark is the S&P 500.

Sector rotation – An investment strategy in which an investor constantly shifts his assets to the best performing sectors of the market

Selling at discount – The market price is lower than the actual value of the ETF

Selling at premium – The market price is higher than the actual value of the ETF

Sharpe ratio – A ratio that indicates whether a portfolio's returns are the result of smart investment decisions or of excess risk

Short position – A situation in which an investor has borrowed shares of an ETF and sold them with the expectation that the price will soon go down and that the shares can be bought back at the lower price and returned to the lender

Short selling – A trading strategy in which an investor borrows shares of an ETF and sells them with the expectation that the price will soon go down and he or she can buy the shares back at the lower price

Small-cap – Stocks are generally classified as small-cap if their capitalization is between $250 million and $1 billion

Sovereign risk – The risk that a government will default on its bonds

Spot price – The price for which a commodity is currently selling

Spread – The difference in price between an asset that is being sold and one that is being bought

Standard & Poor's 500 – An index of 500 stocks chosen for market size, liquidity, and industry grouping, among other factors. The S&P 500 is one of the most commonly used benchmarks for the overall U.S. stock market.

Standard deviation – The amount by which the price of a stock or an ETF deviates from its mean over a period of time

Stop order – An order to sell shares of an ETF when the prices drop to a specified level

Striking price – The price at which an option is exercised or a buy or sell limit order is activated

Style box – A grid that provides a visual characterization of the style of a stock, an ETF, or an entire portfolio

Style drift – The tendency of an actively managed fund portfolio to deviate over time from its stated investment objectives

Style – The characteristics by which a security is classified when it is evaluated for inclusion in a portfolio or index

Swing trade – An investment that is bought and sold again within approximately two weeks

Systemic risk – The risk associated with the stock market and economy as a whole

Top-down analysis – A method that looks at the entire global economy for macroeconomic trends

Total return indexes – Indexes that factor in the total returns of an investment over time, including interest, dividends, returns from reinvestment of cash, and fees from loaning securities

Top ten – The ten securities that have the most weight in an index or an ETF

Tracking error – The discrepancy between the returns of an ETF and the returns of the index it is tracking

Trailing earnings growth – Most recent earnings growth, usually from the most recent 3-, 6-, or 12-month period

Trend line – A straight line drawn on a price chart to demonstrate an upward or downward trend

Turnover – The selling of stocks or ETFs in a portfolio and their replacement with new investments

Unit investment trust (UIT) – An investment company that offers a fixed, unmanaged portfolio, generally of stocks and bonds, and does not reinvest the dividends

Value stocks – Stocks, generally of a company whose size has remained steady, that are considered to be a good value compared to the stock of other, similar companies

Value-weighted index – An index containing a high proportion of value stocks

Volatility – The degree to which a stock or ETF price tends to fluctuate

World mutual funds – ETFs that may hold U.S. stocks along with international stocks

Yankee bonds – Corporate bonds issued by foreign companies but trading in U.S. dollars on U.S. exchanges

o o o o o

Bibliography

Culloton, Dan, *Morningstar ETFs 150: Annual Sourcebook*, Wiley, Hoboken, New Jersey, 2007.

Delfeld, Carl T., *ETF Investing Around the World: A Guide to Building a Global ETF Portfolio*, iUniverse, New York, 2007.

Ferri, Richard A., *The ETF Book: All You Need to Know About Exchange-Traded Funds*, Hoboken, Wiley, New Jersey, 2008.

Gordon, Gary, "All-ETF Portfolios: Keeping It Too Simple May Be Stupid," *ETFExpert.com*, April 9, 2008, <**www.etfexpert.com/etf_expert/2008/04/ vanguard-etfs-k.html**>, Accessed November 16, 2008.

Landis, David, "Own the Market with Index Funds and ETFs," *Kiplinger's Personal Finance*, February 14, 2008, <**www.kiplinger.com/features/ archives/2008/02/index-funds.html**>, Accessed November 16, 2008.

Lofton, Todd, *Getting Started in Exchange Traded Funds (ETFs)*, Wiley, Hoboken, New Jersey, 2007.

Parmar, Neil. "THERE'S A NEW WATCHWORD for the discount-broker business: technology." Smart Money. July 10, 2007.

(http://www.smartmoney.com/investing/economy/online-stock-investing-manage-and-trade-stocks-21519/), Accessed November 16, 2008.

Steinhardt, Michael. "International ETF Bubbles," Hedgefolios.com. May 11, 2006. (http://www.hedgefolios.com/read/international-etf-bubbles)

Updegrave, Walter, "Building the Perfect ETF Portfolio," *CNN Money*, June 6, 2005, <http://money.cnn.com/2005/05/31/funds/etf_portfolio/index.htm>, Accessed November 16, 2008.

Vomund, David, et al., *ETF Trading Strategies Revealed: Trade Secrets*, Marketplace Books, Columbia, Maryland, 2006.

Wasik, John F., "529 College Savings Plans Are Hobbled by Expenses," *Bloomberg.com*, August 11, 2003, <http://www.bloomberg.com/apps/news?pid=10000039&refer=columnist_wasik&sid=aGrSrqqPSzCE>, Accessed November 16, 2008.

Wherry, Rob, "Ready for an All-ETF Portfolio? Here Are Some Models," *Smart Money*, February 13, 2007; updated October 15, 2007, <http://www.smartmoney.com/etffocus/index.cfm?story=20070213&pgnum=2>, Accessed November 16, 2008.

Wild, Russell, *Exchange-Traded Funds for Dummies*, Wiley, Indianapolis, 2007.

ooooo

Dedication

Dedicated to Wilford W. Fraser

○ ○ ○ ○ ○

Author Biography

Martha Maeda is an economic historian who writes on politics, ethics, and modern philosophy. After graduating from Northwestern University, she lived and worked in Australia, Japan, Latin America, and several African countries before settling in the United States. She has a particular interest in microeconomics and in the effects of globalization on the lives and businesses of people all over the world. Maeda's second book *The Complete Guide to Investing in Bonds and Bond Funds: How to Earn High Rates of Return—Safely* will also be released by Atlantic Publishing Company in 2009.

Index